EVERYDAY Slow Cooker & ONE DISH RECIPES

Taste of Home BOOKS

For other *Taste of Home* books and products, visit **ShopTasteofHome.com.**

1610 N. 2nd St., Suite 102, Milwaukee WI 53212-3906

INTERNATIONAL STANDARD BOOK NUMBER:
978-1-61765-317-9

INTERNATIONAL STANDARD SERIAL NUMBER:
1944-6382

COMPONENT NUMBER:
119400030H00

PRINTED IN CHINA.
3 5 7 9 10 8 6 4 2

PICTURED ON THE FRONT COVER:
Slow Cooker Turkey Chili, page 66;
Honey-Butter Peas and Carrots, page 73;
Caramel Fudge Cheesecake, page 228;
Pizza Ring, page 197.

PICTURED ON THE BACK COVER:
Sweet & Spicy Pulled Pork Sandwiches, page 63;
Sweet-and-Sour Beef, page 106;
Honey-Glazed Hens with Fruit Stuffing, page 191.

Table of Contents

Slow Cooker

Stovetop Suppers

Oven Entrees

Bonus Chapter:

Slow Cooking 101

The original slow cooker was introduced in 1971 by Rival. They called it the Crock-Pot, and it's still so successful that the term "slow cooker" and the name Crock-Pot are often used interchangeably—but Crock-Pot is a brand of the beloved slow cooker appliance.

Most slow cookers have two or more settings. Food cooks faster on the high setting, but the low setting is ideal for all-day cooking or working with less tender cuts of meat. Slow cooker recipes in this book refer to cooking on either high or low settings. The warm setting keeps food hot and tasty until it's ready to serve.

In general, one hour of cooking on high equals roughly two hours of cooking on low. Read on for more useful tips and soon you'll be slow-cooker savvy.

Advantages of Slow Cooking

CONVENIENCE. Slow cookers provide people with the ease of safely preparing meals while away from home. The appliances are readily available and budget-friendly.

HEALTH. As more people turn, more nutritious food choices to improve their health, slow cooking has gained popularity. Low-temperature cooking retains more vitamins in foods, and leaner cuts of meat become tender in the slow cooker without added fats. Lower-sodium and lower-fat versions of many canned goods are available, which can help you create even lighter, healthier meals. And, for many busy folks, knowing that a healthy meal is waiting at home helps them avoid the temptation of the drive-thru after work.

FINANCIAL SAVINGS. A slow cooker uses very little electricity because of its low wattage. For instance, it would cost roughly 21 cents to operate a slow cooker for a total of 10 hours. If you cook a pork roast for only 2 hours in the oven instead of using the slow cooker for 10 hours, you would spend $2.51 to operate an electric oven or $1.49 to operate a gas one. Also, slow cookers do not heat up the kitchen as ovens do, which saves on summertime cooling costs.

Handy icons throughout the book!

CHICKEN GYROS, PAGE 118

EAT SMART

Recipes are lower in calories, fat and sodium. Most include Diabetic Exchanges. More than 80 recipes offer classic down-home flavor, while being better for you!

APPLE-PEAR COMPOTE, PAGE 88

FREEZE IT

Freezer-friendly recipes include directions for freezing and future use. Stretch your kitchen time with more than 40 recipes that make it a breeze to plan future meals.

TIPS FOR TASTY OUTCOMES

- Be sure the lid is well-placed over the ceramic insert, not tilted or askew. The steam during cooking creates a seal.
- Refrain from lifting the lid while using the slow cooker, unless the recipe instructs you to stir or add ingredients. The loss of steam each time you lift the lid can mean an extra 20 to 30 minutes of cooking time.
- Remember that slow cooking may take longer at higher altitudes.
- When food is finished cooking, remove it from the slow cooker within an hour. Promptly refrigerate any leftovers.
- Use a slow cooker on a buffet table to keep soup, stew, savory dips or mashed potatoes hot.
- Heat cooked food on the stovetop or in the microwave and then put it into a slow cooker to keep it hot for serving. Reheating food in a slow cooker isn't recommended.
- Don't forget your slow cooker when you go camping, if electricity will be available. When space is limited and you want "set-it-and-forget-it" meals, it's a handy appliance.

know when it's **DONE!**

145°F

- Medium-rare beef and lamb roasts
- Fish

160°F

- Medium beef and lamb roasts
- Pork
- Egg dishes

165°F

- Ground chicken and turkey

170°F

- Well-done beef and lamb roasts
- Chicken and turkey that is whole or in pieces

Purchasing a Slow Cooker

Slow cookers range in price from $20 to more than $200 and are available in sizes from 1½ to 7 quarts. Decide on a price range that fits your budget and choose a size appropriate for your family (see chart below).

Most slow cooker inserts are ceramic, but some pricier models have aluminum inserts that let you brown meats in them before slow cooking. For convenience, look for inserts that are dishwasher-safe.

Slow cookers are available in round and oval shapes. If you plan to prepare roasts in the slow cooker, you may wish to consider an oval shape. If stews and soups are your forte, a round slow cooker is perfect for your cooking needs.

SLOW COOKER SIZES

HOUSEHOLD SIZE	SLOW COOKER CAPACITY
1 to 2 people	2 to 3½ quarts
3 to 4 people	3½ to 4½ quarts
4 to 5 people	4½ to 5 quarts
6 or more people	5 to 7 quarts

Cooking Basics

- While slow cooker models vary, they usually have at least two settings, low (about 180°) and high (about 280°). Some models also have a keep-warm setting.
- The keep-warm setting is useful if you plan to use the slow cooker to serve hot foods while entertaining. Some slow cookers will automatically switch to a keep-warm setting after cooking. This provides added convenience and helps you avoid overcooking the food while you're away from home.
- A range in cooking time is provided to account for variables such as thickness of meat, fullness of the slow cooker and desired finished temperature of the food being cooked. As you grow familiar with your slow cooker, you'll be able to judge which end of the range to use.
- New slow cookers tend to heat up more quickly than older ones. If you have an older model and your recipe directs to cook on low, you may wish to cook on high for the first hour to ensure food safety.
- Old slow cookers can lose their efficiency and may not achieve proper cooking temperatures. To confirm safe cooking temperatures, review the steps of Slow Cooker Temperature Check on page 9.
- To learn more about specific models, check online or in reputable consumer magazines for product reviews.

Preparing Foods for the Slow Cooker

BEANS. Dried beans can be tricky to cook in a slow cooker. Minerals in the water and variations in voltage affect various type of beans in different ways. Always soak dried beans prior to cooking. Soak them overnight or place them in a Dutch oven and add enough water to cover by 2 inches. Bring to a boil and boil for 2 minutes. Remove from the heat, cover and let stand for 1 to 4 hours or until softened. Drain and rinse beans, discarding liquid. Sugar, salt and acidic ingredients, such as vinegar, interfere with the beans' ability to cook and become tender. Add these ingredients only after the beans are fully cooked. Lentils and split peas do not need soaking.

COUSCOUS. Couscous is best cooked on the stovetop rather than in the slow cooker.

DAIRY. Milk-based products tend to break down during slow cooking. Items like milk, cream, sour cream or cream cheese are best added during the last hour of cooking. Cheeses don't generally hold up during the slow cooker's extended cooking time and should be added near the end of cooking. Condensed cream soups generally hold up well in the slow cooker..

FISH & SEAFOOD. Fish and seafood cook quickly and can break down if cooked too long. They are generally added to the slow cooker toward the end of the cooking time to keep them at optimal quality.

MEATS. Meat may be browned before adding to the slow cooker. While browning is not necessary, it adds to the flavor and appearance of the meat and allows you to drain off the fat. Cut roasts over 3 pounds in half before placing in the slow cooker to ensure even cooking. Trim off any excess fat. Fat retains heat, and large amounts of fat could raise the temperature of the cooking liquid, causing the meat to overcook.

OATS. Quick-cooking and old-fashioned oats are often interchangeable in recipes. However, old-fashioned oats hold up better in the slow cooker.

PASTA. If added to a slow cooker when dry, pasta tends to become very sticky. It's better to cook it according to the package directions and stir it into the slow cooker just before serving. Small pastas such as orzo and ditalini may be cooked in the slow cooker, however. To keep them from becoming mushy, add during the last hour of cooking.

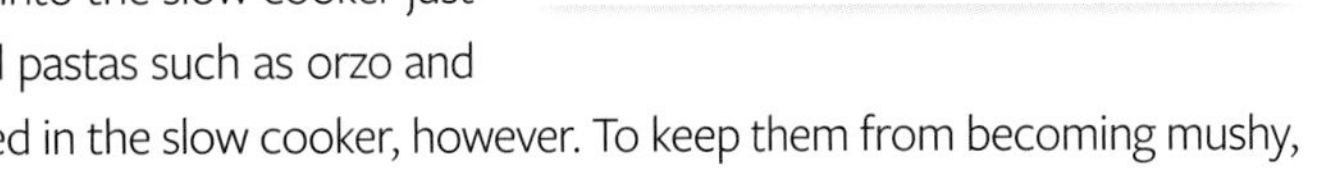

RICE. Converted rice is ideal for all-day cooking. If using instant rice, add it during the last 30 minutes of cooking.

VEGETABLES. Firm vegetables like potatoes and carrots tend to cook more slowly than meat. Cut these foods into uniform pieces and place on the bottom and around the sides of the slow cooker. Place the meat over the vegetables. During the last 15 to 60 minutes of cooking, add tender vegetables, like peas and zucchini, or ones you'd prefer to be crisp-tender.

COOK TIMES

Conventional Oven	Slow Cooker
15 to 30 minutes	Low: 4 to 6 hours High: 1½ to 2 hours
35 to 45 minutes	Low: 6 to 8 hours High: 3 to 4 hours
50 minutes or more	Low: 8 to 10 hours High: 4 to 6 hours

Thickening Stews & Sauces

Quick-cooking tapioca can be used as a thickener for stews. Add it along with other ingredients at the beginning of cooking.

To thicken juices at the end of cooking, use flour or cornstarch. Mix flour or cornstarch with some cold water until smooth. Stir into the slow cooker. Cover and cook on high for 30 minutes or until the cooking juices are thickened.

Or, strain cooking juices and place in a saucepan. Mix flour or cornstarch with some cold water until smooth. Stir into juices. Bring to a boil; cook and stir for 2 minutes or until thickened.

Converting Recipes for the Slow Cooker

Almost any recipe that bakes in the oven or simmers on the stovetop can be converted for the slow cooker. Here are some guidelines.

- Before converting recipes, check the manufacturer's guidelines for your particular slow cooker. Find a recipe that is similar to the one you want to convert and use it as a guide. Note the amount and size of meat and vegetables, heat setting, cooking time and amount of liquid.
- Since there is no evaporation, adjusting the amount of liquid in your recipe may be necessary. If a recipe calls for 6 to 8 cups of water, try starting with 5 cups. Conversely, recipes should include at least a little liquid. If a recipe does not include liquid, add ½ cup of water or broth.
- In general, 1 hour of simmering on the stove or baking at 350°F in the oven is equal to 8-10 hours on low or 4-6 hours on high in a slow cooker. Check the chart at top left.
- Cornstarch, flour and tapioca are often used to thicken stews and sauces in the slow cooker. See the information at left for more details.

Useful Handles for Lifting Food

Layered dishes or meat loaves are easier to get out of the slow cooker with foil handles. Here's how:

1 For a 3-qt. slow cooker, cut three 20x3-in. strips of heavy-duty foil (or 25x3-in. for larger slow cookers). Or cut 6-in.-wide strips from regular foil and fold in half lengthwise. Crisscross the strips so they resemble the spokes of a wheel.

2 Place the strips on the bottom and up the sides of the slow cooker insert. Let strips hang over the edge of the slow cooker. Coat strips with cooking spray.

3 Place food in the center of the strips and lower until the food rests on the bottom of the slow cooker.

4 After cooking, grasp the foil strips and carefully lift food up. Remove food from foil strips and serve.

Slow Cooker Temperature Check

To be considered safe, a slow cooker must be able to cook slowly enough that it can be left unattended, yet fast enough to keep the food at a proper temperature. Here's how to check your slow cooker:

1. Fill the slow cooker ½ to ⅔ full with room-temperature water.
2. Cover and heat on low for 8 hours.
3. Using a thermometer, check the temperature of the water quickly, since the temperature can drop once the lid is removed.
4. The temperature should be at least 185°. If it's too hot, a meal cooked for 8 hours would likely be overdone. If the temperature is below 185°, the slow cooker is not safe to use and should be discarded.

Power Outage Solutions

If the power goes out while you are using a slow cooker, the U.S. Department of Agriculture offers the following recommendations:

- Fully cooked foods are safe at room temperature for up to 2 hours. If the food has been sitting for 2 hours or longer, or for an unknown period of time, it should be discarded.
- If the food is not fully cooked and you're home when the power goes out, immediately finish cooking it with another method, such as with a gas stove or grill.

CLEANING TIPS

- Removable inserts make cleanup a breeze. Be sure to cool the insert before rinsing or cleaning with water to avoid cracking or warping. Do not immerse the metal base in water. Clean it with a damp sponge.
- If the insert is dishwasher-safe, place it in the dishwasher. Otherwise, wash it in warm soapy water. Avoid using abrasive cleansers, since they may scratch the surface.
- To remove mineral stains on a ceramic insert, fill the cooker with hot water and 1 cup of white vinegar; cover. Turn the heat to high for 2 hours, then empty. When cool, wash the insert with hot soapy water and a cloth or sponge. Rinse well and dry with a towel.
- To remove water marks from a highly glazed ceramic insert, rub the surface with canola oil and allow to stand for 2 hours before washing with hot soapy water.

CAJUN PORK AND RICE, PAGE 48

"I created this recipe after returning home from traveling when I had little food in the house. I used ingredients already available in the refrigerator and pantry. My husband loves this pork dish because it's tasty, and I love it because it's easy."

—**ALLISON GAPINSKI** CARY, NC
about her recipe, Cajun Pork and Rice, on page 48

Slow Cooker

Beef & Ground Beef

From family-pleasing **classics** like barbecue meat loaf and chili mac to **exciting new dishes** such as Cuban picadillo or Korean beef, you'll **discover dozens** of heartwarming recipes here. With so **much variety**, it's no wonder that slow-cooked beef is so popular with **busy cooks**!

Tomato-Basil Steak

I use basil and bell peppers from my herb and vegetable garden to make this dish. It's so easy to prepare and so rich and delicious.

—SHERYL LITTLE SHERWOOD, AR

PREP: 15 MIN. • **COOK:** 6 HOURS
MAKES: 4 SERVINGS

- **1¼ pounds boneless beef shoulder top blade or flat iron steaks**
- **½ pound whole fresh mushrooms, quartered**
- **1 medium sweet yellow pepper, julienned**
- **1 can (14½ ounces) stewed tomatoes, undrained**
- **1 can (8 ounces) tomato sauce**
- **1 envelope onion soup mix**
- **2 tablespoons minced fresh basil**
- **Hot cooked rice**

1. Place steaks in a 4-qt slow cooker. Add mushrooms and pepper. In a small bowl, mix tomatoes, tomato sauce, soup mix and basil; pour over top.

2. Cook, covered, on low 6-8 hours or until beef and vegetables are tender. Serve with rice.

TOMATO-BASIL STEAK

"On cool days, which we get plenty of in Saskatchewan, I like to get out my slow cooker and make a big batch of this comforting stew. Trying to appeal to 10 picky eaters in our large household isn't easy, but everyone asks for seconds with this recipe."

—BARB SMITH REGINA, SK

Barley Beef Stew

PREP: 20 MIN. • **COOK:** 6 HOURS
MAKES: 6-8 SERVINGS

- **1½ pounds beef stew meat, cut into 1-inch pieces**
- **1 medium onion, chopped**
- **2 tablespoons canola oil**
- **4 cups water**
- **1 can (15 ounces) tomato sauce**
- **5 medium carrots, cut into ½-inch pieces**
- **1 celery rib, thinly sliced**
- **2 teaspoons salt**
- **½ teaspoon dried oregano**
- **½ teaspoon paprika**
- **¼ teaspoon pepper**
- **2 cups fresh or frozen green beans, thawed**
- **2 cups fresh or frozen corn, thawed**
- **¾ cup medium pearl barley**

1. In a large skillet, brown beef and onion in oil until meat is no longer pink; drain. Transfer to a 5-qt. slow cooker. Add water, tomato sauce, carrots, celery, salt, oregano, paprika and pepper.

2. Cover and cook on low for 4-5 hours. Add the beans, corn and barley; cover and cook on low 2 hours longer or until barley, beef and vegetables are tender.

FREEZE OPTION *Place individual portions of cooled stew in freezer containers and freeze. To use, partially thaw in refrigerator overnight. Heat through in a saucepan, stirring occasionally and adding a little water if necessary.*

MEDITERRANEAN POT ROAST DINNER

EAT SMART

Mediterranean Pot Roast Dinner

I first made this recipe one winter day. My family (adults, kids and dogs) were having a blast sledding and playing in the snow all day, and when we came inside, supper was ready! The pot roast is perfect served with mashed potatoes, rice or crusty dinner rolls.

—**HOLLY BATTISTE** BARRINGTON, NJ

PREP: 30 MIN. • **COOK:** 8 HOURS
MAKES: 8 SERVINGS

- **2 pounds potatoes (about 6 medium), peeled and cut into 2-inch pieces**
- **5 medium carrots (about ¾ pound), cut into 1-inch pieces**
- **2 tablespoons all-purpose flour**
- **1 boneless beef chuck roast (3 to 4 pounds)**
- **1 tablespoon olive oil**
- **8 whole fresh mushrooms, quartered**
- **2 celery ribs, chopped**
- **1 medium onion, thinly sliced**
- **¼ cup sliced Greek olives**
- **½ cup minced fresh parsley, divided**
- **1 can (14½ ounces) fire-roasted diced tomatoes, undrained**
- **1 tablespoon minced fresh oregano or 1 teaspoon dried oregano**
- **1 tablespoon lemon juice**
- **2 teaspoons minced fresh rosemary or ½ teaspoon dried rosemary, crushed**
- **2 garlic cloves, minced**
- **¾ teaspoon salt**
- **¼ teaspoon pepper**
- **¼ teaspoon crushed red pepper flakes, optional**

1. Place potatoes and carrots in a 6-qt. slow cooker. Sprinkle flour over all surfaces of roast. In a large skillet, heat oil over medium-high heat. Brown roast on all sides. Place over vegetables.

2. Add mushrooms, celery, onion, olives and 1/4 cup parsley to slow cooker. In a small bowl, mix remaining ingredients; pour over top.

3. Cook, covered, on low 8-10 hours or until meat and vegetables are tender. Remove beef. Stir remaining parsley into vegetables. Serve beef with vegetables.

PER SERVING *422 cal., 18 g fat (6 g sat. fat), 111 mg chol., 538 mg sodium, 28 g carb., 4 g fiber, 37 g pro.* ***Diabetic Exchanges:*** *5 lean meat, 1½ starch, 1 vegetable, ½ fat.*

Steak Strips with Dumplings

Take in a parade on the Fourth or spend a day by the lake and come home to this delicious slow-cooked specialty! Homemade dumplings make it unique.

—**JOHN SMALLDRIDGE** PRINCETON, ID

PREP: 25 MIN. • **COOK:** 5 HOURS
MAKES: 2 SERVINGS

- **¾ pound beef top round steak, cut into ½-inch strips**
- **¼ teaspoon pepper**
- **2 teaspoons canola oil**
- **⅔ cup condensed cream of chicken soup, undiluted**
- **½ cup beef broth**
- **4 large fresh mushrooms, sliced**
- **¼ cup each chopped onion, green pepper and celery**

DUMPLINGS

- **½ cup all-purpose flour**
- **¾ teaspoon baking powder**
- **¼ teaspoon salt**
- **2 tablespoons beaten egg**
- **3 tablespoons 2% milk**
- **½ teaspoon dried parsley flakes**

1. Sprinkle steak with pepper. In a small skillet, brown steak in oil over medium-high heat. Transfer to a 1½-qt. slow cooker. Combine the soup, broth and vegetables; pour over steak. Cover and cook on low for 4-5 hours.

2. For dumplings, in a small bowl, combine the flour, baking powder and salt. Stir in egg and milk just until blended. Drop by tablespoonfuls onto meat mixture. Sprinkle with parsley.

3. Cover and cook on high for 1 hour or until a toothpick inserted in a dumpling comes out clean (do not lift the cover while cooking).

It's easy to **double the recipe** for steak and dumplings. Use a whole can of **chicken soup** and a **3-qt. slow cooker.**

EAT SMART FREEZE IT

Chipotle Shredded Beef

This beef is delicious all rolled up in a tortilla, served with corn salsa and eaten as a burrito. You could also serve it over rice or mashed potatoes or in buns.

—**DARCY WILLIAMS** OMAHA, NE

PREP: 25 MIN. • **COOK:** 8 HOURS
MAKES: 10 SERVINGS

- **1 small onion, chopped**
- **1 teaspoon canola oil**
- **1 can (28 ounces) diced tomatoes, undrained**
- **¼ cup cider vinegar**
- **6 garlic cloves, minced**
- **2 chipotle peppers in adobo sauce, chopped**
- **2 tablespoons brown sugar**
- **2 bay leaves**
- **2 teaspoons adobo sauce**
- **½ teaspoon ground cumin**
- **½ teaspoon paprika**
- **½ teaspoon pepper**
- **¼ teaspoon ground cinnamon**
- **1 boneless beef chuck roast (2½ pounds)**
- **5 cups cooked brown rice**
- **Shredded reduced-fat cheddar cheese and reduced-fat sour cream, optional**

1. In a large skillet coated with cooking spray, saute onion in oil until tender. Stir in the tomatoes, vinegar, garlic, peppers, brown sugar, bay leaves, adobo sauce and seasonings. Bring to a boil; reduce heat, simmer, uncovered for 4-6 minutes or until thickened.

2. Place roast in a 5-qt. slow cooker; add tomato mixture. Cover and cook on low heat for 8-9 hours or until meat is tender.

3. Discard bay leaves. Remove meat and shred with two forks. Skim fat from juices; return meat to slow cooker. Using a slotted spoon, serve meat with rice. Top with cheese and sour cream if desired.

FREEZE OPTION *Freeze cooled meat mixture and juices in freezer containers. To use, partially thaw in refrigerator overnight. Heat through in a saucepan, stirring occasionally and adding a little broth if necessary. Serve over rice with cheese and sour cream if desired.*

PER SERVING *345 cal., 13 g fat (4 g sat. fat), 74 mg chol., 194 mg sodium, 31 g carb., 3 g fiber, 26 g pro.* ***Diabetic Exchanges:*** *3 lean meat, 2 starch.*

CHIPOTLE SHREDDED BEEF

Picadillo

Most traditional recipes out there have numerous variations... and picadillo is no exception. This is my take on the Cuban classic. For added convenience, I adapted it for the slow cooker.

—**SANFORD BROWN** COVINGTON, GA

PREP: 30 MIN. • **COOK:** 4½ HOURS
MAKES: 8 SERVINGS

- **2 large onions, chopped**
- **2 tablespoons olive oil**
- **¾ cup white wine or beef broth**
- **2 pounds lean ground beef (90% lean)**
- **1¼ cups crushed tomatoes**
- **1 can (8 ounces) tomato sauce**
- **⅓ cup tomato paste**
- **4 garlic cloves, minced**
- **2 teaspoons dried oregano**
- **½ teaspoon salt**
- **½ teaspoon ground cinnamon**
- **½ teaspoon ground cloves**
- **½ teaspoon pepper**
- **1 cup raisins**
- **1 medium green pepper, chopped**
- **¾ cup pimiento-stuffed olives, coarsely chopped**
- **2 tablespoons chopped seeded jalapeno pepper**
- **Hot cooked brown rice**

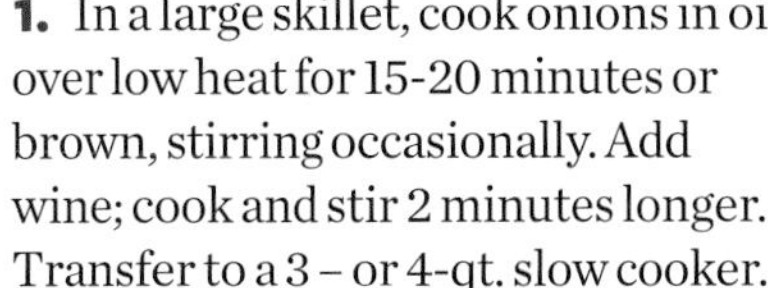

1. In a large skillet, cook onions in oil over low heat for 15-20 minutes or brown, stirring occasionally. Add wine; cook and stir 2 minutes longer. Transfer to a 3 – or 4-qt. slow cooker.

2. In the same skillet, cook beef over medium heat until no longer pink. Add to slow cooker. Combine the tomatoes, tomato sauce, tomato paste, garlic and seasonings; pour over top. Cover and cook on low for 4-6 hours or until heated through.

3. Place raisins in a small bowl and cover with boiling water; let stand for 5 minutes. Drain.

4. Stir the green pepper, olives, jalapeno and raisins into the slow cooker. Cover and cook 30 minutes longer. Serve with rice.

NOTE *Wear disposable gloves when cutting hot peppers; the oils can burn skin. Avoid touching your face.*

"My family loves the bold barbecue flavor of this tender meat loaf. I like that it's such an easy recipe to prepare in the slow cooker."
—DAVID SNODGRASS COLUMBIA, MO

CHEDDAR-TOPPED BARBECUE MEAT LOAF

Cheddar-Topped Barbecue Meat Loaf

PREP: 20 MIN. • **COOK:** 3¼ HOURS
MAKES: 8 SERVINGS

- **3 eggs, lightly beaten**
- **¾ cup old-fashioned oats**
- **1 large sweet red or green pepper, chopped (about 1½ cups)**
- **1 small onion, finely chopped**
- **1 envelope onion soup mix**
- **3 garlic cloves, minced**
- **½ teaspoon salt**
- **¼ teaspoon pepper**
- **2 pounds lean ground beef (90% lean)**
- **1 cup ketchup**
- **2 tablespoons brown sugar**
- **1 tablespoon barbecue seasoning**
- **1 teaspoon ground mustard**
- **1 cup (4 ounces) shredded cheddar cheese**

1. Cut three 18x3-in. strips of heavy-duty foil; crisscross so they resemble spokes of a wheel. Place strips on bottom and up sides of a 3-qt. slow cooker. Coat strips with cooking spray.
2. In a large bowl, combine eggs, oats, chopped pepper, onion, soup mix, garlic, salt and pepper. Add beef; mix lightly but thoroughly. Shape into a 7-in. round loaf.
3. Place loaf in center of strips in slow cooker. Cook, covered, on low 3-4 hours or until a thermometer reads at least 160°.
4. In a small bowl, mix ketchup, brown sugar, barbecue seasoning and mustard; pour over meat loaf and sprinkle with cheese. Cook, covered, on low 15 minutes longer or until cheese is melted. Let stand 5 minutes.
5. Using foil strips as handles, remove meat loaf to a platter.

BEEFY CABBAGE BEAN STEW

Beefy Cabbage Bean Stew

While on one of our small group quilting retreats, one of my friends served this wonderful recipe for dinner. We all loved it and have since passed it around for others to enjoy—and now I'm passing it on to you.
—MELISSA GLANCY LA GRANGE, KY

PREP: 20 MIN. • **COOK:** 6 HOURS
MAKES: 6 SERVINGS

- **½ pound lean ground beef (90% lean)**
- **3 cups shredded cabbage or angel hair coleslaw mix**
- **1 can (16 ounces) red beans, rinsed and drained**
- **1 can (14½ ounces) diced tomatoes, undrained**
- **1 can (8 ounces) tomato sauce**
- **¾ cup salsa or picante sauce**
- **1 medium green pepper, chopped**
- **1 small onion, chopped**
- **3 garlic cloves, minced**
- **1 teaspoon ground cumin**
- **½ teaspoon pepper**

1. In a large skillet, cook beef over medium heat 4-6 minutes or until no longer pink, breaking into crumbles; drain.
2. Transfer meat to a 4-qt. slow cooker. Stir in remaining ingredients. Cook, covered, on low 6-8 hours or until cabbage is tender.

GERMAN-STYLE SHORT RIBS

German-Style Short Ribs

Our whole family is excited when I plug in the slow cooker to make these amazing ribs. We like them served over rice or egg noodles.

—**BREGITTE RUGMAN** SHANTY BAY, ON

PREP: 15 MIN. • **COOK:** 8 HOURS
MAKES: 8 SERVINGS

- **¾ cup dry red wine or beef broth**
- **½ cup mango chutney**
- **3 tablespoons quick-cooking tapioca**
- **¼ cup water**
- **3 tablespoons brown sugar**
- **3 tablespoons cider vinegar**
- **1 tablespoon Worcestershire sauce**
- **½ teaspoon salt**
- **½ teaspoon ground mustard**
- **½ teaspoon chili powder**
- **½ teaspoon pepper**
- **4 pounds bone-in beef short ribs**
- **2 medium onions, sliced**
- **Hot cooked egg noodles**

1. In a 5-qt. slow cooker, combine the first 11 ingredients. Add ribs and turn to coat. Top with onions.

2. Cover and cook on low for 8-10 hours or until meat is tender. Remove ribs from slow cooker. Skim fat from cooking juices; serve with ribs and noodles.

Brown sugar, cider **vinegar** and a hint of spicy ground **mustard** create a classic flavor combination that's both **sweet and sour**. The sauce would also be tasty with **pork chops** or smoked **kielbasa.**

Creamy Beef and Pasta

When my children were young, I often made this set-it-and-forget-it meal when my husband and I went out for date night. Even the babysitters commented on how much they liked it.

—**CAROL LOSIER** BALDWINSVILLE, NY

PREP: 15 MIN. • **COOK:** 2½ HOURS
MAKES: 4-6 SERVINGS

- **2 cans (10¾ ounces each) condensed cream of mushroom soup, undiluted**
- **2 cups (8 ounces) shredded cheddar or part-skim mozzarella cheese**
- **1 pound ground beef, cooked and drained**
- **2 cups uncooked small pasta**
- **2 cups milk**
- **½ to 1 teaspoon onion powder**
- **½ to 1 teaspoon salt**
- **¼ to ½ teaspoon pepper**

In a 3-qt. slow cooker, combine all ingredients. Cover and cook on low for 2½ to 3½ hours or until the pasta is tender.

Simple Tortilla Stack

Just add crispy tortilla chips and a green salad to turn this easy entree into a fun and festive meal. It's one of my go-to favorites for busy days.

—**DENISE WALLER** OMAHA, NE

PREP: 20 MIN. • **COOK:** 6 HOURS
MAKES: 6 SERVINGS

- **1 pound ground beef**
- **2 cans (10 ounces each) enchilada sauce**
- **1 can (10¾ ounces) condensed cream of onion soup, undiluted**
- **¼ teaspoon salt**
- **1 package (8½ ounces) flour tortillas, torn**
- **3 cups (12 ounces) shredded cheddar cheese**

1. In a skillet, cook beef over medium heat until no longer pink; drain. Stir in enchilada sauce, soup and salt.

2. In a 3-qt. slow cooker, layer a third of the beef mixture, tortillas and cheese. Repeat the layers twice. Cover and cook on low for 6-8 hours or until heated through.

Beer-Braised Roast with Root Vegetables

My nephew is an avid hunter and makes an effort to share his bounty with family members. I like the combination of seasoned vegetables and lean venison in this recipe, and my wife likes how the seasonings complement the meat. I serve the roast with a garden salad and crusty multigrain bread.

—**MALCOLM CIESZKO** WASHINGTON, NC

PREP: 35 MIN. • **COOK:** 8 HOURS
MAKES: 6 SERVINGS

- **2 tablespoons olive oil**
- **1 boneless beef chuck or venison roast (3 to 3½ pounds), trimmed**
- **2 large onions, sliced**
- **3 celery ribs, cut into 1-inch pieces**
- **3 medium carrots, cut into 1-inch pieces**
- **1 medium sweet potato, peeled and cut into 1-inch cubes**
- **½ pound fresh whole mushrooms, quartered**
- **1 bottle (12 ounces) dark beer or 1½ cups beef broth**
- **4 tablespoons minced fresh parsley, divided**
- **3 tablespoons Worcestershire sauce**
- **3 tablespoons seedless blackberry spreadable fruit**
- **1 teaspoon salt**
- **1 teaspoon pepper**
- **2 tablespoons cornstarch**
- **½ cup cold water**

BEER-BRAISED ROAST WITH ROOT VEGETABLES

1. In a large skillet, heat oil over medium heat. Brown roast on all sides. Place vegetables in a 6-qt. slow cooker. Place roast over vegetables.

2. In a small bowl, combine the beer, 2 tablespoons parsley, Worcestershire sauce, spreadable fruit, salt and pepper; pour over meat. Cook, covered, on low 8-10 hours or until meat and vegetables are tender.

3. Remove roast to a serving platter. Using a slotted spoon, remove vegetables to platter; keep warm. Pour cooking juices into a small saucepan; skim fat and bring to a boil.

4. Mix cornstarch and cold water until smooth; stir into cooking juices. Return to a boil; cook and stir 1-2 minutes or until thickened. Serve with roast and vegetables; sprinkle with remaining parsley.

Shortcut Meatball Stew

I came up with this hearty meal as another way to use convenient frozen meatballs. It's quick to put together in the morning and ready when my husband gets home in the evening.

—**IRIS SCHULTZ** MIAMISBURG, OH

PREP: 20 MIN. • **COOK:** 9 HOURS
MAKES: 6 SERVINGS

- **3 medium potatoes, peeled and cut into ½-inch cubes**
- **1 pound fresh baby carrots, quartered**
- **1 large onion, chopped**
- **3 celery ribs, sliced**
- **1 package (12 ounces) frozen fully cooked homestyle meatballs**
- **1 can (10¾ ounces) condensed tomato soup, undiluted**
- **1 can (10½ ounces) beef gravy**
- **1 cup water**
- **1 envelope onion soup mix**
- **2 teaspoons beef bouillon granules**

1. Place the potatoes, carrots, onion, celery and meatballs in a 5-qt. slow cooker. Combine the remaining ingredients; pour over meatball mixture.

2. Cover and cook on low for 9-10 hours or until the vegetables are crisp-tender.

BRAISED SHORT RIBS

Braised Short Ribs

I've been relying on this recipe ever since I bought my first slow cooker some 19 years ago. The fall-off-the-bone-tender ribs are so good to come home to after a busy day.

—**PEGGY EDWARDS** HEBER CITY, UT

PREP: 20 MIN. • **COOK:** 6 HOURS
MAKES: 7 SERVINGS

- **½ cup all-purpaose flour**
- **1½ teaspoons salt**
- **1½ teaspoons paprika**
- **½ teaspoon ground mustard**
- **4 pounds bone-in beef short ribs**
- **2 tablespoons canola oil**
- **2 medium onions, sliced**
- **1 cup beer or beef broth**
- **1 garlic clove, minced**

GRAVY

- **2 teaspoons all-purpose flour**
- **1 tablespoon cold water**

1. In a large resealable plastic bag, combine the flour, salt, paprika and mustard. Add ribs in batches and shake to coat. In a large skillet, brown ribs in oil; drain.

2. Place onions in a 5-qt. slow cooker; add ribs. Top with beer and garlic. Cover and cook on low for 6-7 hours or until meat is tender.

3. Remove ribs and onions to a serving platter; keep warm. Skim fat from cooking juices; transfer to a small saucepan. Bring to a boil.

4. Combine flour and water until smooth; gradually stir into the pan. Return to a boil; cook and stir for 2 minutes or until thickened. Serve with ribs.

Slow Cooker Garlic-Sesame Beef

My mom received this marinade recipe from a neighbor while she lived in Seoul, South Korea, which is where I was adopted from. Mom created heritage night for my brother and me, and she served Korean bulgogi with sticky rice, kimchi and chopsticks. As a busy mom of four, I keep her tradition alive but let the slow cooker do the work!

—**JACKIE BROWN** FAIRVIEW, NC

PREP: 15 MIN. + MARINATING
COOK: 5 HOURS • **MAKES:** 6 SERVINGS

- **6 green onions, sliced**
- **½ cup sugar**
- **½ cup water**
- **½ cup reduced-sodium soy sauce**
- **¼ cup sesame oil**
- **3 tablespoons sesame seeds, toasted**
- **2 tablespoons all-purpose flour**
- **4 garlic cloves, minced**
- **1 beef sirloin tip roast (3 pounds), thinly sliced**
- **Additional sliced green onions and toasted sesame seeds**
- **Hot cooked rice**

1. In a large resealable plastic bag, mix the first eight ingredients. Add beef; seal bag and turn to coat. Refrigerate 8 hours or overnight.

2. Pour beef and marinade into a 3-qt. slow cooker. Cook, covered, on low 5-7 hours or until meat is tender.

3. Using a slotted spoon, remove beef to a serving platter; sprinkle with additional green onions and sesame seeds. Serve with rice.

Traditional Korean **bulgogi** is **grilled** after marinating in the soy mixture. Try the **leftover beef** tucked into **lettuce roll-ups**.

SLOW COOKER GARLIC-SESAME BEEF

Slow-Cooked Beef Stroganoff

I've been preparing Stroganoff in the slow cooker for more than 30 years. Once you've done it this way, you'll never cook it on the stovetop again. It's great for family or company.

—**KAREN HERBERT** PLACERVILLE, CA

PREP: 20 MIN. **COOK:** 5 HOURS
MAKES: 8-10 SERVINGS

- 2 **beef top round steaks (about ¾ inch thick and 1½ pounds each)**
- ½ **cup all-purpose flour**
- 1½ **teaspoons salt**
- ½ **teaspoon ground mustard**
- ⅛ **teaspoon pepper**
- 1 **medium onion, sliced and separated into rings**
- 1 **can (8 ounces) mushroom stems and pieces, drained**
- 1 **can (10½ ounces) condensed beef broth, undiluted**
- 1½ **cups (12 ounces) sour cream**
- **Hot cooked noodles**

1. Cut round steaks into 3x½-in. strips. In a shallow bowl, mix flour, salt, mustard and pepper. Add beef in batches; toss to coat.

2. In a 5-qt. slow cooker, layer onion, mushrooms and beef. Pour broth over top. Cook, covered, on low 5-7 hours or until meat is tender. Just before serving, stir in sour cream. Serve with noodles.

You can **customize** this recipe by doubling the **onion**, substituing ½ pound sliced **baby portobello** mushrooms or tossing in a julienned **red pepper**.

SLOW-COOKED BEEF STROGANOFF

Slow Cooker Enchiladas

When you're craving Southwestern food but don't want to spend time preparing it in the evening, try my recipe. I simply fill the slow cooker in the morning, then come home to a sensational supper.

—**MARY LUEBBERT** BENTON, KS

PREP: 30 MIN. • **COOK:** 5 HOURS
MAKES: 4 SERVINGS

- **1 pound ground beef**
- **1 cup chopped onion**
- **½ cup chopped green pepper**
- **1 can (16 ounces) pinto or kidney beans, rinsed and drained**
- **1 can (15 ounces) black beans, rinsed and drained**
- **1 can (10 ounces) diced tomatoes and green chilies, undrained**
- **⅓ cup water**
- **1 teaspoon chili powder**
- **½ teaspoon ground cumin**
- **½ teaspoon salt**
- **¼ teaspoon pepper**
- **1 cup (4 ounces) shredded sharp cheddar cheese**
- **1 cup (4 ounces) shredded Monterey Jack cheese**
- **6 flour tortillas (6 inches)**

1. In a large skillet, cook the beef, onion and green pepper until meat is no longer pink; drain. Add the next eight ingredients; bring to a boil. Reduce heat; cover and simmer for 10 minutes. Combine cheeses.

2. In a 5-qt. slow cooker, layer about 3/4 cup beef mixture, one tortilla and about 1/3 cup cheese. Repeat layers. Cover and cook on low for 5-7 hours or until heated through.

EAT SMART **FREEZE IT**

Tender Salsa Beef

Few ingredients, few steps, BIG taste results! This is my Mexican-style twist on comfort food.

—**STACIE STAMPER** NORTH WILKESBORO, NC

PREP: 15 MIN. • **COOK:** 8 HOURS
MAKES: 8 SERVINGS

- **1½ pounds beef stew meat, cut into ¾-inch cubes**
- **2 cups salsa**
- **1 tablespoon brown sugar**
- **1 tablespoon reduced-sodium soy sauce**
- **1 garlic clove, minced**
- **4 cups hot cooked brown rice**

In a 3-qt. slow cooker, combine the beef, salsa, brown sugar, soy sauce and garlic. Cover and cook on low for 8-10 hours or until meat is tender. Using a slotted spoon, serve beef with rice.

FREEZE OPTION *Freeze individual portions of cooled beef mixture in freezer containers. To use, partially thaw in refrigerator overnight. Heat through in a saucepan, stirring occasionally and adding a little water if necessary.*

PER SERVING *259 cal., 7 g fat (2 g sat. fat), 53 mg chol., 356 mg sodium, 28 g carb., 2 g fiber, 19 g pro.* ***Diabetic Exchanges:*** *2 starch, 2 lean meat.*

TENDER SALSA BEEF

"This flavorful, tender beef dish has been a go-to recipe for many years; it's a meal lifesaver on days when I'm going to be late getting home."
—**ANNIE MERRILL** CROGHAN, NY

SLOW-COOKED TEX-MEX FLANK STEAK

Slow-Cooked Tex-Mex Flank Steak

PREP: 15 MIN. • **COOK:** 6 HOURS
MAKES: 4 SERVINGS

- **1 tablespoon canola oil**
- **1 beef flank steak (1½ pounds)**
- **1 large onion, sliced**
- **⅓ cup water**
- **1 can (4 ounces) chopped green chilies**
- **2 tablespoons cider vinegar**
- **2 to 3 teaspoons chili powder**
- **1 teaspoon garlic powder**
- **1 teaspoon sugar**
- **½ teaspoon salt**
- **⅛ teaspoon pepper**

1. In a large skillet, heat oil over medium-high heat; brown steak 1-2 minutes on each side. Transfer to a 3-qt. slow cooker.
2. Add onion to the skillet; cook and stir 1-2 minutes or until crisp-tender. Add water to pan; cook 30 seconds, stirring to loosen browned bits from the pan.
3. Stir in remaining ingredients; return to a boil. Pour over steak. Cook, covered, on low 6-8 hours or until meat is tender. Slice steak across the grain; serve with onion mixture.

BEEF OSSO BUCCO

Beef Osso Bucco

Treat holiday guests to elegant comfort food at its best. Our beef osso bucco is complimented by gremolata, a fresh-tasting herb condiment that's the classic companion to this savory dish.
—TASTE OF HOME TEST KITCHEN

PREP: 30 MIN. • **COOK:** 7 HOURS
MAKES: 6 SERVINGS

- **½ cup all-purpose flour**
- **½ teaspoon pepper**
- **¾ teaspoon salt, divided**
- **6 beef shanks (14 ounces each)**
- **2 tablespoons butter**
- **1 tablespoon olive oil**
- **½ cup white wine or beef broth**
- **1 can (14½ ounces) diced tomatoes, undrained**
- **1½ cups beef broth**
- **2 medium carrots, chopped**
- **1 medium onion, chopped**
- **1 celery rib, sliced**
- **1 tablespoon dried thyme**
- **1 tablespoon dried oregano**
- **2 bay leaves**
- **3 tablespoons cornstarch**
- **¼ cup cold water**

GREMOLATA
- **⅓ cup minced fresh parsley**
- **1 tablespoon grated lemon peel**
- **1 tablespoon grated orange peel**
- **2 garlic cloves, minced**

1. In a large resealable plastic bag, combine the flour, pepper and ½ teaspoon salt. Add beef, a few pieces at a time, and shake to coat.
2. In a large skillet, brown beef in butter and oil. Transfer meat and drippings to a 6-qt. slow cooker. Add wine to skillet, stirring to loosen browned bits from pan; pour over meat. Add the tomatoes, broth, carrots, onion, celery, thyme, oregano, bay leaves and remaining salt.
3. Cook, covered, on low 7-9 hours or until meat is tender. Discard bay leaves.
4. Skim fat from cooking juices; transfer juices to a large saucepan. Bring to a boil. Combine cornstarch and water until smooth; gradually stir into the pan. Bring to a boil; cook and stir for 2 minutes or until thickened.
5. In a small bowl, combine the gremolata ingredients. Serve beef with gremolata and sauce.

BEEF ROAST WITH CRANBERRY GRAVY

Beef Roast with Cranberry Gravy

I can easily get this recipe ready in the morning and let it cook all day so that it's ready for dinner when I get home at night. The hearty beef dish is also good for the weekends when we want to spend time outdoors or on day trips.

—**DIANE NEMITZ** LUDINGTON, MI

PREP: 40 MIN. • **COOK:** 7 HOURS
MAKES: 6 SERVINGS (2¾ CUPS GRAVY)

- **1 boneless beef chuck roast (3 to 4 pounds)**
- **2 teaspoons salt**
- **1 teaspoon pepper**
- **2 tablespoons canola oil**
- **2 medium carrots, finely chopped**
- **1 medium onion, chopped**
- **2 garlic cloves, minced**
- **1 cup cranberry juice**
- **¾ cup water**
- **½ cup fresh or frozen cranberries**
- **½ cup balsamic vinegar**
- **2 fresh thyme sprigs**
- **1 bay leaf**
- **3 tablespoons cornstarch**
- **3 tablespoons cold water**

1. Sprinkle beef with salt and pepper. In a large skillet, heat oil over medium heat. Brown roast on all sides. Transfer to a 5-qt. slow cooker.
2. Add carrots and onion to drippings; cook and stir over medium heat 4-5 minutes or until tender. Add garlic; cook 1 minute longer. Spoon vegetables around roast; add cranberry juice, 3/4 cup water, cranberries, balsamic vinegar, thyme and bay leaf. Cook, covered, on low 7-9 hours or until meat is tender. Discard thyme sprigs and bay leaf.
3. Remove meat to a serving platter; keep warm. Pour cooking juices into a small saucepan; skim fat and bring to a boil. In a small bowl, mix cornstarch and water until smooth; gradually stir into pan. Return to a boil, stirring constantly; cook and stir 1-2 minutes or until thickened. Serve with roast.

FREEZE IT

Melt-in-Your-Mouth Pot Roast

Slow-simmered with rosemary, mustard and thyme, this irresistible pot roast is easy to make. Substitute red wine or brandy plus a half cup of water for the broth...the aroma is wonderful!

—**JEANNIE KLUGH** LANCASTER, PA

PREP: 10 MIN. • **COOK:** 6 HOURS
MAKES: 6-8 SERVINGS

- **1 pound medium red potatoes, quartered**
- **1 cup fresh baby carrots**
- **1 boneless beef chuck roast (3 to 4 pounds)**
- **¼ cup Dijon mustard**
- **2 teaspoons dried rosemary, crushed**
- **1 teaspoon garlic salt**
- **½ teaspoon dried thyme**
- **½ teaspoon pepper**
- **⅓ cup chopped onion**
- **1½ cups beef broth**

1. Place potatoes and carrots in a 5-qt. slow cooker. Cut roast in half. Combine the mustard, rosemary, garlic salt, thyme and pepper; rub over roast.
2. Place in slow cooker; top with onion and broth. Cover and cook on low for 6-8 hours or until meat and vegetables are tender.

FREEZE OPTION *Place sliced pot roast and vegetables in freezer containers; top with cooking juices. Cool and freeze. To use, partially thaw in refrigerator overnight. Heat through in a covered saucepan, gently stirring and adding a little water if necessary.*

Thai Brisket

Here's an unusual take on brisket that will have you hooked. Peanut butter, soy sauce, crisp-tender veggies and zesty seasonings give it the authentic Thai flavor we crave.
—**TERI RASEY** CADILLAC, MI

PREP: 1 HOUR • **COOK:** 8½ HOURS
MAKES: 6-8 SERVINGS

- **1 fresh beef brisket (3 to 4 pounds), cut in half**
- **3 tablespoons olive oil, divided**
- **1 cup chunky peanut butter**
- **⅔ cup soy sauce**
- **4 teaspoons sesame oil**
- **1 tablespoon minced fresh cilantro**
- **1 tablespoon lemon juice**
- **1 teaspoon garlic powder**
- **1 teaspoon crushed red pepper flakes**
- **1 teaspoon pepper**
- **1 tablespoon cornstarch**
- **1 cup water**
- **1¼ cups julienned carrots**
- **1 medium sweet red pepper, sliced**
- **1 medium green pepper, sliced**
- **½ cup chopped green onions**
- **1 cup unsalted peanuts, optional**
- **Hot cooked rice**

1. In a large skillet over medium-high heat, brown brisket on both sides in 2 tablespoons olive oil. Transfer to a 5-qt. slow cooker. Combine the peanut butter, soy sauce, sesame oil, cilantro, lemon juice, garlic, pepper flakes and pepper; pour over brisket. Cover and cook on low for 8-9 hours or until meat is tender.

2. Remove brisket and keep warm. Combine cornstarch and water until smooth; stir into cooking juices. Cover and cook on high for 30 minutes or until thickened. Meanwhile, in a large skillet or wok, stir-fry the carrots, peppers and onions in remaining olive oil until crisp-tender. Add peanuts if desired. Stir cooking juices; add to vegetable mixture.

3. Thinly slice meat across the grain; serve with rice and vegetable mixture.

NOTE *This is a fresh beef brisket, not corned beef.*

CHILI MAC

Chili Mac

This recipe has regularly appeared on my family menus for more than 40 years, and it's never failed to please at potlucks and bring-a-dish gatherings. Sometimes I turn it into soup by adding a can of beef broth.
—**MARIE POSAVEC** BERWYN, IL

PREP: 15 MIN. • **COOK:** 6 HOURS
MAKES: 4-6 SERVINGS

- **1 pound ground beef, cooked and drained**
- **2 cans (16 ounces each) hot chili beans, undrained**
- **2 large green peppers, chopped**
- **1 large onion, chopped**
- **4 celery ribs, chopped**
- **1 can (8 ounces) tomato sauce**
- **1 envelope chili seasoning**
- **2 garlic cloves, minced**
- **1 package (7 ounces) elbow macaroni, cooked and drained**
- **Salt and pepper to taste**

In a 5-qt. slow cooker, combine the first eight ingredients. Cover and cook on low for 6 hours or until heated through. Stir in macaroni. Season with salt and pepper.

Top the **Chili Mac** with shredded **cheddar** cheese, your favorite **hot sauce**, chopped tomatoes and **green onions**, or a cool dollop of **sour cream**.

Poultry

When you're craving **down-home flavor**, turn to the **heartwarming** chicken and turkey dishes on these pages. From old-fashioned **corn bread casserole** and **family-favorite tacos** to **innovative stews** and **summertime turkey**, you'll find a meal to suit every occasion and taste.

CARIBBEAN CHICKEN STEW

EAT SMART

Caribbean Chicken Stew

I lived with a West Indian family for awhile and enjoyed watching them cook. I lightened up this recipe by leaving out the oil and sugar, removing the skin from the chicken and using chicken sausage.

—JOANNE IOVINO KINGS PARK, NY

PREP: 25 MIN. + MARINATING
COOK: 6 HOURS • **MAKES:** 8 SERVINGS

- **¼ cup ketchup**
- **3 garlic cloves, minced**
- **1 tablespoon sugar**
- **1 tablespoon hot pepper sauce**
- **1 teaspoon browning sauce, optional**
- **1 teaspoon dried basil**
- **1 teaspoon dried thyme**
- **1 teaspoon paprika**
- **½ teaspoon salt**
- **½ teaspoon dried oregano**
- **½ teaspoon ground allspice**
- **½ teaspoon pepper**
- **8 bone-in chicken thighs (about 3 pounds), skin removed**
- **1 pound fully cooked andouille chicken sausage links, sliced**
- **1 medium onion, finely chopped**
- **2 medium carrots, finely chopped**
- **2 celery ribs, finely chopped**

1. In a large resealable plastic bag, combine ketchup, garlic, sugar, pepper sauce and, if desired, browning sauce; stir in seasonings. Add chicken thighs, sausage and vegetables. Seal bag and turn to coat. Refrigerate 8 hours or overnight.
2. Transfer contents of bag to a 4- or 5-qt. slow cooker. Cook, covered, on low 6-8 hours or until chicken is tender.

PER SERVING *309 cal., 14 g fat (4 g sat. fat), 131 mg chol., 666 mg sodium, 9 g carb., 1 g fiber, 35 g pro.* ***Diabetic Exchanges:*** *5 lean meat, 1/2 starch.*

Slow 'n' Easy Barbecued Chicken

I rely on this yummy recipe often during the summer and fall when I know I'm going to be out working in the yard all day. I just pair it with a vegetable and side salad...and supper is served!

—DREAMA HUGHES LONDON, KY

PREP: 20 MIN. • **COOK:** 3 HOURS
MAKES: 4 SERVINGS

- **¼ cup water**
- **3 tablespoons brown sugar**
- **3 tablespoons white vinegar**
- **3 tablespoons ketchup**
- **2 tablespoons butter**
- **2 tablespoons Worcestershire sauce**
- **1 tablespoon lemon juice**
- **1 teaspoon salt**
- **1 teaspoon paprika**
- **1 teaspoon ground mustard**
- **½ teaspoon cayenne pepper**
- **1 broiler/fryer chicken (3 pounds), cut up and skin removed**
- **4 teaspoons cornstarch**
- **1 tablespoon cold water**

1. In a small saucepan, combine the first 11 ingredients. Bring to a boil. Reduce heat; simmer, uncovered, for 5 minutes. Remove from the heat.
2. Place the chicken in a 3-qt. slow cooker. Top with sauce. Cover and cook on low for 3-4 hours or until chicken juices run clear.
3. Remove chicken to a serving platter; keep warm. Skim fat from cooking juices; transfer to a small saucepan. Bring liquid to a boil. Combine cornstarch and water until smooth. Gradually stir into the pan. Bring to a boil; cook and stir for 2 minutes or until thickened. Spoon some of the sauce over chicken and serve the remaining sauce on the side.

CHIPOTLE-MARMALADE CHICKEN

EAT SMART FREEZE IT

Chipotle-Marmalade Chicken

Big on flavor and easy on the cook's time, my chicken recipe is so appealing. The sweet-hot sauce gets its heat from chipotle pepper. I like to serve the chicken with a side of rice to use up every delectable drop of sauce.

—**CITTIE,** TASTE OF HOME ONLINE COMMUNITY

PREP: 15 MIN. • **COOK:** 4 HOURS
MAKES: 4 SERVINGS

- **4 boneless skinless chicken breast halves (6 ounces each)**
- **¼ teaspoon salt**
- **Dash pepper**
- **½ cup chicken broth**
- **⅓ cup orange marmalade**
- **1 tablespoon canola oil**
- **1 tablespoon balsamic vinegar**
- **1 tablespoon minced chipotle pepper in adobo sauce**
- **1 tablespoon honey**
- **1 teaspoon chili powder**
- **¼ teaspoon garlic powder**
- **4 teaspoons cornstarch**
- **2 tablespoons cold water**

1. Sprinkle chicken with salt and pepper. Transfer to a 3-qt. slow cooker. In a small bowl, combine the broth, marmalade, oil, vinegar, chipotle pepper, honey, chili powder and garlic powder; pour over chicken. Cover and cook on low for 4-5 hours or until a thermometer reads 170°.

2. Remove chicken to a serving platter and keep warm. Place cooking juices in a small saucepan; bring to a boil. Combine cornstarch and water until smooth. Gradually stir into the pan. Bring to a boil; cook and stir for 2 minutes or until thickened. Serve with chicken.

EDITOR'S NOTE *Freeze leftover chipotle peppers in adobo sauce in 1- or 2-pepper portions for use in other recipes.*

FREEZE OPTION: *Cool chicken mixture. Freeze in freezer containers. To use, partially thaw in refrigerator overnight. Heat through slowly in a covered skillet until a thermometer inserted in chicken reads 165°, stirring occasionally and adding a little broth or water if necessary.*

PER SERVING *315 cal., 8 g fat (1 g sat. fat), 95 mg chol., 400 mg sodium, 26 g carb., 1 g fiber, 35 g pro.* ***Diabetic Exchanges:*** *5 lean meat, 2 starch, ½ fat.*

EAT SMART

Slow Cooker Chicken & Black Bean Tacos

PREP: 20 MIN. • **COOK:** 4¼ HOURS
MAKES: 6 SERVINGS

- **1 can (8 ounces) crushed pineapple**
- **½ cup salsa**
- **2 green onions, sliced**
- **1 teaspoon grated lime peel**
- **¼ cup lime juice**
- **½ teaspoon chili powder**
- **¼ teaspoon garlic powder**
- **¼ teaspoon ground cumin**
- **⅛ teaspoon each salt, cayenne pepper and pepper**
- **1 pound boneless skinless chicken thighs**
- **1 can (15 ounces) black beans, rinsed and drained**
- **12 flour tortillas (6 inches), warmed**
- **Toppings: shredded Mexican cheese blend, shredded lettuce and chopped avocado**

1. Combine the first five ingredients; stir in seasonings. Place chicken in a 3-qt. slow cooker; add pineapple mixture. Cook, covered, on low 4-5 hours or until chicken is tender.

2. Remove chicken; cool slightly. Shred meat with two forks; return to slow cooker. Stir in beans.

3. Cook, covered, on low 15-20 minutes longer or until heated through. Using a slotted spoon, serve chicken mixture in tortillas with toppings.

PER SERVING *387 cal., 12 g fat (2 g sat. fat), 50 mg chol., 757 mg sodium, 47 g carb., 3 g fiber, 24 g pro.* ***Diabetic Exchanges:*** *3 starch, 3 lean meat.*

Boneless skinless **chicken thighs** work well in the **slow cooker**. The meat shreds easily, yet **stays moist** due its slightly higher fat content.

"My husband and I love Mexican food, and these tacos have become one of our top meals. Try setting out the toppings in different bowls on the table so everyone can help themselves to their favorites."
—**LAURA RODRIGUEZ** WILLOUGHBY, OH

SLOW COOKER CHICKEN & BLACK BEAN TACOS

FREEZE IT

Honey Pineapple Chicken

I adapted a dinnertime favorite for my slow cooker because it's so much easier to do the preparation in advance, then let the chicken cook on its own while I do other things. Your family will love the combination of sweet and savory flavors.
—CAROL GILLESPIE CHAMBERSBURG, PA

PREP: 15 MIN. • **COOK:** 3 HOURS
MAKES: 8 SERVINGS

- **3 pounds boneless skinless chicken breast halves**
- **2 tablespoons canola oil**
- **1 can (8 ounces) unsweetened crushed pineapple, undrained**
- **1 cup packed brown sugar**
- **½ cup honey**
- **⅓ cup lemon juice**
- **¼ cup butter, melted**
- **2 tablespoons prepared mustard**
- **2 teaspoons reduced-sodium soy sauce**

1. In a large skillet, brown chicken in oil in batches on both sides; transfer to a 5-qt. slow cooker. In a small bowl, combine the remaining ingredients; pour over chicken.
2. Cover and cook on low for 3-4 hours or until meat is tender. Strain cooking liquid, reserving pineapple. Serve pineapple with the chicken.
FREEZE OPTION *Cool chicken mixture. Freeze in freezer containers. To use, partially thaw in refrigerator overnight. Heat through slowly in a covered skillet until a thermometer inserted in chicken reads 165°, stirring occasionally and adding a little water if necessary.*

HONEY PINEAPPLE CHICKEN

"I created this recipe for my boys, who love dark meat. It reminds me of our traditional holiday turkey that's seasoned with sage. But this is more convenient than cooking a whole turkey."
—NATALIE SWANSON BALTIMORE, MD

EAT SMART

Sage Turkey Thighs

PREP: 15 MIN. • **COOK:** 6 HOURS
MAKES: 4 SERVINGS

- **4 medium carrots, halved**
- **1 medium onion, chopped**
- **½ cup water**
- **2 garlic cloves, minced**
- **1½ teaspoons rubbed sage, divided**
- **2 turkey thighs or turkey drumsticks (2 pounds total), skin removed**
- **1 tablespoon cornstarch**
- **¼ cup cold water**
- **¼ teaspoon salt**
- **⅛ teaspoon pepper**
- **1 teaspoon browning sauce, optional**

1. In a 3-qt. slow cooker, combine the carrots, onion, water, garlic and 1 teaspoon sage. Top with turkey. Sprinkle with remaining sage. Cover and cook on low for 6-8 hours or until a meat thermometer reads 180°.
2. Remove turkey to a serving platter; keep warm. Strain broth, reserving vegetables. Skim fat from cooking juices; transfer to a small saucepan.
3. Place vegetables in a food processor; cover and process until smooth. Add to cooking juices. Bring to a boil. Combine cornstarch and water until smooth. Gradually stir into the pan. Add salt, pepper and, if desired, browning sauce. Bring to a boil; cook and stir for 2 minutes or until thickened. Serve with turkey.
PER SERVING *277 cal., 8 g fat (3 g sat. fat), 96 mg chol., 280 mg sodium, 15 g carb., 3 g fiber, 34 g pro.* ***Diabetic Exchanges:*** *4 lean meat, 3 vegetable.*

FIESTA-TWISTED BRUNSWICK STEW

Fiesta-Twisted Brunswick Stew

Traditionally made with game, my updated Brunswick stew that uses chicken and spicy sausage is a modern mom's best friend.

—**DONNA MARIE RYAN** TOPSFIELD, MA

PREP: 20 MIN. • **COOK:** 5 HOURS
MAKES: 9 SERVINGS (3½ QUARTS)

- **½ pound uncooked chorizo or bulk spicy pork sausage**
- **1 large potato, cubed**
- **1 large onion, chopped**
- **1 large green pepper, chopped**
- **3 jalapeno peppers, seeded and chopped**
- **1 can (28 ounces) crushed tomatoes**
- **1 jar (26 ounces) marinara sauce**
- **1 can (14¾ ounces) cream-style corn**
- **1 tablespoon Cajun seasoning**
- **1 garlic clove, minced**
- **½ teaspoon sugar**
- **½ teaspoon pepper**
- **¼ teaspoon salt**
- **⅓ cup all-purpose flour**
- **1 can (14½ ounces) chicken broth**
- **2 pounds bone-in chicken breast halves, skin removed**
- **1 cup cut fresh green beans**
- **2 tablespoons minced fresh cilantro**
- **Shredded Asiago cheese**

1. Crumble chorizo into a small skillet; cook over medium heat for 6-8 minutes or until fully cooked. Drain. Transfer to a 6-qt. slow cooker. Add the potato, onion, green pepper, jalapenos, tomatoes, marinara sauce, corn, Cajun seasoning, garlic, sugar, pepper and salt.

2. In a small bowl, combine flour and broth until smooth; stir into slow cooker. Add the chicken. Cover and cook on low for 5-6 hours or until chicken and vegetables are tender, adding green beans and cilantro during the last 2 hours of cooking.

3. Remove chicken from slow cooker. When cool enough to handle, remove meat from bones; discard bones. Cut meat into bite-size pieces and return to slow cooker; heat through. Sprinkle servings with cheese.

NOTE *Wear disposable gloves when cutting hot peppers; the oils can burn skin. Avoid touching your face.*

EAT SMART

Southern Barbecue Spaghetti Sauce

I revamped our favorite sloppy joe recipe into this thick spaghetti sauce that simmers in the slow cooker. The flavor is jazzy enough to be interesting to adults, yet mild enough for the kids to enjoy.

—**RHONDA MELANSON** SARNIA, ON

PREP: 20 MIN. • **COOK:** 4 HOURS
MAKES: 12 SERVINGS

- **1 pound lean ground turkey**
- **2 medium onions, chopped**
- **1½ cups sliced fresh mushrooms**
- **1 medium green pepper, chopped**
- **2 garlic cloves, minced**
- **1 can (14½ ounces) diced tomatoes, undrained**
- **1 can (12 ounces) tomato paste**
- **1 can (8 ounces) tomato sauce**
- **1 cup ketchup**
- **½ cup beef broth**
- **2 tablespoons Worcestershire sauce**
- **2 tablespoons brown sugar**
- **1 tablespoon ground cumin**
- **2 teaspoons chili powder**
- **12 cups hot cooked spaghetti**

1. In a large nonstick skillet, cook the turkey, onions, mushrooms and green pepper over medium heat until meat is no longer pink. Add garlic; cook 1 minute longer. Drain.

2. Transfer to a 3-qt. slow cooker. Stir in the tomatoes, tomato paste, tomato sauce, ketchup, broth, Worcestershire sauce, brown sugar, cumin and chili powder. Cover and cook on low for 4-5 hours or until vegetables are tender. Serve with spaghetti.

PER SERVING *342 cal., 4 g fat (1 g sat. fat), 30 mg chol., 491 mg sodium, 60 g carb., 5 g fiber, 17 g pro.*

Green peppers are unripened versions of **red, yellow** or **orange** peppers. Use one of these for more **sweetness.**

CHICKEN CORN BREAD CASSEROLE

"I love this super-easy chicken recipe because it tastes like Thanksgiving, but without all the hassle. It's such a hearty, delicious meal for the fall or winter season."
—**NANCY BARKER** PEORIA, AZ

Chicken Corn Bread Casserole

PREP: 40 MIN. • **COOK:** 3 HOURS
MAKES: 6 SERVINGS

- **5 cups cubed corn bread**
- **¼ cup butter, cubed**
- **1 large onion, chopped (about 2 cups)**
- **4 celery ribs, chopped (about 2 cups)**
- **3 cups shredded cooked chicken**
- **1 can (10¾ ounces) condensed cream of chicken soup, undiluted**
- **1 can (10¾ ounces) condensed cream of mushroom soup, undiluted**
- **½ cup reduced-sodium chicken broth**
- **1 teaspoon poultry seasoning**
- **½ teaspoon salt**
- **½ teaspoon rubbed sage**
- **¼ teaspoon pepper**

1. Preheat oven to 350°. Place bread cubes in an ungreased 15x10x1-in. baking pan. Bake 20-25 minutes or until toasted. Cool on baking pan.
2. In a large skillet, heat butter over medium-high heat. Add onion and celery; cook and stir 6-8 minutes or until tender. Transfer to a greased 4-qt. slow cooker. Stir in corn bread, chicken, soups, broth and seasonings.
3. Cook, covered, on low 3-4 hours or until heated through.

The corn bread casserole is a great way to use up dry, stale **corn bread**. Bake a large pan of corn bread and **enjoy it fresh** with your favorite chili. Use the leftovers to prepare this **tasty** recipe later on.

PEPPERY CHICKEN WITH POTATOES

Peppery Chicken with Potatoes

I like to start this recipe early on Sunday. Later, after we have come home from church, the perfectly cooked chicken is ready for us. It makes an excellent lunch for family or company.
—LORI DRAVES HIGHLAND, WI

PREP: 20 MIN.
COOK: 5 HOURS + STANDING
MAKES: 4 SERVINGS

- **1 pound red potatoes (about 6 medium), cut into wedges**
- **1 large onion, chopped**
- **2 teaspoons salt**
- **1 teaspoon paprika**
- **½ teaspoon onion powder**
- **½ teaspoon garlic powder**
- **½ teaspoon dried thyme**
- **½ teaspoon white pepper**
- **½ teaspoon cayenne pepper**
- **¼ teaspoon pepper**
- **1 broiler/fryer chicken (3½ to 4 pounds)**

1. Place potatoes and onion in a 6-qt. slow cooker. In a small bowl, mix seasonings. Tuck wings under chicken; tie drumsticks together. Rub seasoning mixture over outside and inside of chicken. Place chicken over vegetables.
2. Cook, covered, on low 5-6 hours or until a thermometer inserted in thickest part of thigh reads 170°-175°. Remove chicken from slow cooker; tent with foil. Let stand 15 minutes before carving.
3. Transfer vegetables to a platter; keep warm. If desired, skim fat and thicken cooking juices for gravy. Serve with chicken.

CHICKEN ATHENA

EAT SMART

Chicken Athena

With olives, sun-dried tomatoes, lemon juice and garlic, Greek flavors abound in my easy chicken dish that's prepared in the slow cooker. Serve it with orzo or couscous for a tasty accompaniment.

—RADELLE KNAPPENBERGER OVIEDO, FL

PREP: 15 MIN. • **COOK:** 4 HOURS
MAKES: 6 SERVINGS

- **6 boneless skinless chicken breast halves (6 ounces each)**
- **2 medium onions, chopped**
- **⅓ cup sun-dried tomatoes (not packed in oil), chopped**
- **⅓ cup pitted Greek olives, chopped**
- **2 tablespoons lemon juice**
- **1 tablespoon balsamic vinegar**
- **3 garlic cloves, minced**
- **½ teaspoon salt**

Place chicken in a 3-qt. slow cooker. Add the remaining ingredients. Cover and cook on low for 4 hours or until a thermometer reads 170°.

PER SERVING *237 cal., 6 g fat (1 g sat. fat), 94 mg chol., 467 mg sodium, 8 g carb., 1 g fiber, 36 g pro.* ***Diabetic Exchanges:*** *4 lean meat, 1 vegetable, 1 fat.*

EAT SMART

Greek Garlic Chicken

Lively flavors of the Greek Isles come through in this chicken entree. I created it so my husband and I could have a nice dinner after a busy day out and about.

—MARGEE BERRY WHITE SALMON, WA

PREP: 20 MIN. • **COOK:** 3½ HOURS
MAKES: 6 SERVINGS

- **½ cup chopped onion**
- **1 tablespoon plus 1 teaspoon olive oil, divided**
- **3 tablespoons minced garlic**
- **2½ cups chicken broth, divided**
- **¼ cup pitted Greek olives, chopped**
- **3 tablespoons chopped sun-dried tomatoes (not packed in oil)**
- **1 tablespoon quick-cooking tapioca**
- **2 teaspoons grated lemon peel**
- **1 teaspoon dried oregano**
- **6 boneless skinless chicken breast halves (6 ounces each)**
- **1¾ cups uncooked couscous**
- **½ cup crumbled feta cheese**

1. In a small skillet, saute onion in 1 tablespoon oil until crisp-tender. Add garlic; cook 1 minute longer.

2. Transfer to a 5-qt. slow cooker. Stir in ¾ cup broth, olives, tomatoes, tapioca, lemon peel and oregano. Add chicken. Cover and cook on low for 3½ to 4 hours or until chicken is tender.

3. In a large saucepan, bring remaining oil and broth to a boil. Stir in couscous. Cover and remove from the heat; let stand for 5 minutes or until broth is absorbed. Serve with chicken; sprinkle with feta cheese.

PER SERVING *318 cal., 8 g fat (2 g sat. fat), 21 mg chol., 625 mg sodium, 47 g carb., 3 g fiber, 16 g pro.*

EAT SMART

Slow Cooker Chicken Cacciatore

My husband and I milk 125 cows. There are days when there's just no time left for cooking! It's really nice to be able to come into the house at night and smell this wonderful dinner simmering.

—**AGGIE ARNOLD-NORMAN** LIBERTY, PA

PREP: 10 MIN. • **COOK:** 6 HOURS
MAKES: 6 SERVINGS

- **2 medium onions, thinly sliced**
- **1 broiler/fryer chicken (3 to 4 pounds), cut up and skin removed**
- **2 garlic cloves, minced**
- **1 to 2 teaspoons dried oregano**
- **1 teaspoon salt**
- **½ teaspoon dried basil**
- **¼ teaspoon pepper**
- **1 bay leaf**
- **1 can (14½ ounces) diced tomatoes, undrained**
- **1 can (8 ounces) tomato sauce**
- **1 can (4 ounces) mushroom stems and pieces, drained or 1 cup sliced fresh mushrooms**
- **¼ cup white wine or water**
- **Hot cooked pasta**

Place sliced onions in a 5-qt. slow cooker. Add the chicken, seasonings, tomatoes, tomato sauce, mushrooms and wine or water. Cover and cook on low for 6-8 hours or until chicken juices run clear. Discard bay leaf. Serve chicken with sauce over pasta.

PER SERVING *207 cal., 6 g fat (2 g sat. fat), 73 mg chol., 787 mg sodium, 11 g carb., 3 g fiber, 27 g pro.* ***Diabetic Exchanges:*** *4 lean meat, 2 vegetable.*

LOUISIANA RED BEANS AND RICE

FREEZE IT

Louisiana Red Beans and Rice

Smoked turkey sausage and red pepper flakes add zip to this slow-cooked version of the New Orleans classic. For extra heat, add red pepper sauce at the table.

—**JULIA BUSHREE** COMMERCE CITY, CO

PREP: 20 MIN. • **COOK:** 8 HOURS
MAKES: 8 SERVINGS

- **4 cans (16 ounces each) kidney beans, rinsed and drained**
- **1 can (14½ ounces) diced tomatoes, undrained**
- **1 package (14 ounces) smoked turkey sausage, sliced**
- **3 celery ribs, chopped**
- **1 large onion, chopped**
- **1 cup chicken broth**
- **1 medium green pepper, chopped**
- **1 small sweet red pepper, chopped**
- **6 garlic cloves, minced**
- **1 bay leaf**
- **½ teaspoon crushed red pepper flakes**
- **2 green onions, chopped**
- **Hot cooked rice**

1. In a 4- or 5-qt. slow cooker, combine the first 11 ingredients. Cook, covered, on low 8-10 hours or until vegetables are tender.

2. Stir before serving. Remove bay leaf. Serve with green onions and rice.

FREEZE OPTION *Discard bay leaf and freeze cooled bean mixture in freezer containers. To use, partially thaw in refrigerator overnight. Heat through in a saucepan, stirring occasionally and adding a little broth or water if necessary. Serve as directed.*

FREEZE IT

Slow-Cooked Southwest Chicken

With just 15 minutes of prep, you'll be out of the kitchen in no time. This delicious low-fat dish gets even better with a garnish of reduced-fat sour cream and fresh cilantro.

—BRANDI CASTILLO SANTA MARIA, CA

PREP: 15 MIN. • **COOK:** 6 HOURS
MAKES: 6 SERVINGS

- **2 cans (15 ounces each) black beans, rinsed and drained**
- **1 can (14½ ounces) reduced-sodium chicken broth**
- **1 can (14½ ounces) diced tomatoes with mild green chilies, undrained**
- **½ pound boneless skinless chicken breast**
- **1 jar (8 ounces) chunky salsa**
- **1 cup frozen corn**
- **1 tablespoon dried parsley flakes**
- **1 teaspoon ground cumin**
- **¼ teaspoon pepper**
- **3 cups hot cooked rice**

1. In a 2- or 3-qt. slow cooker, combine the beans, broth, tomatoes, chicken, salsa, corn and seasonings. Cover and cook on low for 6-8 hours or until a thermometer reads 170°.
2. Shred chicken with two forks and return to the slow cooker; heat through. Serve with rice.

FREEZE OPTION *After shredding chicken, freeze cooled mixture in freezer containers. To use, partially thaw in refrigerator overnight. Heat through in a saucepan, stirring occasionally and adding a little broth or water if necessary.*

SLOW-COOKED SOUTHWEST CHICKEN

EAT SMART

Chicken a la King

When I know I'll be having a busy day with little time to prepare meals, I use my slow cooker to make Chicken a la King. It smells so good while it's cooking.

—ELEANOR MIELKE SNOHOMISH, WA

PREP: 10 MIN. • **COOK:** 7½ HOURS
MAKES: 6 SERVINGS

- **1 can (10¾ ounces) reduced-fat reduced-sodium condensed cream of chicken soup, undiluted**
- **3 tablespoons all-purpose flour**
- **¼ teaspoon pepper**
- **Dash cayenne pepper**
- **1 pound boneless skinless chicken breasts, cubed**
- **1 celery rib, chopped**
- **½ cup chopped green pepper**
- **¼ cup chopped onion**
- **1 package (10 ounces) frozen peas, thawed**
- **2 tablespoons diced pimientos, drained**
- **Hot cooked rice**

1. In a 3-qt. slow cooker, combine soup, flour, pepper and cayenne until smooth. Stir in chicken, celery, green pepper and onion.
2. Cover and cook on low for 7-8 hours or until meat juices run clear. Stir in peas and pimientos. Cook 30 minutes longer or until heated through. Serve with rice.

PER SERVING *183 cal., 3 g fat (0 sat. fat), 52 mg chol., 284 mg sodium, 16 g carb., 0 fiber, 22 g pro.* ***Diabetic Exchanges:*** *2 lean meat, 1 starch.*

Slow-Cooked Turkey Stroganoff

PREP: 20 MIN. • **COOK:** 6 HOURS
MAKES: 6 SERVINGS

- **4 turkey thighs (about 4 pounds)**
- **1 large onion, halved and thinly sliced**
- **1 can (10¾ ounces) condensed cream of celery soup, undiluted**
- **⅓ cup water**
- **3 garlic cloves, minced**
- **2 teaspoons dried tarragon**
- **½ teaspoon salt**
- **½ teaspoon pepper**
- **½ cup sour cream**
- **Hot cooked egg noodles**

1. Place turkey and onion in a 5-qt. slow cooker. In a large bowl, whisk soup, water, garlic, tarragon, salt and pepper until blended; pour over top. Cook, covered, on low 6-8 hours or until meat is tender.

2. Remove turkey from slow cooker. When cool enough to handle, remove meat from bones; discard bones. Shred meat with two forks. Whisk sour cream into the cooking juices; return meat to slow cooker. Serve with egg noodles.

"I have been making this tasty dish for 30-plus years. Our family loves turkey and I make a variety of turkey dishes, but this is our favorite. I love it because I can put it in my slow cooker before I leave for work and come home to a hot, delicious dinner. It's great served over cooked noodles, rice, mashed potatoes or polenta." —CINDY ADAMS TRACY, CA

SLOW-COOKED TURKEY STROGANOFF

FREEZE IT

Fruited Chicken

I've worked full time for more than 30 years, and this convenient recipe has been a lifesaver. It smells heavenly when I walk in the door in the evening.

—MIRIEN CHURCH AURORA, CO

PREP: 10 MIN. • **COOK:** 4 HOURS
MAKES: 6 SERVINGS

- **1 large onion, sliced**
- **6 boneless skinless chicken breast halves (6 ounces each)**
- **⅓ cup orange juice**
- **2 tablespoons soy sauce**
- **2 tablespoons Worcestershire sauce**
- **2 tablespoons Dijon mustard**
- **1 tablespoon grated orange peel**
- **2 garlic cloves, minced**
- **½ cup chopped dried apricots**
- **½ cup dried cranberries**
- **Hot cooked rice**

1. Place onion and chicken in a 5-qt. slow cooker. In a small bowl, combine the orange juice, soy sauce, Worcestershire sauce, mustard, orange peel and garlic; pour over chicken. Sprinkle with apricots and cranberries.

2. Cover and cook on low for 4-5 hours or until a meat thermometer reads 170°. Serve with rice.

FREEZE OPTION *Freeze cooled chicken mixture in freezer containers. To use, partially thaw in refrigerator overnight. Heat through in a covered saucepan, gently stirring and adding a little broth or water if necessary.*

SPICY CHICKEN AND RICE

Spicy Chicken and Rice

As a working mom with two kids, I have little time to prepare something hearty during the week. This recipe is easily tossed together in the morning and fabulous to come home to at night. Both my picky eaters love it!

—JESSICA COSTELLO FITCHBURG, MA

PREP: 20 MIN. • **COOK:** 5½ HOURS
MAKES: 8 SERVINGS

- **1½ pounds boneless skinless chicken breast halves**
- **2 cans (14½ ounces each) diced tomatoes with mild green chilies, undrained**
- **2 medium green peppers, chopped**
- **1 medium onion, chopped**
- **1 garlic clove, minced**
- **1 teaspoon smoked paprika**
- **¾ teaspoon salt**
- **½ teaspoon ground cumin**
- **½ teaspoon ground chipotle pepper**
- **6 cups cooked brown rice**
- **1 can (15 ounces) black beans, rinsed and drained**
- **½ cup shredded cheddar cheese**
- **½ cup reduced-fat sour cream**

1. Place chicken in a 4 – or 5-qt. slow cooker. In a large bowl, combine the tomatoes, green peppers, onion, garlic, paprika, salt, cumin and chipotle pepper; pour over chicken. Cover and cook on low for 5-6 hours or until chicken is tender.

2. Remove chicken; cool slightly. Shred with two forks and return to the slow cooker. Stir in rice and beans; heat through. Garnish with cheese and sour cream.

Beans pack a nutritional one-two punch of **protein and fiber**, which helps you feel fuller longer. They're an **economical** way to stretch the **meat** in a recipe.

Curry Chicken Stew

My Grandma Inky grew up in India and passed down this recipe to my mother, who then passed it down to me. The recipe brings back fond memories of the family gathered around the table, enjoying this delicious meal and catching up on one another's day. I tweaked the ingredients a bit to fit my toddler's taste buds, but it's just as scrumptious as Grandma's own.

—TERESA FLOWERS SACRAMENTO, CA

PREP: 15 MIN. • **COOK:** 4 HOURS
MAKES: 6 SERVINGS

- **2 cans (14½ ounces each) chicken broth**
- **1 can (10¾ ounces) condensed cream of chicken soup, undiluted**
- **1 tub Knorr concentrated chicken stock**
- **4 garlic cloves, minced**
- **1 tablespoon curry powder**
- **¼ teaspoon salt**
- **¼ teaspoon cayenne pepper**
- **¼ teaspoon pepper**
- **6 boneless skinless chicken breasts (6 ounces each)**
- **1 medium green pepper, cut into thin strips**
- **1 medium onion, thinly sliced**
- **Hot cooked rice**
- **Chopped fresh cilantro and chutney, optional**

1. In a large bowl, combine the first eight ingredients. Place chicken, green pepper and onion in a 5- or 6-qt. slow cooker; pour broth mixture over top. Cook, covered, on low 4-5 hours or until chicken and vegetables are tender.

2. Remove chicken and cool slightly. Cut or shred meat into bite-size pieces and return to slow cooker; heat through. Serve with rice. If desired, top with cilantro and chutney.

CURRY CHICKEN STEW

Slow-Cooked Lemon Chicken

Garlic, oregano and lemon juice give spark to this memorable main dish. It's easy to fix— just brown the chicken in a skillet, then let the slow cooker do the work.

—WALTER POWELL WILMINGTON, DE

PREP: 20 MIN. • **COOK:** 5¼ HOURS
MAKES: 6 SERVINGS

- **6 bone-in chicken breast halves (12 ounces each), skin removed**
- **1 teaspoon dried oregano**
- **½ teaspoon seasoned salt**
- **¼ teaspoon pepper**
- **2 tablespoons butter**
- **¼ cup water**
- **3 tablespoons lemon juice**
- **2 garlic cloves, minced**
- **1 teaspoon chicken bouillon granules**
- **2 teaspoons minced fresh parsley**
- **Hot cooked rice**

1. Pat chicken dry with paper towels. Combine the oregano, seasoned salt and pepper; rub over chicken. In a skillet over medium heat, brown the chicken in butter; transfer to a 5-qt. slow cooker. Add water, lemon juice, garlic and bouillon to the skillet; bring to a boil, stirring to loosen browned bits. Pour over chicken.

2. Cover and cook on low for 5-6 hours. Baste chicken with cooking juices. Add parsley. Cover and cook 15-30 minutes longer or until meat juices run clear. If desired, remove chicken to a platter and keep warm; thicken cooking juices. Serve over chicken and rice.

CREAMY GARLIC-LEMON CHICKEN

Creamy Garlic-Lemon Chicken

I needed an easy way to prepare my family's favorite meal, lemon chicken, and this recipe is it! My entire family loves this rich slow-cooker dish, and everyone who eats it asks for the recipe—it's a keeper. I serve the chicken over a bed of rice or couscous and spoon some of the creamy sauce over the top.

—**NAN SLAUGHTER** SAMMAMISH, WA

PREP: 15 MIN. • **COOK:** 3 HOURS
MAKES: 6 SERVINGS

- **1 cup vegetable broth**
- **1½ teaspoons grated lemon peel**
- **3 tablespoons lemon juice**
- **2 tablespoons capers, drained**
- **3 garlic cloves, minced**
- **½ teaspoon pepper**
- **6 boneless skinless chicken breast halves (6 ounces each)**
- **2 tablespoons butter**
- **2 tablespoons all-purpose flour**
- **½ cup heavy whipping cream**
- **Hot cooked rice**

1. In a small bowl, combine the first six ingredients. Place chicken in a 5-qt. slow cooker; pour broth mixture over chicken. Cook, covered, on low 3-4 hours or until chicken is tender.
2. Remove chicken from slow cooker; keep warm. In a large saucepan, melt butter over medium heat. Stir in flour until smooth; gradually whisk in cooking juices. Bring to a boil, stirring constantly; cook and stir 1-2 minutes or until thickened. Remove from heat and stir in cream. Serve chicken and rice with sauce.

EAT SMART

Slow-Cooked Turkey with Berry Compote

We love to eat turkey at our house and this delicious dish is a great way to get all that yummy flavor without heating up the house; the berries make the perfect summer chutney. For browner turkey, broil for a few minutes before serving.

—**MARGARET BRACHER** ROBERTSDALE, AL

PREP: 35 MIN. • **COOK:** 3 HOURS
MAKES: 12 SERVINGS (3¼ CUPS COMPOTE)

- **1 teaspoon salt**
- **½ teaspoon garlic powder**
- **½ teaspoon dried thyme**
- **½ teaspoon pepper**
- **2 boneless turkey breast halves (2 pounds each)**
- **⅓ cup water**

COMPOTE

- **2 medium apples, peeled and finely chopped**
- **2 cups fresh raspberries**
- **2 cups fresh blueberries**
- **1 cup white grape juice**
- **¼ teaspoon crushed red pepper flakes**
- **¼ teaspoon ground ginger**

1. Mix salt, garlic powder, thyme and pepper; rub over turkey breasts. Place in a 5- or 6-qt. slow cooker. Pour water around turkey. Cook, covered, on low 3-4 hours (a thermometer inserted in turkey should read at least 165°).
2. Remove turkey from slow cooker; tent with foil. Let stand 10 minutes before slicing.
3. Meanwhile, in a large saucepan, combine compote ingredients. Bring to a boil. Reduce heat to medium; cook, uncovered, 15-20 minutes or until slightly thickened and apples are tender, stirring occasionally. Serve turkey with compote.

PER SERVING *215 cal., 1 g fat (trace sat. fat), 94 mg chol., 272 mg sodium, 12 g carb., 2 g fiber, 38 g pro.* ***Diabetic Exchanges:*** *5 lean meat, 1 starch.*

SLOW-COOKED TURKEY WITH BERRY COMPOTE

Other Entrees

With the **tempting recipes** that follow, it's easy to cook up something new with your slow cooker. Prepare hearty **meatless stews**, beautiful **brunch** dishes, savory **pork, ham and lamb**—even **satisfying seafood** entrees—all in this **superstar** appliance.

Pork Chop Potato Dinner

This meal of tender pork chops with creamy potatoes is a snap to assemble—and my family loves it!

—DAWN HUIZINGA OWATONNA, MN

PREP: 10 MIN. • **COOK:** 5¼ HOURS
MAKES: 6 SERVINGS

- **6 bone-in pork loin chops (8 ounces each)**
- **1 tablespoon canola oil**
- **1 package (30 ounces) frozen shredded hash brown potatoes, thawed**
- **1½ cups (6 ounces) shredded cheddar cheese, divided**
- **1 can (10¾ ounces) condensed cream of celery soup, undiluted**
- **½ cup milk**
- **½ cup sour cream**
- **½ teaspoon seasoned salt**
- **⅛ teaspoon pepper**
- **1 can (2.8 ounces) French-fried onions, divided**

1. In a large skillet, brown chops in oil on both sides; set aside. In a large bowl, combine the potatoes, 1 cup cheese, soup, milk, sour cream, seasoned salt and pepper. Stir in half of the onions.

2. Transfer to a greased 5-qt. slow cooker; top with pork chops. Cover and cook on low for 5-6 hours or until meat is tender. Sprinkle with remaining cheese and onions. Cover and cook 15 minutes longer or until cheese is melted.

Nutmeg is the secret spice in many dishes. It's commonly used in white **sauces, pasta and potato** dishes. Be careful not to overdo it...a **small amount** goes a long way.

BUFFALO SHRIMP MAC & CHEESE

Buffalo Shrimp Mac & Cheese

For a rich and slightly spicy shrimp and pasta recipe, you can't beat this crowd-pleasing slow cooker dish. It's a nice new twist on popular Buffalo chicken dishes.

—ROBIN HAAS CRANSTON, RI

PREP: 15 MIN. • **COOK:** 3½ HOURS
MAKES: 6 SERVINGS

- **2 cups 2% milk**
- **1 cup half-and-half cream**
- **2 tablespoons Louisiana-style hot sauce**
- **1 tablespoon butter**
- **1 teaspoon ground mustard**
- **½ teaspoon onion powder**
- **¼ teaspoon white pepper**
- **¼ teaspoon ground nutmeg**
- **2 cups (8 ounces) finely shredded cheddar cheese**
- **1 cup (4 ounces) shredded Gouda or Swiss cheese**
- **1½ cups uncooked elbow macaroni**
- **¾ pound frozen cooked salad shrimp, thawed**
- **1 cup (4 ounces) crumbled blue cheese**
- **2 tablespoons minced fresh chives**
- **2 tablespoons minced fresh parsley**
- **Additional Louisiana-style hot sauce, optional**

1. In a 3-qt. slow cooker, combine the first eight ingredients; stir in shredded cheeses and macaroni. Cook, covered, on low 3 to 3½ hours or until macaroni is almost tender.

2. Stir in shrimp and blue cheese; cook, covered, 30-35 minutes longer or until heated through. Just before serving, stir in chives, parsley and, if desired, additional hot sauce.

SLOW COOKER FRITTATA PROVENCAL

EAT SMART

Slow Cooker Frittata Provencal

This amazing recipe means that a delectable dinner is ready when I walk in the door. The slow cooker meal also makes an elegant breakfast for holiday mornings.

—**CONNIE EATON** PITTSBURGH, PA

PREP: 30 MIN. • **COOK:** 3 HOURS
MAKES: 6 SERVINGS

- **½ cup water**
- **1 tablespoon olive oil**
- **1 medium Yukon Gold potato, peeled and sliced**
- **1 small onion, thinly sliced**
- **½ teaspoon smoked paprika**
- **12 eggs**
- **1 teaspoon minced fresh thyme or ¼ teaspoon dried thyme**
- **1 teaspoon hot pepper sauce**
- **½ teaspoon salt**
- **¼ teaspoon pepper**
- **1 log (4 ounces) fresh goat cheese, coarsely crumbled, divided**
- **½ cup chopped soft sun-dried tomatoes (not packed in oil)**

1. Layer two 24-in. pieces of aluminum foil; starting with a long side, fold up foil to create a 1-in. wide strip. Shape strip into a coil to make a rack for bottom of a 6-qt. oval slow cooker. Add water to slow cooker; set foil rack in water.

2. In a large skillet, heat oil over medium-high heat. Add potato and onion; cook and stir 5-7 minutes or until potato is lightly browned. Stir in paprika. Transfer to a greased 1½-qt. baking dish (dish must fit in slow cooker).

3. In a large bowl, whisk eggs, thyme, pepper sauce, salt and pepper; stir in 2 ounces cheese. Pour over potato mixture. Top with tomatoes and remaining goat cheese. Place dish on foil rack.

4. Cook, covered, on low 3 hours or until eggs are set and a knife inserted near the center comes out clean.

EDITOR'S NOTE *This recipe was tested with sun-dried tomatoes that are ready-to-use without soaking. When using other sun-dried tomatoes that are not oil-packed, cover with boiling water and let stand until soft. Drain before using.*

PER SERVING *245 cal., 14 g fat (5 g sat. fat), 385 mg chol., 338 mg sodium, 12 g carb., 2 g fiber, 15 g pro.* ***Diabetic Exchanges:*** *2 medium-fat meat, 1 starch, ½ fat.*

Ham and Bean Stew

You only need five ingredients to fix this thick and flavorful stew. It's always a favorite with my family ... and with me, because it's so easy to make! I top bowls of it with a sprinkling of grated cheese.

—**TERESA D'AMATO** EAST GRANBY, CT

PREP: 5 MIN. • **COOK:** 7 HOURS
MAKES: 6 SERVINGS

- **2 cans (16 ounces each) baked beans**
- **2 medium potatoes, peeled and cubed**
- **2 cups cubed fully cooked ham**
- **1 celery rib, chopped**
- **½ cup water**

In a 3-qt. slow cooker, combine all ingredients; mix well. Cover and cook on low for 7 hours or until the potatoes are tender.

Spaghetti Pork Chops

Tender pork chops are simmered to perfection in a tangy sauce and then served over pasta. This was one of my mother's most-loved recipes.

—**ELLEN GALLAVAN** MIDLAND, MI

PREP: 20 MIN. • **COOK:** 6 HOURS
MAKES: 6 SERVINGS

- **3 cans (8 ounces each) tomato sauce**
- **1 can (10¾ ounces) condensed tomato soup, undiluted**
- **1 small onion, finely chopped**
- **1 bay leaf**
- **1 teaspoon celery seed**
- **½ teaspoon Italian seasoning**
- **6 bone-in pork loin chops (8 ounces each)**
- **2 tablespoons olive oil**
- **Hot cooked spaghetti**

1. In a 5-qt. slow cooker, combine the tomato sauce, soup, onion, bay leaf, celery seed and Italian seasoning.

2. In a large skillet, brown pork chops in oil. Add to the slow cooker. Cover and cook on low for 6-8 hours or until meat is tender. Discard bay leaf. Serve chops and sauce over spaghetti.

"My roast with a hint of orange is popular with adults and children alike. It's an excellent take-along meal for potlucks."
—RADELLE KNAPPENBERGER OVIEDO, FL

EAT SMART

Light Glazed Pork Roast

PREP: 30 MIN. • **COOK:** 4 HOURS
MAKES: 16 SERVINGS

- **1 boneless pork loin roast (4 pounds), trimmed**
- **1 tablespoon olive oil**
- **1 tablespoon butter, melted**
- **⅔ cup thawed orange juice concentrate**
- **⅓ cup water**
- **3 garlic cloves, minced**
- **1½ teaspoons salt**
- **½ teaspoon pepper**

GLAZE

- **¼ cup packed brown sugar**
- **2 tablespoons balsamic vinegar**
- **1 tablespoon thawed orange juice concentrate**
- **1 garlic clove, minced**
- **1 can (11 ounces) mandarin oranges, drained, optional**

1. Cut roast in half. In a large skillet, brown roast in oil and butter on all sides.
2. Transfer to a 5-qt. slow cooker. Add the orange juice concentrate, water, garlic, salt and pepper. Cover and cook on low for 4-6 hours or until meat is tender.
3. For glaze, in a small saucepan, combine the brown sugar, vinegar, orange juice concentrate and garlic. Bring to a boil. Reduce heat; simmer, uncovered, for 3-5 minutes or until reduced to about 1/4 cup. Brush over roast. Garnish with oranges if desired.
PER SERVING *190 cal., 7 g fat (2 g sat. fat), 58 mg chol., 263 mg sodium, 9 g carb., trace fiber, 22 g pro.* ***Diabetic Exchanges:*** *3 lean meat, 1/2 starch.*

Cheesy Tater Tots & Canadian Bacon

This slow cooker meal was created to pay homage to my favorite style of pizza—Hawaiian with bacon and pineapple. The Tater Tots in this recipe make it family-friendly.
—LISA RENSHAW KANSAS CITY, MO

PREP: 15 MIN.
COOK: 4 HOURS + STANDING
MAKES: 8 SERVINGS

- **1 package (32 ounces) frozen Tater Tots, thawed**
- **8 ounces Canadian bacon, chopped**
- **1 cup frozen pepper strips, thawed and chopped**
- **1 medium onion, finely chopped**
- **1 can (8 ounces) pineapple tidbits, drained**
- **2 eggs**
- **3 cans (5 ounces each) evaporated milk**
- **1 can (15 ounces) pizza sauce**
- **1 cup (4 ounces) shredded provolone cheese**
- **½ cup grated Parmesan cheese, optional**

1. Place half of the Tater Tots in a greased 5-qt. slow cooker. Layer with Canadian bacon, peppers, onion and pineapple. Top with remaining Tater Tots. In a large bowl, whisk eggs, milk and pizza sauce; pour over top. Sprinkle with provolone cheese.
2. Cook, covered, on low 4-5 hours or until heated through. If desired, sprinkle with Parmesan cheese; let stand, covered, 20 minutes.

CHEESY TATER TOTS & CANADIAN BACON

PIZZA IN A POT

FREEZE IT

Pizza in a Pot

Since most kids will try anything to do with pizza, I rely on this recipe when one of my two teenage sons has a friend stay for dinner. It's always a hit with them.
—**ANITA DOUGHTY** WEST DES MOINES, IA

PREP: 15 MIN. • **COOK:** 8 HOURS
MAKES: 6 SERVINGS

- **1 pound bulk Italian sausage**
- **1 can (28 ounces) crushed tomatoes**
- **1 can (16 ounces) chili beans, undrained**
- **1 can (15 ounces) black beans, rinsed and drained**
- **1 can (2¼ ounces) sliced ripe olives, drained**
- **1 medium onion, chopped**
- **1 small green pepper, chopped**
- **2 garlic cloves, minced**
- **¼ cup grated Parmesan cheese**
- **1 tablespoon quick-cooking tapioca**
- **1 tablespoon dried basil**
- **1 bay leaf**
- **1 teaspoon salt**
- **½ teaspoon sugar**
- **Hot cooked pasta**
- **Shredded part-skim mozzarella cheese, optional**

1. In a large skillet over medium heat, cook the sausage until no longer pink; drain. Transfer to a 5-qt. slow cooker. Stir in the next 13 ingredients.
2. Cover and cook on low for 8-9 hours or until slightly thickened. Discard bay leaf. Stir before serving with pasta. Sprinkle with mozzarella cheese if desired.
FREEZE OPTION *Do not cook or add pasta. Freeze cooled sausage mixture in freezer containers. To use, partially thaw in refrigerator overnight. Cook pasta according to package directions. Place sausage mixture in a large skillet; heat through, stirring occasionally and adding a little water if necessary. Serve with pasta and, if desired, mozzarella cheese.*

Cajun Pork and Rice

PREP: 20 MIN. • **COOK:** 4¼ HOURS
MAKES: 4 SERVINGS

- **1½ teaspoons ground cumin**
- **1½ teaspoons chili powder**
- **1½ pounds boneless pork loin chops**
- **1 can (14½ ounces) petite diced tomatoes, undrained**
- **1 small onion, finely chopped**
- **1 celery rib, finely chopped**
- **1 small carrot, shredded**
- **1 garlic clove, minced**
- **½ teaspoon Louisiana-style hot sauce**
- **¼ teaspoon salt**
- **1½ cups uncooked instant rice**
- **1 cup reduced-sodium chicken broth**
- **1 teaspoon olive oil**
- **1 medium green pepper, julienned**

1. Mix cumin and chili powder; sprinkle pork chops with 2 teaspoon spice mixture. Transfer to a 4-qt. slow cooker.
2. In a small bowl, mix tomatoes, onion, celery, carrot, garlic, hot sauce, salt and remaining spice mixture; pour over chops. Cook, covered, on low 4-5 hours or until meat is tender.
3. Stir in rice and chicken broth, breaking up pork into pieces. Cook, covered, on low 10-15 minutes longer or until rice is tender. In a small skillet, heat oil over medium-high heat. Add green pepper; cook and stir 5-7 minutes or until crisp-tender. Serve with pork mixture.

To keep **pasta** from sticking together when cooking, use a large pot with **plenty of water**. Add a little cooking **oil** if desired (this also prevents boiling over).

CAJUN PORK AND RICE

This hearty Tex-Mex egg casserole is great outside of breakfast. I add a salad and dinner is on!
—**GAIL WATKINS** NORWALK, CA

CHILI & CHEESE CRUSTLESS QUICHE

Chili & Cheese Crustless Quiche

PREP: 15 MIN.
COOK: 3 HOURS + STANDING
MAKES: 6 SERVINGS

- **3 corn tortillas (6 inches)**
- **2 cans (4 ounces each) whole green chilies**
- **1 can (15 ounces) chili con carne**
- **1½ cups (6 ounces) shredded cheddar cheese, divided**
- **4 eggs**
- **1½ cups 2% milk**
- **1 cup biscuit/baking mix**
- **¼ teaspoon salt**
- **¼ teaspoon pepper**
- **1 teaspoon hot pepper sauce, optional**
- **1 can (4 ounces) chopped green chilies**
- **2 medium tomatoes, sliced**
- **Sour cream, optional**

1. In a greased 4- or 5-qt. slow cooker, layer tortillas, whole green chilies, chili con carne and 1 cup cheese.
2. In a small bowl, whisk eggs, milk, biscuit mix, salt, pepper and, if desired, pepper sauce until blended; pour into slow cooker. Top with chopped green chilies and tomatoes.
3. Cook, covered, on low 3-4 hours or until a thermometer reads 160°, sprinkling with remaining cheese during the last 30 minutes of cooking. Turn off slow cooker; remove insert and let stand 15 minutes before serving. If desired, top with sour cream.

FREEZE IT

Pork Burritos

As a working mother, I depend on my slow cooker to help feed my family. We all love the spicy but slightly sweet flavor of these tender burritos.
—**KELLY GENGLER** THERESA, WI

PREP: 25 MIN. • **COOK:** 8 HOURS
MAKES: 10 BURRITOS

- **1 boneless pork shoulder butt roast (3 to 4 pounds)**
- **1 can (14½ ounces) diced tomatoes with mild green chilies, undrained**
- **¼ cup chili powder**
- **3 tablespoons minced garlic**
- **2 tablespoons lime juice**
- **2 tablespoons honey**
- **1 tablespoon chopped seeded jalapeno pepper**
- **1 teaspoon salt**
- **10 flour tortillas (8 inches), warmed**
- **Sliced avocado and sour cream, optional**

1. Cut roast in half; place in a 5-qt. slow cooker. In a blender, combine the tomatoes, chili powder, garlic, lime juice, honey, jalapeno and salt; cover and process until smooth. Pour over pork. Cover and cook on low for 8-10 hours or until meat is tender.
2. Remove roast; cool slightly. Shred pork with two forks and return to slow cooker. Using a slotted spoon, place about 1/2 cup pork mixture down the center of each tortilla; top with avocado and sour cream if desired. Fold sides and ends over filling and roll up.

FREEZE OPTION *Omit avocado and sour cream. Individually wrap cooled burritos in paper towels and foil; freeze in a resealable plastic freezer bag. To use, remove foil; place paper towel-wrapped burrito on a microwave-safe plate. Microwave on high for 3-4 minutes or until heated through, turning once. Let stand 20 seconds. Serve with avocado and sour cream if desired.*

NOTE *Wear disposable gloves when cutting hot peppers; the oils can burn skin. Avoid touching your face.*

EAT SMART

Cranberry-Mustard Pork Loin

This dressed-up pork loin is easy because you only have to spend a few minutes preparing it. The roast is a family favorite because it's so tasty, and a favorite of mine because it's so fast to get started!
—LAURA COOK WILDWOOD, MO

PREP: 15 MIN. • **COOK:** 4 HOURS
MAKES: 8 SERVINGS

- **1 boneless pork loin roast (2 pounds)**
- **1 can (14 ounces) whole-berry cranberry sauce**
- **¼ cup Dijon mustard**
- **3 tablespoons brown sugar**
- **3 tablespoons lemon juice**
- **1 tablespoon cornstarch**
- **¼ cup cold water**

1. Place roast in a 3-qt. slow cooker. Combine the cranberry sauce, mustard, brown sugar and lemon juice; pour over roast. Cover and cook on low for 4 to 5 hours or until meat is tender. Remove roast and keep warm.
2. Strain cooking juices into a 2-cup measuring cup; add enough water to measure 2 cups. In a small saucepan, combine cornstarch and cold water until smooth; stir in cooking juices. Bring to a boil; cook and stir for 2 minutes or until thickened. Serve with pork.

PER SERVING *255 cal., 6 g fat (2 g sat. fat), 56 mg chol., 236 mg sodium, 28 g carb., 1 g fiber, 22 g pro.*

ZESTY SAUSAGE & BEANS

FREEZE IT

Zesty Sausage & Beans

You will love this hearty and delicious dish for feeding your hungry family. Packed with sausage, beans and bacon, it's guaranteed to satisfy the heftiest appetites.
—MELISSA JUST MINNEAPOLIS, MN

PREP: 30 MIN. • **COOK:** 5 HOURS
MAKES: 10 SERVINGS

- **2 pounds smoked kielbasa or Polish sausage, halved and sliced**
- **2 cans (15 ounces each) black beans, rinsed and drained**
- **1 can (15 ounces) great northern beans, rinsed and drained**
- **1 can (15 ounces) thick and zesty tomato sauce**
- **1 medium green pepper, chopped**
- **1 medium onion, chopped**
- **5 bacon strips, cooked and crumbled**
- **3 tablespoons brown sugar**
- **2 tablespoons cider vinegar**
- **3 garlic cloves, minced**
- **¼ teaspoon dried thyme**
- **¼ teaspoon dried marjoram**
- **¼ teaspoon cayenne pepper**
- **Hot cooked rice**

In a large skillet, brown the sausage. Transfer to a 4-qt. slow cooker; add the beans, tomato sauce, green pepper, onion, bacon, brown sugar, vinegar, garlic, thyme, marjoram and cayenne. Cover and cook on low for 5-6 hours or until vegetables are tender. Serve with rice.

FREEZE OPTION *Freeze cooled sausage mixture in freezer containers. To use, partially thaw in refrigerator overnight. Heat through in a saucepan, stirring occasionally and adding a little broth or water if necessary.*

"Our family loves to eat Indian food, and this recipe is quick and easy to do with jarred korma sauce and fresh spring vegetables. If you want it hotter, add cayenne pepper to taste. Sometimes I add grilled chicken to the recipe. I serve this dish with naan bread, chutney and flaked coconut for condiments. So good!"

—**NANCY HEISHMAN** LAS VEGAS, NV

CREAMY CURRY VEGETABLE STEW

Creamy Curry Vegetable Stew

PREP: 25 MIN. • **COOK:** 7 HOURS
MAKES: 6 SERVINGS

- **2 jars (15 ounces each) korma curry sauce**
- **2 tablespoons curry powder**
- **2 teaspoons garam masala**
- **1½ teaspoons ground mustard**
- **2 pounds red potatoes (about 6 medium), cubed**
- **2 cups small fresh mushrooms**
- **2 cups fresh baby carrots**
- **1½ cups frozen corn, thawed**
- **5 green onions, chopped**
- **2 cups cut fresh asparagus (2-inch pieces)**
- **2 tablespoons water**
- **1½ cups frozen peas, thawed**
- **¼ cup chopped fresh parsley**
- **Naan flatbreads or cooked basmati rice, optional**

1. In a greased 5-qt. slow cooker, combine curry sauce, curry powder, garam masala and mustard. Stir in potatoes, mushrooms, carrots, corn and green onions. Cook, covered, on low 7-9 hours or until vegetables are tender.
2. In a microwave-safe bowl, combine asparagus and water; microwave, covered, on high for 2-3 minutes or until crisp-tender. Drain. Stir asparagus and peas into slow cooker; heat through. Sprinkle with parsley. If desired, serve with naan.
NOTE *Look for garam masala in the spice aisle.*

Slow-Cooked Blueberry French Toast

Your slow cooker can be your best friend on a busy morning. Just get this recipe going, run some errands and come back to the aroma of French toast ready to eat.
—ELIZABETH LORENZ PERU, IN

PREP: 30 MIN. + CHILLING • **COOK:** 3 HOURS
MAKES: 12 SERVINGS (2 CUPS SYRUP)

- **8 eggs**
- **½ cup plain yogurt**
- **⅓ cup sour cream**
- **1 teaspoon vanilla extract**
- **½ teaspoon ground cinnamon**
- **1 cup 2% milk**
- **⅓ cup maple syrup**
- **1 loaf (1 pound) French bread, cubed**
- **1½ cups fresh or frozen blueberries**
- **12 ounces cream cheese, cubed**

BLUEBERRY SYRUP

- **1 cup sugar**
- **2 tablespoons cornstarch**
- **1 cup cold water**
- **¾ cup fresh or frozen blueberries, divided**
- **1 tablespoon butter**
- **1 tablespoon lemon juice**

1. In a large bowl, whisk eggs, yogurt, sour cream, vanilla and cinnamon. Gradually whisk in milk and maple syrup until blended.
2. Place half of the bread in a greased 5- or 6-qt. slow cooker; layer with half of the blueberries, cream cheese and egg mixture. Repeat layers. Refrigerate, covered, overnight.
3. Remove from refrigerator 30 minutes before cooking. Cook, covered, on low 3-4 hours or until a knife inserted near the center comes out clean.
4. For syrup, in a small saucepan, mix sugar and cornstarch; stir in water until smooth. Stir in ¼ cup blueberries. Bring to a boil; cook and stir until berries pop, about 3 minutes. Remove from heat; stir in butter, lemon juice and remaining berries. Serve warm with French toast.

SLOW-COOKED BLUEBERRY FRENCH TOAST

PORK TENDERLOIN WITH CRAN-APPLE SAUERKRAUT

Pork Tenderloin with Cran-Apple Sauerkraut

I love all the ingredients in this recipe because together they're perfect for Oktoberfest, a fun festival during my favorite time of the year. Serve the pork and sauerkraut with a hearty dark bread, such as rye or pumpernickel, along with an ice-cold beer. Delicious!

—BARBARA LENTO HOUSTON, PA

PREP: 25 MIN.
COOK: 2 HOURS + STANDING
MAKES: 4 SERVINGS

- **¼ pound center-cut bacon strips, chopped**
- **1 cup sliced leeks (white portion only)**
- **1 cup cubed peeled sweet potato**
- **1 tablespoon water**
- **1 can (14 ounces) sauerkraut, rinsed and well drained**
- **1 medium apple, peeled and finely chopped**
- **½ cup frozen cranberries**
- **½ cup sweet white wine or unsweetened apple juice**
- **¼ cup packed brown sugar**
- **1 teaspoon caraway seeds**
- **¾ teaspoon salt, divided**
- **1 pork tenderloin (1 pound)**
- **¼ teaspoon pepper**

1. In a large skillet, cook bacon and leeks over medium heat 6-8 minutes or until bacon is crisp, stirring occasionally. Remove with a slotted spoon; drain on paper towels.
2. Place sweet potato and water in a large microwave-safe dish. Microwave, covered, on high for 2-3 minutes or until potatoes are almost tender; drain. Stir in bacon mixture, sauerkraut, apple, cranberries, wine, brown sugar, caraway seeds and 1/4 teaspoon salt.
3. Transfer half of the sauerkraut mixture to a greased 4-qt. slow cooker. Sprinkle pork with pepper and remaining salt; place in slow cooker. Top with the remaining sauerkraut mixture.
4. Cover and cook on low for 2-3 hours or until pork is tender.
5. Remove pork from slow cooker; tent with foil. Let stand 10 minutes before slicing. Serve pork with the sauerkraut mixture.

Burgundy Lamb Shanks

For those who love fall-from-the-bone lamb, this recipe fills the bill. Burgundy wine adds a special touch to the sauce that's served alongside.

—F. W. CREUTZ SOUTHOLD, NY

PREP: 10 MIN. • **COOK:** 8¼ HOURS
MAKES: 4 SERVINGS

- **4 lamb shanks (about 20 ounces each)**
- **Salt and pepper to taste**
- **2 tablespoons dried parsley flakes**
- **2 teaspoons minced garlic**
- **½ teaspoon dried oregano**
- **½ teaspoon grated lemon peel**
- **½ cup chopped onion**
- **1 medium carrot, chopped**
- **1 teaspoon olive oil**
- **1 cup Burgundy wine**
- **1 teaspoon beef bouillon granules**

1. Sprinkle lamb with salt and pepper. Place in a 5-qt. slow cooker. Sprinkle with the parsley, garlic, oregano and lemon peel.
2. In a small saucepan, saute onion and carrot in oil for 3-4 minutes or until tender. Stir in wine and bouillon. Bring to a boil, stirring occasionally. Pour over lamb. Cover and cook on low for 8 hours or until meat is tender.
3. Remove lamb and keep warm. Strain cooking juices and skim fat. In a small saucepan, bring juices to a boil; cook until liquid is reduced by half. Serve with lamb.

Apple-Cranberry Grains

While on my quest to lose 130 pounds, I had to make some changes in my diet, such as reducing sugar and increasing my fiber and protein intake. These delicious slow-cooker grains are perfect because even my husband, who is a picky eater, loves them, as do my children. I set my slow cooker to start automatically overnight and a hearty breakfast is ready in the morning, making this quick and healthy recipe a favorite in my home.

—**SHERISSE DAWE** BLACK DIAMOND, AB

PREP: 10 MIN. • **COOK:** 4 HOURS
MAKES: 10 SERVINGS

- **2 medium apples, peeled and chopped**
- **1 cup sugar**
- **1 cup fresh cranberries**
- **½ cup wheat berries**
- **½ cup quinoa, rinsed**
- **½ cup oat bran**
- **½ cup medium pearl barley**
- **½ cup chopped walnuts**
- **½ cup packed brown sugar**
- **1½ to 2 teaspoons ground cinnamon**
- **6 cups water**
- **Milk**

In a 3-qt. slow cooker, combine the first 11 ingredients. Cook, covered, on low 4-5 hours or until grains are tender. Serve with milk.

NOTE *Look for oat bran cereal near the hot cereals or in the natural foods section. Look for quinoa in the cereal, rice or organic food aisle.*

Quinoa is sometimes called the perfect grain because it offers a complete **protein**. It's a great choice for **meatless** dishes, which can otherwise be low in protein.

APPLE-CRANBERRY GRAINS

EAT SMART

Teriyaki Pork Roast

I'm always looking for no-fuss recipes, so I was thrilled to find this one. The tender teriyaki pork is a real family-pleaser.

—**ROXANNE HULSEY** GAINESVILLE, GA

PREP: 10 MIN. • **COOK:** 7 HOURS
MAKES: 8 SERVINGS

- **¾ cup unsweetened apple juice**
- **2 tablespoons sugar**
- **2 tablespoons reduced-sodium soy sauce**
- **1 tablespoon white vinegar**
- **1 teaspoon ground ginger**
- **¼ teaspoon garlic powder**
- **⅛ teaspoon pepper**
- **1 boneless pork loin roast (about 3 pounds), halved**
- **7½ teaspoons cornstarch**
- **3 tablespoons cold water**

1. In a greased 3-qt. slow cooker, combine the first seven ingredients. Add roast and turn to coat. Cover and cook on low for 7-8 hours or until meat is tender.

2. Remove pork to a serving platter; keep warm. Skim fat from cooking juices; transfer to a small saucepan. Bring to a boil. Combine cornstarch and water until smooth. Gradually stir into the pan. Bring to a boil; cook and stir for 2 minutes or until thickened. Serve with meat.

PER SERVING *292 cal., 12 g fat (0 sat. fat), 101 mg chol., 212 mg sodium, 9 g carb., trace fiber, 36 g pro.* ***Diabetic Exchanges:*** *4½ lean meat, ½ starch.*

FREEZE IT

Savory Mushroom & Herb Pork Roast

For an extra treat with this tender pork, brown some canned French-fried onions in a dry skillet and sprinkle them over the top just before serving. Round out the meal with mashed potatoes or fluffy noodles.

—**JUDY CLARK** ADDISON, MI

PREP: 25 MIN. • **COOK:** 5 HOURS
MAKES: 8 SERVINGS

- **2 medium onions, chopped**
- **16 fresh baby carrots**
- **1 boneless pork shoulder butt roast (3 to 4 pounds)**
- **1 can (10¾ ounces) condensed cream of mushroom soup, undiluted**
- **¾ cup chicken broth**
- **1 can (4 ounces) mushroom stems and pieces, drained**
- **½ teaspoon dried thyme**
- **½ teaspoon Worcestershire sauce**
- **¼ teaspoon dried rosemary, crushed**
- **¼ teaspoon dried marjoram**
- **¼ teaspoon pepper**
- **1 tablespoon cornstarch**
- **2 tablespoons cold water**
- **French-fried onions, optional**

1. Place onions and carrots in a 5-qt. slow cooker. Cut roast in half; add to slow cooker. In a small bowl, combine the soup, broth, mushrooms, thyme, Worcestershire sauce, rosemary, marjoram and pepper; pour over pork. Cover and cook on low for 5-6 hours or until meat is tender.

2. Remove pork to a serving platter; keep warm. Skim fat from cooking juices; transfer to a large saucepan. Bring liquid to a boil. Combine cornstarch and water until smooth; gradually stir into the pan. Bring to a boil; cook and stir for 2 minutes or until thickened.

3. Serve pork with gravy. Sprinkle servings with French-fried onions if desired.

FREEZE OPTION *Place individual portions of cooled meat mixture in freezer containers. To use, partially thaw in refrigerator overnight. Microwave, covered, on high in a microwave-safe dish until heated through, gently stirring and adding a little water if necessary.*

SAVORY MUSHROOM & HERB PORK ROAST

Spicy Lentil & Chickpea Stew

PREP: 25 MIN. • **COOK:** 8 HOURS
MAKES: 8 SERVINGS (2¾ QUARTS)

- **2 teaspoons olive oil**
- **1 medium onion, thinly sliced**
- **1 teaspoon dried oregano**
- **½ teaspoon crushed red pepper flakes**
- **2 cans (15 ounces each) chickpeas or garbanzo beans, rinsed and drained**
- **1 cup dried lentils, rinsed**
- **1 can (2¼ ounces) sliced ripe olives, drained**
- **3 teaspoons smoked paprika**
- **4 cups vegetable broth**
- **4 cans (8 ounces each) no-salt-added tomato sauce**
- **4 cups fresh baby spinach**
- **¾ cup fat-free plain yogurt**

1. In a small skillet, heat oil over medium-high heat. Add onion, oregano and pepper flakes; cook and stir 8-10 minutes or until onion is tender. Transfer to a 5- or 6-qt. slow cooker.

2. Add chickpeas, lentils, olives and paprika; stir in broth and tomato sauce. Cook, covered, on low 8-10 hours or until lentils are tender. Stir in spinach. Top servings with yogurt.

Smoked paprika adds a **rich, meaty** flavor to lentil and bean dishes. You could also use the spice in recipes that call for **ground chipotle pepper**. Just add cayenne or chili powder if needed to **boost the heat**.

SPICY LENTIL & CHICKPEA STEW

Slow-Cooked Fish Stew

PREP: 25 MIN. • **COOK:** 6½ HOURS
MAKES: 8 SERVINGS (3 QUARTS)

- **1 pound potatoes (about 2 medium), peeled and finely chopped**
- **1 package (10 ounces) frozen corn, thawed**
- **1½ cups frozen lima beans, thawed**
- **1 large onion, finely chopped**
- **1 celery rib, finely chopped**
- **1 medium carrot, finely chopped**
- **4 garlic cloves, minced**
- **1 bay leaf**
- **1 teaspoon lemon-pepper seasoning**
- **1 teaspoon dried parsley flakes**
- **1 teaspoon dried rosemary, crushed**
- **½ teaspoon salt**
- **1½ cups vegetable or chicken broth**
- **1 can (10¾ ounces) condensed cream of celery soup, undiluted**
- **½ cup white wine or additional vegetable broth**
- **1 pound cod fillets, cut into 1-inch pieces**
- **1 can (14½ ounces) diced tomatoes, undrained**
- **1 can (12 ounces) fat-free evaporated milk**

1. In a 5-qt. slow cooker, combine the first 15 ingredients. Cook, covered, on low 6-8 hours or until potatoes are tender.

2. Remove bay leaf. Stir in cod, tomatoes and milk; cook, covered, 30-35 minutes longer or until fish just begins to flake easily with a fork.

SLOW-COOKED FISH STEW

EAT SMART

Chinese Pork Chops

These delicious pork chops are so saucy and tender. I got the recipe years ago and it's been a family favorite ever since.
—SHARON CRIDER JUNCTION CITY, KS

PREP: 15 MIN. • **COOK:** 3 HOURS
MAKES: 6 SERVINGS

- **6 boneless pork loin chops (4 ounces each)**
- **1 small onion, finely chopped**
- **⅓ cup ketchup**
- **3 tablespoons brown sugar**
- **3 tablespoons water**
- **3 tablespoons reduced-sodium soy sauce**
- **1 garlic clove, minced**
- **1 teaspoon ground ginger**
- **3 cups hot cooked rice**

Place pork chops in a 3-qt. slow cooker coated with cooking spray. In a small bowl, combine the onion, ketchup, brown sugar, water, soy sauce, garlic and ginger. Pour over chops. Cover and cook on low for 3-4 hours or until meat is tender. Serve with rice and cooking juices.

PER SERVING *305 cal., 7 g fat (2 g sat. fat), 55 mg chol., 496 mg sodium, 34 g carb., 1 g fiber, 25 g pro.* ***Diabetic Exchanges:*** *3 lean meat, 2 starch.*

Easy Chili Verde

I LOVE chili verde and order it whenever I can at restaurants! I figured out how to make an easy, tasty version at home. People have the option to eat the chili verde with a fork or in tortillas with a variety of toppings such as cheese, cilantro, minced onions or lime wedges. There are never leftovers at my house.
—JULIE ROWLAND SALT LAKE CITY, UT

PREP: 10 MIN. • **COOK:** 5 HOURS
MAKES: 12 SERVINGS (3 QUARTS)

- **1 boneless pork shoulder roast (4 to 5 pounds), cut into 1-inch pieces**
- **3 cans (10 ounces each) green enchilada sauce**
- **1 cup salsa verde**
- **1 can (4 ounces) chopped green chilies**
- **½ teaspoon salt**
- **Hot cooked rice**
- **Sour cream, optional**

In a 5-qt. slow cooker, combine pork, enchilada sauce, salsa verde, green chilies and salt. Cook, covered, on low 5-6 hours or until pork is tender. Serve with rice. If desired, top with sour cream.

EASY CHILI VERDE

Soups, Sides & Sandwiches

Experience the joy of coming home to a heartwarming crock of **slow-simmered soup**. Share a big **batch of** crowd-pleasing **sandwiche**s at your next get-together. And, make **holidays** a breeze with **smart side dishes** that cook and serve right out of your **favorite appliance**.

Bacon & Sausage Stuffing

This recipe was inspired by my mother's stuffing recipe. It smells like heaven while you're making it, and people can never seem to get enough.

—**SCOTT RUGH** PORTLAND, OR

PREP: 25 MIN.
COOK: 4 HOURS + STANDING
MAKES: 20 SERVINGS (¾ CUP EACH)

- **1 pound bulk pork sausage**
- **1 pound thick-sliced bacon strips, chopped**
- **½ cup butter, cubed**
- **1 large onion, chopped**
- **3 celery ribs, sliced**
- **10½ cups unseasoned stuffing cubes**
- **1 cup sliced fresh mushrooms**
- **1 cup chopped fresh parsley**
- **4 teaspoons dried sage leaves**
- **4 teaspoons dried thyme**
- **6 eggs**
- **2 cans (10¾ ounces each) condensed cream of chicken soup, undiluted**
- **1¼ cups chicken stock**

1. In a large skillet, cook sausage over medium heat for 6-8 minutes or until no longer pink, breaking into crumbles. Remove with a slotted spoon; drain on paper towels. Discard drippings.
2. Add bacon to pan; cook over medium heat until crisp. Remove to paper towels to drain. Discard drippings. Wipe out pan. In same pan, heat butter over medium-high heat. Add onion and celery; cook and stir 6-8 minutes or until tender. Remove from heat.
3. In a large bowl, combine stuffing cubes, sausage, bacon, onion mixture, mushrooms, parsley, sage and thyme. In a small bowl, whisk eggs, soup and stock; pour over stuffing mixture and toss to coat.
4. Transfer to a greased 6-qt. slow cooker. Cook, covered, on low 4-5 hours or until a thermometer reads 160°. Remove lid; let stand 15 minutes before serving.

BACON & SAUSAGE STUFFING

"These party-sized sandwiches eat like a meal! Just add your favorite Italian salad on the side. If you'd like, top the sandwiches off with sliced provolone."
—**TROY PARKOS** VERONA, WI

Easy Italian Beef Sandwiches

PREP: 20 MIN. • **COOK:** 5 HOURS
MAKES: 12 SERVINGS

- **1 boneless beef chuck roast (3 pounds)**
- **1 teaspoon Italian seasoning**
- **¼ teaspoon cayenne pepper**
- **¼ teaspoon pepper**
- **¼ cup water**
- **1 jar (16 ounces) sliced pepperoncini, undrained**
- **1 medium sweet red pepper, julienned**
- **1 medium green pepper, julienned**
- **1 garlic clove, minced**
- **1 envelope reduced-sodium onion soup mix**
- **2 tablespoons Worcestershire sauce**
- **2 loaves (1 pound each) Italian bread, split**

1. Cut roast in half; place in a 5-qt. slow cooker. Sprinkle with the Italian seasoning, cayenne and pepper. Add water. Cover and cook on high for 4 hours or until meat is tender.
2. Remove roast; shred meat with two forks and return to the slow cooker.
3. In a large bowl, combine the pepperoncini, peppers, garlic, soup mix and Worcestershire sauce; pour over meat. Cover and cook on high for 1 hour longer or until peppers are tender.
4. Spoon beef mixture over the bottom halves of bread; replace bread tops. Cut each loaf into six sandwiches.

"I threw some always-available condiments into my slow cooker with a pork roast to create this fantastic pulled pork. It has become a staple sandwich filler for large get-togethers. Serve with rolls, on top of toasted crostini or as a filling for empanadas. The flavor of the pork goes well with a cold glass of white wine."

—**LORI TERRY** CHICAGO, IL

SWEET & SPICY PULLED PORK SANDWICHES

Sweet & Spicy Pulled Pork Sandwiches

PREP: 30 MIN. • **COOK:** 8 HOURS
MAKES: 10 SERVINGS

- **2 medium onions, sliced (about 2 cups)**
- **2 tablespoons brown sugar**
- **1 tablespoon smoked paprika**
- **1½ teaspoons salt**
- **½ teaspoon pepper**
- **1 boneless pork shoulder roast (4 to 5 pounds)**
- **½ cup chicken or vegetable broth**
- **¼ cup cider vinegar**
- **3 tablespoons reduced-sodium soy sauce**
- **3 tablespoons Worcestershire sauce**
- **2 tablespoons Sriracha Asian hot chili sauce**
- **1 tablespoon molasses**
- **2 garlic cloves, minced**
- **2 teaspoons Dijon mustard**
- **3 cups coleslaw mix**
- **3 tablespoons lime juice**
- **10 kaiser or onion rolls, split**

1. Place onions in a 4- or 5-qt. slow cooker. Mix brown sugar, paprika, salt and pepper; rub over roast. Place over onions.
2. In a small bowl, mix broth, vinegar, soy sauce, Worcestershire sauce, chili sauce, molasses, garlic and mustard; pour over roast. Cook, covered, on low 8-10 hours or until meat is tender.
3. Remove roast; cool slightly. Skim fat from cooking juices. In a small bowl, toss coleslaw mix with lime juice. Shred pork with two forks. Return pork to slow cooker; heat through. Serve on rolls with coleslaw.

If you don't have Sriracha, improvise with a moderately spicy **hot sauce**. Add some **pepper flakes, lime** juice or extra **molasses** to suit your taste.

FREEZE IT

Tex-Mex Chili

Hearty, spicy and loaded with meat, this is a man's chili for sure. You can also simmer it up on the stovetop—the longer you cook it, the better!
—**ERIC HAYES** ANTIOCH, CA

PREP: 20 MIN. • **COOK:** 6 HOURS
MAKES: 12 SERVINGS (1⅓ CUPS EACH)

- **3 pounds beef stew meat**
- **1 tablespoon canola oil**
- **3 garlic cloves, minced**
- **3 cans (16 ounces each) kidney beans, rinsed and drained**
- **3 cans (15 ounces each) tomato sauce**
- **1 can (14½ ounces) diced tomatoes, undrained**
- **1 cup water**
- **1 can (6 ounces) tomato paste**
- **¾ cup salsa verde**
- **1 envelope chili seasoning**
- **2 teaspoons dried minced onion**
- **1 teaspoon chili powder**
- **½ teaspoon crushed red pepper flakes**
- **½ teaspoon ground cumin**
- **½ teaspoon cayenne pepper**
- **Shredded cheddar cheese and minced fresh cilantro**

1. In a large skillet, brown beef in oil in batches. Add garlic; cook 1 minute longer. Transfer to a 6-qt. slow cooker.
2. Stir in the beans, tomato sauce, tomatoes, water, tomato paste, salsa verde and seasonings. Cover and cook on low for 6-8 hours or until meat is tender. Garnish each serving with cheese and cilantro.
FREEZE OPTION *Before adding toppings, cool chili. Freeze chili in freezer containers. To use, partially thaw in refrigerator overnight. Heat through in a saucepan, stirring occasionally and adding a little broth or water if necessary. Sprinkle each serving with cheese and cilantro.*

TEX-MEX CHILI

CHICKEN BEAN SOUP

Brats with Sauerkraut

I've made many variations of brats and kraut over the years. The bratwurst can be plain or smoked, served whole or cut into slices, with a bun or without. It's popular at parties and potlucks.
—**DARLENE DIXON** HANOVER, MN

PREP: 10 MIN. • **COOK:** 6 HOURS
MAKES: 8 SERVINGS

- **8 uncooked bratwurst links**
- **1 can (14 ounces) sauerkraut, rinsed and well drained**
- **2 medium apples, peeled and finely chopped**
- **3 bacon strips, cooked and crumbled**
- **¼ cup packed brown sugar**
- **¼ cup finely chopped onion**
- **1 teaspoon ground mustard**
- **8 brat buns, split**

1. Place the bratwurst in a 5-qt. slow cooker. In a large bowl, combine the sauerkraut, apples, bacon, brown sugar, onion and mustard; spoon over bratwurst.
2. Cover and cook on low for 6-8 hours or until a thermometer inserted in the sausage reads 160°.
3. Place brats in buns; using a slotted spoon, top with sauerkraut mixture.

EAT SMART

Chicken Bean Soup

This easy soup is tasty and nutritious, too. I like to top individual bowls with a few sprigs of fresh parsley. Home-baked rolls—I use the ones that start with frozen dough— are an added treat.
—**PHYLLIS SHAUGHNESSY** LIVONIA, NY

PREP: 10 MIN. • **COOK:** 4 HOURS
MAKES: 12 SERVINGS (3 QUARTS)

- **1 pound boneless skinless chicken breasts, cubed**
- **2 cans (14½ ounces each) chicken broth**
- **2 cans (14½ ounces each) Italian diced tomatoes, undrained**
- **1 can (16 ounces) kidney beans, rinsed and drained**
- **1 can (15¼ ounces) whole kernel corn, drained or 1½ cups frozen corn**
- **1 can (15 ounces) lima beans, rinsed and drained or 1½ cups frozen lima beans**
- **1 cup frozen peas and pearl onions**
- **1 tablespoon snipped fresh dill or 1 teaspoon dill weed**
- **½ teaspoon ground ginger, optional**

In a 5-qt. slow cooker, combine all ingredients. Cover and cook on low for 4-5 hours or until chicken is no longer pink.

PER SERVING *159 cal., 1 g fat (trace sat. fat), 22 mg chol., 624 mg sodium, 22 g carb., 5 g fiber, 13 g pro.* ***Diabetic Exchanges:*** *1 starch, 1 lean meat, 1 vegetable.*

NAVY BEAN VEGETABLE SOUP

Navy Bean Vegetable Soup

My family enjoys bean soup, so I came up with this hearty version. The leftovers are even better the next day.

—**ELEANOR MIELKE** MITCHELL, SD

PREP: 15 MIN. • **COOK:** 9 HOURS
MAKES: 12 SERVINGS (3 QUARTS)

- **4 medium carrots, thinly sliced**
- **2 celery ribs, chopped**
- **1 medium onion, chopped**
- **2 cups cubed fully cooked ham**
- **1½ cups dried navy beans**
- **1 envelope vegetable recipe mix (Knorr)**
- **1 envelope onion soup mix**
- **1 bay leaf**
- **½ teaspoon pepper**
- **8 cups water**

In a 5-qt. slow cooker, combine the first nine ingredients. Stir in water. Cover and cook on low for 9-10 hours or until beans are tender. Discard the bay leaf.

Slow-Simmered Kidney Beans

My husband always signs us up to bring a side dish when we're invited to a potluck. Canned beans cut down on prep time yet get plenty of zip from bacon, apple, red pepper and onion. I like how the slow cooker blends the flavors and I don't have to stand over the stove.

—**SHEILA VAIL** LONG BEACH, CA

PREP: 15 MIN. • **COOK:** 6 HOURS
MAKES: 16 SERVINGS (¾ CUP EACH)

- **6 bacon strips, diced**
- **½ pound smoked Polish sausage or kielbasa**
- **4 cans (16 ounces each) kidney beans, rinsed and drained**
- **1 can (28 ounces) diced tomatoes, drained**
- **2 medium sweet red peppers, chopped**
- **1 large onion, chopped**
- **1 cup ketchup**
- **½ cup packed brown sugar**
- **¼ cup honey**
- **¼ cup molasses**
- **1 tablespoon Worcestershire sauce**
- **1 teaspoon salt**
- **1 teaspoon ground mustard**
- **2 medium unpeeled red apples, cubed**

1. In a large skillet, cook bacon until crisp. Remove with a slotted spoon to paper towels. Add sausage to drippings; cook and stir for 5 minutes. Drain and set aside.

2. In a 5-qt. slow cooker, combine the beans, tomatoes, red peppers, onion, ketchup, brown sugar, honey, molasses, Worcestershire sauce, salt and mustard. Stir in the bacon and sausage.

3. Cover and cook on low for 4-6 hours. Stir in apples. Cover and cook 2 hours longer or until bubbly.

For easy cleanup, **spritz** the measuring cup with a little **cooking spray** before measuring sticky ingredients like **honey** and **molasses**.

Maple-Walnut Sweet Potatoes

Sweet potatoes with dried cherries and walnuts make this a holiday-worthy dish.
—**SARAH HERSE** BROOKLYN, NY

PREP: 10 MIN. • **COOK:** 5 HOURS
MAKES: 12 SERVINGS (¾ CUP EACH)

- **4 pounds sweet potatoes (about 8 medium)**
- **¾ cup coarsely chopped walnuts, divided**
- **½ cup packed light brown sugar**
- **½ cup dried cherries, coarsely chopped**
- **½ cup maple syrup**
- **¼ cup apple cider or juice**
- **¼ teaspoon salt**

1. Peel and cut sweet potatoes lengthwise in half; cut crosswise into ½-in. slices. Place in a 5-qt. slow cooker. Add ½ cup walnuts, brown sugar, cherries, syrup, cider and salt; toss to combine.
2. Cook, covered, on low 5-6 hours or until potatoes are tender. Sprinkle with remaining walnuts.

MAPLE-WALNUT SWEET POTATOES

Slow Cooker Turkey Chili

PREP: 30 MIN. • **COOK:** 7¼ HOURS
MAKES: 8 SERVINGS (2¾ QUARTS)

- **2 tablespoons olive oil**
- **1½ pounds ground turkey**
- **1 medium onion, chopped**
- **2 tablespoons ground ancho chili pepper**
- **1 tablespoon chili powder**
- **1½ teaspoons salt**
- **1½ teaspoons ground cumin**
- **1½ teaspoons paprika**
- **2 cans (14½ ounces each) fire-roasted diced tomatoes, undrained**
- **1 medium sweet yellow pepper, chopped**
- **1 medium sweet red pepper, chopped**
- **1 can (4 ounces) chopped green chilies**
- **1 garlic clove, minced**
- **1 cup brewed coffee**
- **¾ cup dry red wine or chicken broth**
- **1 can (16 ounces) kidney beans, rinsed and drained**
- **1 can (15 ounces) white kidney or cannellini beans, rinsed and drained**
- **Sliced avocado and chopped green onions**

1. In a large skillet, heat oil over medium heat. Add turkey and onion; cook 8-10 minutes or until meat is no longer pink, breaking up turkey into crumbles.
2. Transfer to a 5-qt. slow cooker; stir in seasonings. Add tomatoes, sweet peppers, chilies and garlic; stir in coffee and wine.
3. Cook, covered, on low 7-9 hours. Stir in beans; cook 15-20 minutes longer or until heated through. Top servings with avocado and green onions.

FREEZE OPTION *Freeze cooled chili in freezer containers. To use, partially thaw in refrigerator overnight. Heat through in a saucepan, stirring occasionally and adding broth or water if necessary. Serve with toppings.*

SLOW COOKER TURKEY CHILI

Pulled Brisket Sandwiches

Don't let the number of ingredients in this recipe scare you; I'll bet you have most of them in your pantry already. The sauce is what makes this dish so special. It's hard not to like ketchup, brown sugar and a little butter drizzled over tender beef brisket.

—**JANE GUILBEAU** NEW ORLEANS, LA

PREP: 25 MIN. • **COOK:** 8 HOURS
MAKES: 12 SERVINGS

- **1 fresh beef brisket (4 to 5 pounds)**
- **1½ cups water**
- **½ cup Worcestershire sauce**
- **2 tablespoons cider vinegar**
- **2 garlic cloves, minced**
- **1½ teaspoons beef bouillon granules**
- **1½ teaspoons chili powder**
- **1 teaspoon ground mustard**
- **½ teaspoon cayenne pepper**
- **¼ teaspoon garlic salt**
- **½ cup ketchup**
- **2 tablespoons brown sugar**
- **2 tablespoons butter**
- **½ teaspoon hot pepper sauce**
- **12 kaiser rolls, split**

1. Cut brisket in half; place in a 5-qt. slow cooker. In a small bowl, combine the water, Worcestershire sauce, vinegar, garlic, bouillon, chili powder, mustard, cayenne and garlic salt. Cover and refrigerate 1/2 cup mixture for sauce; pour remaining mixture over beef. Cover and cook on low for 8-10 hours or until meat is tender.

2. Remove beef; cool slightly. Skim fat from cooking juices. Shred meat with two forks and return to the slow cooker; heat through.

3. In a small saucepan, combine the ketchup, brown sugar, butter, pepper sauce and reserved water mixture. Bring to a boil; reduce heat. Simmer, uncovered, for 2-3 minutes to allow flavors to blend. Using a slotted spoon, place beef on rolls; drizzle with sauce.

NOTE *This is a fresh beef brisket, not corned beef.*

PULLED BRISKET SANDWICHES

EAT SMART

Onion-Garlic Hash Browns

Quick to assemble, this is a simple recipe I've served many times. Stir in hot sauce if you like a bit of heat. I often top the finished dish with a sprinkling of shredded cheddar cheese.

—**CINDI HAYWARD-BOGER** ARDMORE, AL

PREP: 20 MIN. • **COOK:** 3 HOURS
MAKES: 12 SERVINGS (½ CUP EACH)

- **1 large red onion, chopped**
- **1 small sweet red pepper, chopped**
- **1 small green pepper, chopped**
- **¼ cup butter, cubed**
- **1 tablespoon olive oil**
- **4 garlic cloves, minced**
- **1 package (30 ounces) frozen shredded hash brown potatoes**
- **½ teaspoon salt**
- **½ teaspoon pepper**
- **3 drops hot pepper sauce, optional**
- **2 teaspoons minced fresh parsley**

1. In a large skillet, saute onion and peppers in butter and oil until crisp-tender. Add garlic; cook 1 minute longer. Stir in the hash browns, salt, pepper and pepper sauce if desired.

2. Transfer to a 5-qt. slow cooker coated with cooking spray. Cover and cook on low for 3-4 hours or until heated through. Sprinkle with parsley before serving.

PER SERVING *110 cal., 5 g fat (3 g sat. fat), 10 mg chol., 136 mg sodium, 15 g carb., 1 g fiber, 2 g pro.* ***Diabetic Exchanges:*** *1 starch, 1 fat.*

FREEZE IT

Hearty Minestrone

I picked up this recipe in California in the '80s and have been making it ever since. I love it partly because it's simple to put together and partly because the flavor is so wonderful!

—**BONNIE HOSMAN** YOUNG, AZ

PREP: 25 MIN. • **COOK:** 6¼ HOURS
MAKES: 7 SERVINGS (ABOUT 2½ QUARTS)

- **2 cans (one 28 ounces, one 14½ ounces) diced tomatoes, undrained**
- **2 cups water**
- **2 medium carrots, sliced**
- **1 medium onion, chopped**
- **1 medium zucchini, chopped**
- **1 package (3½ ounces) sliced pepperoni**
- **2 teaspoons minced garlic**
- **2 teaspoons chicken bouillon granules**
- **½ teaspoon dried basil**
- **½ teaspoon dried oregano**
- **2 cans (16 ounces each) kidney beans, rinsed and drained**
- **1 package (10 ounces) frozen chopped spinach, thawed and squeezed dry**
- **1¼ cups cooked elbow macaroni**
- **Shredded Parmesan cheese**

1. In a 5-qt. slow cooker, combine the first 10 ingredients. Cover and cook on low for 6-8 hours or until vegetables are tender.

2. Stir in the beans, spinach and macaroni. Cover and cook 15 minutes longer or until heated through. Sprinkle with cheese.

FREEZE OPTION *Cool soup and transfer to freezer containers. Freeze for up to 3 months. To use frozen soup, thaw in the refrigerator overnight. Transfer to a saucepan. Cover and cook over medium heat until heated through. Sprinkle with cheese.*

HEARTY MINESTRONE

PORK & RICE NOODLE SOUP

Pork & Rice Noodle Soup

My husband and I are crazy over the Korean noodle bowls at our favorite restaurant. I created this recipe to enjoy the same flavors in a quick and easy meal. You can find rice noodles in the Asian section of the grocery store.

—**LISA RENSHAW** KANSAS CITY, MO

PREP: 15 MIN. • **COOK:** 6½ HOURS
MAKES: 8 SERVINGS (3 QUARTS)

- **1½ pounds boneless country-style pork ribs, cut into 1-inch cubes**
- **6 garlic cloves, minced**
- **2 tablespoons minced fresh gingerroot**
- **2 cans (14½ ounces each) reduced-sodium chicken broth**
- **2 cans (13.66 ounces each) coconut milk**
- **¼ cup reduced-sodium soy sauce**
- **4 ounces uncooked thin rice noodles**
- **2 cups frozen pepper strips, thawed**
- **1 can (8 ounces) sliced water chestnuts, drained**
- **¼ cup minced fresh cilantro**
- **2 tablespoons lime juice**

1. In a 5-qt. slow cooker, combine the first six ingredients. Cook, covered, on low 6-8 hours or until meat is tender.
2. Add rice noodles, pepper strips and water chestnuts; cook 30-35 minutes longer or until noodles are tender. If desired, skim soup. Just before serving, stir in cilantro and lime juice.

EAT SMART

Mexican Shredded Beef Wraps

I first served this go-to beef slow cooker recipe following my son's baptism. I made a double batch and fed a crowd of 20!

—**AMY LENTS** GRAND FORKS, ND

PREP: 20 MIN. • **COOK:** 6 HOURS
MAKES: 6 SERVINGS

- **1 small onion, finely chopped**
- **1 jalapeno pepper, seeded and minced**
- **3 garlic cloves, minced**
- **1 boneless beef chuck roast (2 to 3 pounds)**
- **½ teaspoon salt**
- **½ teaspoon pepper**
- **1 can (8 ounces) tomato sauce**
- **¼ cup lime juice**
- **1 tablespoon chili powder**
- **1 teaspoon ground cumin**
- **¼ teaspoon cayenne pepper**
- **6 flour or whole wheat tortillas (8 inches)**
- **Optional toppings: torn romaine, chopped tomatoes and sliced avocado**

1. Place onion, jalapeno and garlic in a 4-qt. slow cooker. Sprinkle roast with salt and pepper; place over vegetables. In a small bowl, mix tomato sauce, lime juice, chili powder, cumin and cayenne; pour over roast.
2. Cook, covered, on low 6-8 hours or until meat is tender. Remove roast; cool slightly. Shred meat with two forks; return to slow cooker. Serve beef on tortillas with toppings of your choice.

NOTE *Wear disposable gloves when cutting hot peppers; the oils can burn skin. Avoid touching your face.*

PER SERVING *428 cal., 18 g fat (6 g sat. fat), 98 mg chol., 696 mg sodium, 31 g carb., 1 g fiber, 35 g pro.* ***Diabetic Exchanges:*** *5 lean meat, 2 starch.*

MEXICAN SHREDDED BEEF WRAPS

CAROLINA-STYLE VINEGAR BBQ CHICKEN

EAT SMART

Carolina-Style Vinegar BBQ Chicken

I live in Georgia, but I appreciate the tangy, sweet and slightly spicy taste of Carolina barbecue. I make my version in the slow cooker. When you walk in the door after being gone all day, the aroma will knock you off your feet!

—RAMONA PARRIS ACWORTH, GA

PREP: 10 MIN. • **COOK:** 4 HOURS
MAKES: 6 SERVINGS

- **2 cups water**
- **1 cup white vinegar**
- **¼ cup sugar**
- **1 tablespoon reduced-sodium chicken base**
- **1 teaspoon crushed red pepper flakes**
- **¾ teaspoon salt**
- **1½ pounds boneless skinless chicken breasts**
- **6 whole wheat hamburger buns, split, optional**

1. In a small bowl, mix the first six ingredients. Place chicken in a 3-qt. slow cooker; add vinegar mixture. Cook, covered, on low 4-5 hours or until chicken is tender.

2. Remove chicken; cool slightly. Reserve 1 cup cooking juices; discard remaining juices. Shred chicken with two forks. Return meat and reserved cooking juices to slow cooker; heat through. If desired, serve chicken mixture on buns.

NOTE *Look for chicken base near the broth and bouillon.*

PER (½-CUP) SERVING *134 cal., 3 g fat (1 g sat. fat), 63 mg chol., 228 mg sodium, 3 g carb., trace fiber, 23 g pro.*

EAT SMART

Pork and Beef Barbecue

It's the combination of beef stew meat and tender pork that keep friends and family asking about these tangy sandwiches. Add a little lettuce and tomato for a crisp contrast.

—CORBIN DETGEN BUCHANAN, MI

PREP: 15 MIN. • **COOK:** 6 HOURS
MAKES: 12 SERVINGS

- **1 can (6 ounces) tomato paste**
- **½ cup packed brown sugar**
- **¼ cup chili powder**
- **¼ cup cider vinegar**
- **2 teaspoons Worcestershire sauce**
- **1 teaspoon salt**
- **1½ pounds beef stew meat, cut into ¾-inch cubes**
- **1½ pounds pork chop suey meat or pork tenderloin, cut into ¾-inch cubes**
- **3 medium green peppers, chopped**
- **2 large onions, chopped**
- **12 sandwich buns, split**
- **Lettuce and tomatoes, optional**

1. In a 5-qt. slow cooker, combine the first six ingredients. Stir in beef, pork, green peppers and onions. Cover and cook on low for 6-8 hours or until meat is tender.

2. Shred meat with two forks. Serve on buns with lettuce and tomatoes if desired.

PER SERVING *444 cal., 12 g fat (4 g sat. fat), 69 mg chol., 684 mg sodium, 52 g carb., 3 g fiber, 32 g pro.*

When setting up a **potluck**, mark the table with **sticky notes** labeled for main dishes, sides, salads, drinks and desserts. Attendees will know **where to place items** and not have to ask.

Slow-Cooked Sauerkraut Soup

We live in Lancaster County, which has a rich heritage of German culture. The dishes often include sauerkraut, potatoes and sausage. We enjoy this soup on cold winter nights with muffins and fresh fruit.

—**LINDA LOHR** LITITZ, PA

PREP: 20 MIN. • **COOK:** 5 HOURS
MAKES: 10-12 SERVINGS (ABOUT 3 QUARTS)

- **1 medium potato, cut into ¼-inch cubes**
- **1 pound smoked kielbasa, cut into ½-inch cubes**
- **1 can (32 ounces) sauerkraut, rinsed and well drained**
- **4 cups chicken broth**
- **1 can (10¾ ounces) condensed cream of mushroom soup, undiluted**
- **½ pound sliced fresh mushrooms**
- **1 cup cubed cooked chicken**
- **2 medium carrots, sliced**
- **2 celery ribs, sliced**
- **2 tablespoons white vinegar**
- **2 teaspoons dill weed**
- **½ teaspoon pepper**
- **3 to 4 bacon strips, cooked and crumbled**

In a 5-qt. slow cooker, combine the first 12 ingredients. Cover and cook on high for 5-6 hours or until the vegetables are tender. Skim fat. Garnish with bacon.

HONEY-BUTTER PEAS AND CARROTS

EAT SMART

Honey-Butter Peas and Carrots

This classic combination of peas and carrots is enriched with a handful of flavor enhancers. Slow-cooking allows the ingredients to meld for maximum richness.

—**THERESA KREYCHE** TUSTIN, CA

PREP: 15 MIN. • **COOK:** 5¼ HOURS
MAKES: 12 SERVINGS (½ CUP EACH)

- **1 pound carrots, sliced**
- **1 large onion, chopped**
- **¼ cup water**
- **¼ cup butter, cubed**
- **¼ cup honey**
- **4 garlic cloves, minced**
- **1 teaspoon salt**
- **1 teaspoon dried marjoram**
- **⅛ teaspoon white pepper**
- **1 package (16 ounces) frozen peas**

In a 3-qt. slow cooker, combine the first nine ingredients. Cook, covered, on low 5 hours. Stir in peas. Cook, covered, on high 15-25 minutes or until vegetables are tender.

PER SERVING *106 cal., 4 g fat (2 g sat. fat), 10 mg chol., 293 mg sodium, 16 g carb., 3 g fiber, 3 g pro.* ***Diabetic Exchanges:*** *1 starch, 1 fat.*

BEEF & VEGGIE SLOPPY JOES

EAT SMART

Beef & Veggie Sloppy Joes

I'm always looking for ways to serve my family healthy and delicious food, so I started experimenting with my favorite veggies and ground beef. I came up with this favorite that my three kids actually request! A bonus is that the healthy take on sloppy joes reminds me of my own childhood.

—MEGAN NIEBUHR YAKIMA, WA

PREP: 35 MIN. • **COOK:** 5 HOURS
MAKES: 12 SERVINGS

- **4 medium carrots, shredded (about 3½ cups)**
- **1 medium yellow summer squash, shredded (about 2 cups)**
- **1 medium zucchini, shredded (about 2 cups)**
- **1 medium sweet red pepper, finely chopped**
- **2 medium tomatoes, seeded and chopped**
- **1 small red onion, finely chopped**
- **½ cup ketchup**
- **3 tablespoons minced fresh basil or 3 teaspoons dried basil**
- **3 tablespoons molasses**
- **2 tablespoons cider vinegar**
- **2 garlic cloves, minced**
- **½ teaspoon salt**
- **½ teaspoon pepper**
- **2 pounds lean ground beef (90% lean)**
- **12 whole wheat hamburger buns, split**

1. In a 5- or 6-qt. slow cooker, combine the first 13 ingredients. In a large skillet, cook beef over medium heat 8-10 minutes or until no longer pink, breaking into crumbles. Drain; transfer beef to slow cooker. Stir to combine.

2. Cook, covered, on low 5-6 hours or until heated through and vegetables are tender. Using a slotted spoon, serve beef mixture on buns.

PER SERVING *282 cal., 8 g fat (3 g sat. fat), 47 mg chol., 490 mg sodium, 34 g carb., 5 g fiber, 19 g pro.* ***Diabetic Exchanges:*** *2 starch, 2 lean meat, 1 vegetable.*

VEGETABLE CHICKEN SOUP

FREEZE IT

Vegetable Chicken Soup

This satisfying veggie soup hits the spot at lunch or dinner. Add a side salad and some whole grain bread for a filling and nutritious meal.

—AMY CHEATHAM SANDUSKY, OH

PREP: 25 MIN. • **COOK:** 5 HOURS
MAKES: 7 SERVINGS (2¾ QUARTS)

- **1 large sweet onion, chopped**
- **1 cup sliced baby portobello mushrooms**
- **½ cup chopped green pepper**
- **½ cup chopped sweet red pepper**
- **1 tablespoon butter**
- **1 tablespoon olive oil**
- **5 garlic cloves, minced**
- **¾ pound boneless skinless chicken breasts, cut into ½-in. cubes**
- **1 can (49½ ounces) chicken broth**
- **1 can (28 ounces) crushed tomatoes, undrained**
- **2 medium carrots, cut into ¼-inch slices**
- **½ cup medium pearl barley**
- **1¾ teaspoons Italian seasoning**
- **1½ teaspoons pepper**
- **½ teaspoon salt**

1. In a large skillet, saute the onion, mushrooms and peppers in butter and oil until tender. Add garlic; cook 1 minute longer.

2. Transfer to a 5-qt. slow cooker. Add the remaining ingredients. Cover and cook on low for 5-6 hours or until chicken and barley are tender.

FREEZE OPTION *Freeze cooled soup in freezer containers. To use, partially thaw in refrigerator overnight. Heat through in a saucepan, stirring occasionally and adding a little broth if necessary.*

Depending on your region, **sweet onions** may only be **available** during the **warmer months** of the year. You can use regular **yellow** onion in the soup recipe.

Jazzed-Up Green Bean Casserole

After trying many variations of this old standby, I decided to give it a little extra kick. The crunchy texture, cheesy goodness and bacon make it a hit at the holiday table.

—**SCOTT RUGH** PORTLAND, OR

PREP: 20 MIN. • **COOK:** 5½ HOURS
MAKES: 10 SERVINGS

- **2 packages (16 ounces each) frozen cut green beans, thawed**
- **2 cans (10¾ ounces each) condensed cream of mushroom soup, undiluted**
- **1 can (8 ounces) sliced water chestnuts, drained**
- **1 cup 2% milk**
- **6 bacon strips, cooked and crumbled**
- **1 teaspoon pepper**
- **⅛ teaspoon paprika**
- **4 ounces process cheese (Velveeta), cubed**
- **1 can (2.8 ounces) French-fried onions**

In a 4-qt. slow cooker, combine the green beans, soup, water chestnuts, milk, bacon, pepper and paprika. Cover and cook on low for 5-6 hours or until beans are tender; stir in cheese. Cover and cook for 30 minutes or until cheese is melted. Sprinkle with onions.

"This is one of my favorite soup recipes to serve in the winter because it's super-easy to make and fills the whole house with a wonderful aroma. My whole family loves it!"

—**BRANDY STANSBURY** EDNA, TX

GINGER CHICKEN NOODLE SOUP

EAT SMART

Ginger Chicken Noodle Soup

PREP: 15 MIN. • **COOK:** 3½ HOURS
MAKES: 8 SERVINGS (2½ QUARTS)

- **1 pound boneless skinless chicken breasts, cubed**
- **2 medium carrots, shredded**
- **3 tablespoons sherry or reduced-sodium chicken broth**
- **2 tablespoons rice vinegar**
- **1 tablespoon reduced-sodium soy sauce**
- **2 to 3 teaspoons minced fresh gingerroot**
- **¼ teaspoon pepper**
- **6 cups reduced-sodium chicken broth**
- **1 cup water**
- **2 cups fresh snow peas, halved**
- **2 ounces uncooked angel hair pasta, broken into thirds**

1. In a 5-qt. slow cooker, combine the first seven ingredients; stir in broth and water. Cook, covered, on low 3-4 hours or until chicken is tender.

2. Stir in snow peas and pasta. Cook, covered, on low 30 minutes longer or until snow peas and pasta are tender.

PER SERVING *126 cal., 2 g fat (trace sat. fat), 31 mg chol., 543 mg sodium, 11 g carb., 2 g fiber, 16 g pro.* ***Diabetic Exchanges:*** *2 lean meat, 1 starch.*

Autumn Pumpkin Chili

Everyone loves this chili, even my most finicky grandchildren. It wouldn't be fall without this savory standby.

—KIMBERLY NAGY PORT HADLOCK, WA

PREP: 20 MIN. • **COOK:** 7 HOURS
MAKES: 4 SERVINGS

- **1 medium onion, chopped**
- **1 small green pepper, chopped**
- **1 small sweet yellow pepper, chopped**
- **1 tablespoon canola oil**
- **1 garlic clove, minced**
- **1 pound ground turkey**
- **1 can (15 ounces) solid-pack pumpkin**
- **1 can (14½ ounces) diced tomatoes, undrained**
- **4½ teaspoons chili powder**
- **¼ teaspoon pepper**
- **¼ teaspoon salt**
- **Optional toppings: shredded cheddar cheese, sour cream and sliced green onions**

1. Saute the onion and green and yellow peppers in oil in a large skillet until tender. Add garlic; cook 1 minute longer. Crumble turkey into skillet. Cook over medium heat until meat is no longer pink.

2. Transfer to a 3-qt. slow cooker. Stir in the pumpkin, tomatoes, chili powder, pepper and salt. Cover and cook on low for 7-9 hours. Serve with toppings of your choice.

COUNTRY RIB SANDWICHES

Country Rib Sandwiches

Perfect for a weekday dinner or casual picnic in the backyard, these sandwiches are packed with delicious flavor.

—MARGARET LUCHSINGER JUPITER, FL

PREP: 30 MIN. • **COOK:** 6 HOURS
MAKES: 8 SERVINGS

- **1 large onion, chopped**
- **2 pounds boneless country-style pork ribs**
- **½ cup ketchup**
- **¼ cup plum sauce**
- **¼ cup chili sauce**
- **2 tablespoons brown sugar**
- **1 teaspoon celery seed**
- **1 teaspoon garlic powder**
- **1 teaspoon liquid smoke, optional**
- **½ teaspoon ground allspice**
- **8 kaiser rolls, split**

1. Place onion in a 3-qt. slow cooker; top with ribs. Combine the ketchup, plum sauce, chili sauce, brown sugar, celery seed, garlic powder, liquid smoke if desired and allspice; pour over ribs.

2. Cover and cook on low for 6-7 hours or until meat is tender. Shred meat with two forks. Serve on rolls.

EAT SMART

Butternut Squash with Whole Grain Pilaf

Fresh thyme really shines in this hearty slow-cooked side dish featuring nutritious Kashi and vitamin-packed spinach and winter squash.

—TASTE OF HOME TEST KITCHEN

PREP: 15 MIN. • **COOK:** 4 HOURS
MAKES: 12 SERVINGS (¾ CUP EACH)

- **1 cup Kashi whole grain pilaf**
- **1 medium butternut squash (about 3 pounds), cut into ½-inch cubes**
- **1 can (14½ ounces) vegetable broth**
- **1 medium onion, chopped**
- **½ cup water**
- **3 garlic cloves, minced**
- **2 teaspoons minced fresh thyme or ½ teaspoon dried thyme**
- **½ teaspoon salt**
- **¼ teaspoon pepper**
- **1 package (6 ounces) fresh baby spinach**

Place pilaf in a 4-qt slow cooker. In a large bowl, combine the squash, broth, onion, water, garlic, thyme, salt and pepper; add to slow cooker. Cover and cook on low for 4-5 hours or until pilaf is tender, adding spinach during the last 30 minutes of cooking.

PER SERVING *97 cal., 1 g fat (trace sat. fat), 0 chol., 280 mg sodium, 20 g carb., 5 g fiber, 3 g pro.* ***Diabetic Exchange:*** *1 starch.*

Creamy Corn

You only need a few ingredients and a slow cooker to make this rich side dish. And with the satisfying accompaniment cooking on its own, you'll have some extra time to prepare the main course.

—**JUDY MCCARTHY** DERBY, KS

PREP: 5 MIN. • **COOK:** 4 HOURS
MAKES: 8 SERVINGS

- **2 packages (16 ounces each) frozen corn**
- **1 package (8 ounces) cream cheese, cubed**
- **⅓ cup butter, cubed**
- **½ teaspoon garlic powder**
- **½ teaspoon salt**
- **¼ teaspoon pepper**

In a 3-qt. slow cooker, combine all ingredients. Cover and cook on low for 4 hours or until heated through and cheese is melted. Stir well before serving.

French Dips

A chuck roast slow-simmered in a beefy broth is delicious when shredded and spooned onto rolls. I serve the cooking juices in individual cups for dipping.

—**CARLA KIMBALL** CALLAWAY, NE

PREP: 5 MIN. • **COOK:** 6 HOURS
MAKES: 10 SERVINGS

- **1 boneless beef chuck roast (3 pounds), trimmed**
- **1 can (10½ ounces) condensed French onion soup, undiluted**
- **1 can (10½ ounces) condensed beef consomme, undiluted**
- **1 can (10½ ounces) condensed beef broth, undiluted**
- **1 teaspoon beef bouillon granules**
- **8 to 10 French or Italian rolls, split**

1. Halve roast and place in a 3-qt. slow cooker. Combine the soup, consomme, broth and bouillon; pour over roast. Cover and cook on low for 6-8 hours or until meat is tender.

2. Remove meat and shred with two forks. Serve on rolls. Skim fat from cooking juices and serve as a dipping sauce.

FREEZE IT

Barbecued Beef Sandwiches

Chuck roast makes delicious shredded beef sandwiches after simmering in a rich homemade sauce all day. The meat really is tender and juicy, and it only takes minutes to prepare. This is a nice meal to enjoy during the workweek.

—**TATINA SMITH** SAN ANGELO, TX

PREP: 20 MIN. • **COOK:** 8¼ HOURS
MAKES: 12 SERVINGS

- **1 boneless beef chuck roast (3 pounds)**
- **1½ cups ketchup**
- **¼ cup packed brown sugar**
- **¼ cup barbecue sauce**
- **2 tablespoons Worcestershire sauce**
- **2 tablespoons Dijon mustard**
- **1 teaspoon Liquid Smoke, optional**
- **½ teaspoon salt**
- **¼ teaspoon garlic powder**
- **¼ teaspoon pepper**
- **12 sandwich buns, split**
- **Sliced onions, dill pickles and pickled jalapenos, optional**

1. Cut roast in half and place in a 3- or 4-qt. slow cooker. In a small bowl, combine the ketchup, brown sugar, barbecue sauce, Worcestershire sauce, mustard, liquid smoke if desired and seasonings. Pour over beef.

2. Cover and cook on low for 8-10 hours or until meat is tender. Remove meat; cool slightly. Skim fat from cooking liquid.

3. Shred beef with two forks; return to the slow cooker. Cover and cook for 15 minutes or until heated through. Using a slotted spoon, place ½ cup on each bun. Serve with onions, pickles and jalapenos if desired.

FREEZE OPTION *Place individual portions of cooled meat mixture in freezer containers. To use, partially thaw in refrigerator overnight. Microwave, covered, on high in a microwave-safe dish until heated through, gently stirring and adding a little broth or water if necessary.*

BARBECUED BEEF SANDWICHES

"I combine ingredients for this hearty chili the night before, start my trusty slow cooker in the morning and come home to a rich, spicy meal at night!"
—**MARJORIE AU** HONOLULU, HI

EAT SMART

Vegetarian Chili Ole!

PREP: 35 MIN. • **COOK:** 6 HOURS
MAKES: 7 SERVINGS

- **1 can (16 ounces) kidney beans, rinsed and drained**
- **1 can (15 ounces) black beans, rinsed and drained**
- **1 can (14½ ounces) diced tomatoes, undrained**
- **1½ cups frozen corn**
- **1 large onion, chopped**
- **1 medium zucchini, chopped**
- **1 medium sweet red pepper, chopped**
- **1 can (4 ounces) chopped green chilies**
- **1 ounce Mexican chocolate, chopped**
- **1 cup water**
- **1 can (6 ounces) tomato paste**
- **1 tablespoon cornmeal**
- **1 tablespoon chili powder**
- **½ teaspoon salt**
- **½ teaspoon dried oregano**
- **½ teaspoon ground cumin**
- **¼ teaspoon hot pepper sauce, optional**
- **Optional toppings: diced tomatoes, chopped green onions and crumbled queso fresco**

1. In a 4-qt. slow cooker, combine the first nine ingredients. Combine the water, tomato paste, cornmeal, chili powder, salt, oregano, cumin and pepper sauce if desired until smooth; stir into slow cooker. Cover and cook on low for 6-8 hours or until vegetables are tender.
2. Serve with toppings of your choice.

PER SERVING *216 cal., 1 g fat (trace sat. fat), 0 chol., 559 mg sodium, 43 g carb., 10 g fiber, 11 g pro.* ***Diabetic Exchanges:*** *2½ starch, 1 lean meat.*

FRENCH ONION SOUP WITH MEATBALLS

French Onion Soup with Meatballs

I got the idea for how to make this soup after I went to a brewhouse restaurant that put ale in their gravy. I make this every time the weather starts to cool down in the fall—it's comfort food for the soul.
—**CRYSTAL HOLSINGER** SURPRISE, AZ

PREP: 15 MIN. • **COOK:** 8 HOURS
MAKES: 6 SERVINGS

- **1 package (12 ounces) frozen fully cooked Italian meatballs**
- **2 large sweet onions, sliced**
- **2 garlic cloves, minced**
- **1 teaspoon beef bouillon granules**
- **½ teaspoon dried thyme**
- **¼ teaspoon salt**
- **¼ teaspoon pepper**
- **5 cups beef broth**
- **1 bottle (12 ounces) pale ale or additional beef broth**
- **18 slices French bread baguette (¼ inch thick)**
- **12 slices Muenster or cheddar cheese**

1. In a 4-qt. slow cooker, combine the first nine ingredients. Cook, covered, on low 8-10 hours or until onions are tender.
2. Ladle soup into six broiler-safe 16-oz. ramekins. Top each with three slices of bread and two slices of cheese. Broil 4-6 in. from heat 2-3 minutes or until cheese is melted. Serve immediately.

Garlic Green Beans with Gorgonzola

I updated the green bean holiday side dish by adding a touch of white wine, fresh thyme and green onions. It's delicious, easy to make and my family looks forward to it!

—**NANCY HEISHMAN** LAS VEGAS, NV

PREP: 20 MIN. • **COOK:** 3 HOURS
MAKES: 10 SERVINGS

- **2 pounds fresh green beans, trimmed and halved**
- **1 can (8 ounces) sliced water chestnuts, drained**
- **4 green onions, chopped**
- **5 bacon strips, cooked and crumbled, divided**
- **⅓ cup white wine or chicken broth**
- **2 tablespoons minced fresh thyme or 2 teaspoons dried thyme**
- **4 garlic cloves, minced**
- **1½ teaspoons seasoned salt**
- **1 cup (8 ounces) sour cream**
- **¾ cup crumbled Gorgonzola cheese**

1. Place green beans, water chestnuts, green onions and 1/4 cup cooked bacon in a 4-qt. slow cooker. In a small bowl, mix wine, thyme, garlic and seasoned salt; pour over top. Cook, covered, on low 3-4 hours or until green beans are crisp-tender. Drain liquid from beans.

2. Just before serving, stir in sour cream; sprinkle with cheese and remaining bacon.

GARLIC GREEN BEANS WITH GORGONZOLA

Parsley Smashed Potatoes

PREP: 20 MIN. • **COOK:** 6 HOURS
MAKES: 8 SERVINGS

- **16 small red potatoes (about 2 pounds)**
- **1 celery rib, sliced**
- **1 medium carrot, sliced**
- **¼ cup finely chopped onion**
- **2 cups chicken broth**
- **1 tablespoon minced fresh parsley**
- **1½ teaspoons salt, divided**
- **1 teaspoon pepper, divided**
- **1 garlic clove, minced**
- **2 tablespoons butter, melted**
- **Additional minced fresh parsley**

1. Place potatoes, celery, carrot and onion in a 4-qt. slow cooker. In a small bowl, mix broth, parsley, 1 teaspoon salt, 1/2 teaspoon pepper and garlic; pour over vegetables. Cook, covered, on low 6-8 hours or until potatoes are tender.

2. Transfer potatoes from slow cooker to a 15x10x1-in. pan; discard cooking liquid and vegetables. Using the bottom of a measuring cup, flatten potatoes slightly. Transfer to a large bowl; drizzle with butter. Sprinkle with remaining salt and pepper; toss to coat. Sprinkle with additional parsley.

PER SERVING *114 cal., 3 g fat (2 g sat. fat), 8 mg chol., 190 mg sodium, 20 g carb., 2 g fiber, 2 g pro.* ***Diabetic Exchanges:*** *1 starch, 1/2 fat.*

For best results, crumble the **Gorgonzola** yourself for the **green beans.** Ready-made crumbles may have additives that affect their **creaminess** and **melting** ability.

"I love potatoes but hate the work involved in making mashed potatoes from scratch. I came up with this simple side dish that was made even easier thanks to my slow cooker. The best part is I can use the leftover broth for soup the next day!" **—KATIE HAGY** BLACKSBURG, SC

PARSLEY SMASHED POTATOES

Snacks & Sweets

87

88

90

Dazzle family and friends with **hot munchies**, cheesy party dips, **over-the-top desserts**, spiced winter drinks and more. They'll be amazed that you made it in your **trusty slow cooker**! Or, keep this **busy-cook's secret** all to yourself.

SOUTHWESTERN PULLED PORK CROSTINI

Southwestern Pulled Pork Crostini

For a unique take on crostini, these hearty appetizers are great for cookouts, tailgating and other casual parties. Everyone enjoys these spicy, sweet and salty bites, which makes the recipe even more special to me.

—RANDY CARTWRIGHT LINDEN, WI

PREP: 45 MIN. • **COOK:** 6 HOURS
MAKES: 32 APPETIZERS

- **1 boneless pork shoulder butt roast (about 2 pounds)**
- **½ cup lime juice**
- **2 envelopes mesquite marinade mix**
- **¼ cup sugar**
- **¼ cup olive oil**

SALSA

- **1 cup frozen corn, thawed**
- **1 cup canned black beans, rinsed and drained**
- **1 small tomato, finely chopped**
- **2 tablespoons finely chopped seeded jalapeno pepper**
- **2 tablespoons lime juice**
- **2 tablespoons olive oil**
- **1½ teaspoons ground cumin**
- **1 teaspoon chili powder**
- **½ teaspoon salt**
- **¼ teaspoon crushed red pepper flakes**

SAUCE

- **1 can (4 ounces) chopped green chilies**
- **⅓ cup apricot preserves**
- **⅛ teaspoon salt**

CROSTINI

- **32 slices French bread baguette (¼ inch thick)**
- **¼ cup olive oil**
- **⅔ cup crumbled queso fresco or feta cheese**
- **Lime wedges, optional**

1. Place roast in a 3-qt. slow cooker. In a small bowl, whisk lime juice, marinade mix, sugar and oil until blended; pour over roast. Cook, covered, on low 6-8 hours or until meat is tender.

2. For salsa, in a small bowl, combine corn, beans, tomato and jalapeno. Stir in lime juice, oil and seasonings. In a small saucepan, combine sauce ingredients; cook and stir over low heat until blended.

3. For crostini, preheat broiler. Brush bread slices on both sides with oil; place on ungreased baking sheets. Broil 3-4 in. from heat 1-2 minutes on each side or until golden brown.

4. Remove roast from slow cooker; cool slightly. Shred pork with two forks. To serve, layer toasts with salsa, pork and cheese. Top with sauce. If desired, serve with lime wedges.

Creamy Cranberry Meatballs

Extras from tonight's rich and juicy appetizers can become tomorrow's entree. Just serve the meatballs over a bed of rice or buttered noodles— if you have any left over.

—AMY WARREN MAINEVILLE, OH

PREP: 10 MIN. • **COOK:** 3 HOURS
MAKES: ABOUT 5 DOZEN

- **2 envelopes brown gravy mix**
- **1 package (32 ounces) frozen fully cooked Swedish meatballs**
- **⅔ cup jellied cranberry sauce**
- **2 teaspoons Dijon mustard**
- **¼ cup heavy whipping cream**

Prepare gravy mix according to package directions. In a 4-qt. slow cooker, combine the meatballs, cranberry sauce, mustard and gravy. Cover and cook on low for 3-4 hours or until heated through, adding cream during the last 30 minutes of cooking.

Queso fresco is sometimes labeled queso blanco. It has a **neutral** but salty flavor. Feta, which is also **salty**, is a good substitute that's easier to find.

Garlic Swiss Fondue

I've been making this recipe for years—everyone flips over the wonderful flavors. When cooled, this cheesy appetizer is also fantastic as a cracker spread.

—CLEO GONSKE REDDING, CA

PREP: 10 MIN. • **COOK:** 2 HOURS
MAKES: 3 CUPS

- **4 cups (16 ounces) shredded Swiss cheese**
- **1 can (10¾ ounces) condensed cheddar cheese soup, undiluted**
- **2 tablespoons sherry or chicken broth**
- **1 tablespoon Dijon mustard**
- **2 garlic cloves, minced**
- **2 teaspoons hot pepper sauce**
- **Cubed French bread baguette, sliced apples and seedless red grapes**

In a 1½-qt. slow cooker, mix the first six ingredients. Cook, covered, on low 2 to 2½ hours or until cheese is melted, stirring every 30 minutes. Serve warm with bread cubes and fruit.

EAT SMART

Apple Pie Oatmeal Dessert

Here's a warm dessert that brings back memories of time spent with my family around the kitchen table. I serve it with sweetened whipped cream or vanilla ice cream as a topper.

—CAROL GREER EARLVILLE, IL

PREP: 15 MIN. • **COOK:** 4 HOURS
MAKES: 6 SERVINGS

- **1 cup quick-cooking oats**
- **½ cup all-purpose flour**
- **⅓ cup packed brown sugar**
- **2 teaspoons baking powder**
- **1½ teaspoons apple pie spice**
- **¼ teaspoon salt**
- **3 eggs**
- **1⅔ cups 2% milk, divided**
- **1½ teaspoons vanilla extract**
- **3 medium apples, peeled and finely chopped**
- **Vanilla ice cream, optional**

1. In a large bowl, whisk oats, flour, brown sugar, baking powder, pie spice and salt. In a small bowl, whisk eggs, 1 cup milk and vanilla until blended. Add to oat mixture, stirring just until moistened. Fold in apples.

2. Transfer to a greased 3-qt. slow cooker. Cook, covered, on low 4-5 hours or until apples are tender and top is set.

3. Stir in remaining milk. Serve warm or cold with ice cream if desired.

PER SERVING *238 cal., 5 g fat (2 g sat. fat), 111 mg chol., 306 mg sodium, 41 g carb., 3 g fiber, 8 g pro.*

APPLE PIE OATMEAL DESSERT

EAT SMART

Warm Spiced Cider Punch

Let the enticing aroma of apple cider, orange juice and sweet spices help get your next party started. I garnish each mug with an orange wheel, which most folks drop into their hot cider.

—SUSAN SMITH FOREST, VA

PREP: 5 MIN. • **COOK:** 4 HOURS
MAKES: 8 SERVINGS

- **4 cups apple cider or unsweetened apple juice**
- **2¼ cups water**
- **¾ cup orange juice concentrate**
- **¾ teaspoon ground nutmeg**
- **¾ teaspoon ground ginger**
- **3 whole cloves**
- **2 cinnamon sticks**
- **Orange slices and additional cinnamon sticks, optional**

1. In a 3-qt. slow cooker, combine the apple cider, water, orange juice concentrate, nutmeg and ginger. Place cloves and cinnamon sticks on a double thickness of cheesecloth; bring up corners of cloth and tie with string to form a bag. Place bag in slow cooker.
2. Cover and cook on low for 4-5 hours or until heated through. Discard spice bag. Garnish with orange slices and additional cinnamon sticks if desired.

PER SERVING *108 cal., trace fat (trace sat. fat), 0 chol., 13 mg sodium, 26 g carb., trace fiber, 1 g pro.* ***Diabetic Exchange:*** *2 fruit.*

Raisin Bread Pudding

My sister gave me the recipe for this delicious bread pudding that's dotted with raisins. It's a big hit with everyone who's tried it. A homemade vanilla sauce goes together quickly on the stovetop and is yummy drizzled over warm servings of this old-fashioned treat.

—SHERRY NIESE MCCOMB, OH

PREP: 20 MIN. • **COOK:** 4 HOURS
MAKES: 6 SERVINGS

- **8 slices bread, cubed**
- **4 eggs**
- **2 cups milk**
- **¼ cup sugar**
- **¼ cup butter, melted**
- **¼ cup raisins**
- **½ teaspoon ground cinnamon**

SAUCE

- **2 tablespoons butter**
- **2 tablespoons all-purpose flour**
- **1 cup water**
- **¾ cup sugar**
- **1 teaspoon vanilla extract**

1. Place bread cubes in a greased 3-qt. slow cooker. In a large bowl, beat eggs and milk; stir in the sugar, butter, raisins and cinnamon. Pour over bread; stir.
2. Cover and cook on high for 1 hour. Reduce heat to low; cook for 3-4 hours or until a thermometer reads 160°.
3. For sauce, melt butter in a small saucepan. Stir in flour until smooth. Gradually add water, sugar and vanilla. Bring to a boil; cook and stir for 2 minutes or until thickened. Serve with warm bread pudding.

RAISIN BREAD PUDDING

"Preparing the pulled turkey in a delicious teriyaki sauce for these snack-size sandwiches is a breeze with the slow cooker. Serve them on lightly toasted sweet dinner rolls for the finishing touch."
—**AMANDA HOOP** SEAMAN, OH

MINI TERIYAKI TURKEY SANDWICHES

Mini Teriyaki Turkey Sandwiches

PREP: 20 MIN. • **COOK:** 5½ HOURS
MAKES: 20 SERVINGS

- **2 boneless skinless turkey breast halves (2 pounds each)**
- **⅔ cup packed brown sugar**
- **⅔ cup reduced-sodium soy sauce**
- **¼ cup cider vinegar**
- **3 garlic cloves, minced**
- **1 tablespoon minced fresh gingerroot**
- **½ teaspoon pepper**
- **2 tablespoons cornstarch**
- **2 tablespoons cold water**
- **20 Hawaiian sweet rolls**
- **2 tablespoons butter, melted**

1. Place turkey in a 5- or 6-qt. slow cooker. In a small bowl, combine brown sugar, soy sauce, vinegar, garlic, ginger and pepper; pour over turkey. Cook, covered, on low 5-6 hours or until meat is tender.

2. Remove turkey from slow cooker. In a small bowl, mix cornstarch and water until smooth; gradually stir into cooking liquid. When cool enough to handle, shred meat with two forks and return meat to slow cooker. Cook, covered, on high 30-35 minutes or until sauce is thickened.

3. Preheat oven to 325°. Split rolls and brush cut sides with butter; place on an ungreased baking sheet, cut side up. Bake 8-10 minutes or until toasted and golden brown. Spoon ⅓ cup turkey mixture on roll bottoms. Replace tops.

Hawaiian sweet rolls are tender and slightly **sweet**. If they're not in your store, use **egg or potato rolls**, which are **softer** and **richer** than regular dinner rolls.

SLOW COOKER CHERRY BUCKLE

Slow Cooker Cherry Buckle

This is my version of a recipe I saw on a cooking show. When the enticing aromas of this down-home dessert drift into the kitchen, it's hard not to take a peek in the slow cooker, but keep that lid on! For a really decadent dessert, top servings off with vanilla ice cream.

—**SHERRI MELOTIK** OAK CREEK, WI

PREP: 10 MIN. • **COOK:** 3 HOURS
MAKES: 6 SERVINGS

- **2 cans (15 ounces each) sliced pears, drained**
- **1 can (21 ounces) cherry pie filling**
- **¼ teaspoon almond extract**
- **1 package yellow cake mix (regular size)**
- **¼ cup old-fashioned oats**
- **¼ cup sliced almonds**
- **1 tablespoon brown sugar**
- **½ cup butter, melted**
- **Vanilla ice cream, optional**

1. In a greased 5-qt. slow cooker, combine pears and pie filling; stir in extract. In a large bowl, combine cake mix, oats, almonds and brown sugar; stir in melted butter. Sprinkle over fruit.

2. Cook, covered, on low 3-4 hours or until topping is golden brown. If desired, serve with ice cream.

Sweet & Spicy Chicken Wings

The meat literally falls off the bones of these wings! Spice lovers will get a kick out of the big sprinkling of red pepper flakes.

—**SUE BAYLESS** PRIOR LAKE, MN

PREP: 25 MIN. • COOK: 5 HOURS
MAKES: ABOUT 2½ DOZEN

- **3 pounds chicken wings**
- **1½ cups ketchup**
- **1 cup packed brown sugar**
- **1 small onion, finely chopped**
- **¼ cup finely chopped sweet red pepper**
- **2 tablespoons chili powder**
- **2 tablespoons Worcestershire sauce**
- **1½ teaspoons crushed red pepper flakes**
- **1 teaspoon ground mustard**
- **1 teaspoon dried basil**
- **1 teaspoon dried thyme**
- **1 teaspoon pepper**

Cut wings into three sections; discard wing tip sections. Place chicken in a 4-qt. slow cooker. In a small bowl, combine the remaining ingredients. Pour over chicken; stir until coated. Cover and cook on low for 5-6 hours or until chicken juices run clear.

NOTE *Uncooked chicken wing sections (wingettes) may be substituted for whole chicken wings.*

FREEZE IT

Apple-Pear Compote

PREP: 20 MIN. • **COOK:** 3¼ HOURS
MAKES: 8 CUPS

- **5 medium apples, peeled and chopped**
- **3 medium pears, chopped**
- **1 medium orange, thinly sliced**
- **½ cup dried cranberries**
- **½ cup packed brown sugar**
- **½ cup maple syrup**
- **⅓ cup butter, cubed**
- **2 tablespoons lemon juice**
- **2 teaspoons ground cinnamon**
- **1 teaspoon ground ginger**
- **5 tablespoons orange juice, divided**
- **4 teaspoons cornstarch**
- **Sweetened whipped cream and toasted chopped pecans, optional**

1. In a 4- or 5-qt. slow cooker, combine the first 10 ingredients. Stir in 2 tablespoons orange juice. Cook, covered, on low 3-4 hours or until fruit is tender.

2. In a small bowl, mix cornstarch and remaining orange juice until smooth; gradually stir into fruit mixture. Cook, covered, on high 15-20 minutes longer or until sauce is thickened. If desired, top with whipped cream and pecans.

FREEZE OPTION *Freeze cooled compote in freezer containers. To use, partially thaw in refrigerator overnight. Heat through in a saucepan, stirring occasionally and adding a little orange juice if necessary.*

"Apples and pears are always popular, so this warm, comforting dessert recipe is great for potlucks or other get-togethers. I also like to add raisins or chopped nuts to the compote. For a more adult flavor I add 1/3 cup brandy or dark rum."
—**NANCY HEISHMAN** LAS VEGAS, NV

APPLE-PEAR COMPOTE

Hot Bacon Cheese Dip

I've tried several appetizer recipes before, but this one is my surefire people-pleaser. The thick dip has lots of bacon and cheese flavor. It always keeps my friends happily munching.
—**SUZANNE WHITAKER** KNOXVILLE, TN

PREP: 15 MIN. • **COOK:** 2 HOURS
MAKES: 4 CUPS

- **2 packages (8 ounces each) cream cheese, cubed**
- **4 cups (16 ounces) shredded cheddar cheese**
- **1 cup half-and-half cream**
- **2 teaspoons Worcestershire sauce**
- **1 teaspoon dried minced onion**
- **1 teaspoon prepared mustard**
- **16 bacon strips, cooked and crumbled**
- **Tortilla chips or French bread slices**

1. In a 1½-qt. slow cooker, combine the first six ingredients. Cover and cook on low for 2-3 hours or until cheeses are melted, stirring occasionally.

2. Just before serving, stir in bacon. Serve warm with tortilla chips or bread.

FREEZE IT

Turkey-Mushroom Egg Rolls

I slow-cook ground turkey in a hoisin, soy and sesame sauce along with fresh veggies for a finger-licking filling for egg rolls. These egg rolls are a favorite appetizer with guests—I never have any leftovers!

—**SARAH HERSE** BROOKLYN, NY

PREP: 1¼ HOURS • **COOK:** 4 HOURS
MAKES: 3½ DOZEN

- **1½ pounds ground turkey**
- **½ pound sliced fresh mushrooms**
- **2 medium leeks (white portion only), thinly sliced**
- **3 celery ribs, thinly sliced**
- **½ cup hoisin sauce**
- **2 tablespoons minced fresh gingerroot**
- **2 tablespoons rice vinegar**
- **2 tablespoons reduced-sodium soy sauce**
- **1 tablespoon packed brown sugar**
- **1 tablespoon sesame oil**
- **2 garlic cloves, minced**
- **½ cup sliced water chestnuts, chopped**
- **3 green onions, thinly sliced**
- **42 egg roll wrappers**
- **Oil for frying**
- **Sweet-and-sour sauce or Chinese-style mustard, optional**

1. In a large skillet, cook turkey over medium heat 8-10 minutes or until no longer pink, breaking into crumbles. Transfer to a 5-qt. slow cooker.

2. Stir in mushrooms, leeks, celery, hoisin sauce, ginger, vinegar, soy sauce, brown sugar, sesame oil and garlic. Cook, covered, on low 4-5 hours or until vegetables are tender. Stir water chestnuts and green onions into turkey mixture; cool slightly.

3. With one corner of an egg roll wrapper facing you, place 2 tablespoons filling just below center of wrapper. (Cover remaining wrappers with a damp paper towel until ready to use.) Fold bottom corner over filling; moisten remaining wrapper edges with water. Fold side corners toward center over filling. Roll egg roll up tightly, pressing at tip to seal. Repeat.

4. In an electric skillet, heat 1/4 in. of oil to 375°. Fry egg rolls, a few at a time, 3-4 minutes or until golden brown, turning occasionally. Drain on paper towels. If desired, serve with sweet-and-sour sauce.

FREEZE OPTION *Cover and freeze unfried egg rolls on waxed paper-lined baking sheets until firm. Transfer to resealable plastic freezer bags; return to freezer. To use, fry egg rolls as recipe directs, increasing cooking time to 4-5 minutes.*

TURKEY-MUSHROOM EGG ROLLS

Cinnamon-Apple Brown Betty

If I had to define the Betty of Apple Brown Betty, she'd be a smart and thrifty Southern gal with a knack for creating simple, soul-comforting desserts. In this sweet dish, spiced apples are layered with cinnamon-raisin bread for a wonderful slow-cooked twist on the baked classic.

—**HEATHER DEMERITTE** SCOTTSDALE, AZ

PREP: 15 MIN. • **COOK:** 2 HOURS
MAKES: 6 SERVINGS

- **5 medium tart apples, cubed**
- **2 tablespoons lemon juice**
- **1 cup packed brown sugar**
- **1 teaspoon ground cinnamon**
- **¼ teaspoon ground nutmeg**
- **6 cups cubed day-old cinnamon-raisin bread (about 10 slices)**
- **6 tablespoons butter, melted**
- **Sweetened whipped cream, optional**

1. In a large bowl, toss apples with lemon juice. In a small bowl, mix brown sugar, cinnamon and nutmeg; add to apple mixture and toss to coat. In a large bowl, drizzle butter over bread cubes; toss to coat.

2. Place 2 cups bread cubes in a greased 3- or 4-qt. slow cooker. Layer with half of the apple mixture and 2 cups bread cubes. Repeat layers. Cook, covered, on low 2-3 hours or until apples are tender. Stir before serving. If desired, top with whipped cream.

Molten Mocha Cake

PREP: 10 MIN. • **COOK:** 2½ HOURS
MAKES: 4 SERVINGS

- **4 eggs**
- **1½ cups sugar**
- **½ cup butter, melted**
- **3 teaspoons vanilla extract**
- **1 cup all-purpose flour**
- **½ cup baking cocoa**
- **1 tablespoon instant coffee granules**
- **¼ teaspoon salt**
- **Fresh raspberries or sliced fresh strawberries and vanilla ice cream, optional**

1. In a large bowl, beat eggs, sugar, butter and vanilla until blended. In another bowl, whisk flour, cocoa, coffee granules and salt; gradually beat into egg mixture.

2. Transfer to greased 1½-qt. slow cooker. Cook, covered, on low 2½ to 3 hours or until a toothpick comes out with moist crumbs. If desired, serve warm cake with berries and ice cream.

"When I first made my slow cooker chocolate cake, my husband and daughter LOVED it. My daughter claims it's one of her MOST favorite desserts! I also shared the cake with my next-door neighbor's son, who liked it so much that he ate the whole thing without telling anyone about it!"
—**AIMEE FORTNEY** FAIRVIEW, TN

MOLTEN MOCHA CAKE

Chocolate Bread Pudding

I'm a big fan of both chocolate and berries, so I was thrilled to come across this recipe that combines the two. I like to use egg bread when making it.
—**BECKY FOSTER** UNION, OR

PREP: 10 MIN. • **COOK:** 2¼ HOURS
MAKES: 6-8 SERVINGS

- **6 cups cubed day-old bread (¾-inch cubes)**
- **1½ cups semisweet chocolate chips**
- **1 cup fresh raspberries**
- **4 eggs**
- **½ cup heavy whipping cream**
- **½ cup milk**
- **¼ cup sugar**
- **1 teaspoon vanilla extract**
- **Whipped cream and additional raspberries, optional**

1. In a greased 3-qt. slow cooker, layer half of the bread cubes, chocolate chips and raspberries. Repeat layers. In a bowl, whisk the eggs, cream, milk, sugar and vanilla. Pour over bread mixture.
2. Cover and cook on high for 2¼ to 2½ hours or until a thermometer reads 160°. Let stand for 5-10 minutes. Serve with whipped cream and additional raspberries if desired.

Slow Cooker Spiced Poached Pears

Some of the many reasons I love this dessert recipe: it's on the healthy side; it's easy to make; the recipe can be mostly prepared in advance of company arriving; and the presentation is lovely.
—**JILL MANT** DENVER, CO

PREP: 25 MIN. • **COOK:** 4 HOURS
MAKES: 8 SERVINGS

- **1½ cups dry red wine or cranberry juice**
- **⅓ cup packed brown sugar**
- **2 tablespoons dried cherries**
- **1 tablespoon ground cinnamon**
- **1 whole star anise**
- **1 dried Sichuan peppercorn, optional**
- **4 ripe Bosc pears**

GANACHE

- **6 ounces bittersweet chocolate, chopped**
- **¼ cup heavy whipping cream**

TOPPINGS

- **2 tablespoons pine nuts**
- **Fresh blackberries**
- **Sweetened whipped cream, optional**

1. In a 3-qt. slow cooker, mix wine, brown sugar, cherries, cinnamon, star anise and, if desired, peppercorn until blended. Peel and cut pears lengthwise in half. Remove cores, leaving a small well in the center of each. Arrange pears in wine mixture.
2. Cook, covered, on low 4-5 hours or until pears are almost tender. Discard star anise and peppercorn.
3. Place chocolate in a small bowl. In a small saucepan, bring cream just to a boil. Pour over chocolate; stir with a whisk until smooth.
4. To serve, remove pears to dessert dishes; drizzle with some of the poaching liquid. Spoon ganache into wells of pears. Top with pine nuts and blackberries. If desired, serve with whipped cream.

SLOW COOKER SPICED POACHED PEARS

CHILI BEEF PASTA, PAGE 108

“Right after I got married, my aunt gave me her cherished recipe for skillet spaghetti. Over the years, I've tinkered with the ingredients and seasonings to create a healthier dish that my family truly loves.”

—KRISTEN KILLIAN DEPEW, NY
about her recipe, Chili Beef Pasta, on page 108

Stovetop Suppers

Beef & Ground Beef

101

106

96

From **quick pasta suppers** to **classic** New England boiled dinners, and from **nutritious** steak stir-fries to **kid-friendly sloppy joes**, you'll find a bounty of **delectable meal ideas** in this chapter.

SNOW PEAS & BEEF STIR FRY

Snow Peas & Beef Stir-Fry

START TO FINISH: 30 MIN.
MAKES: 6 SERVINGS

- **½ cup reduced-sodium soy sauce**
- **½ cup sherry or water**
- **2 tablespoons cornstarch**
- **2 teaspoons sugar**
- **2 tablespoons canola oil, divided**
- **2 garlic cloves, minced**
- **1½ pounds beef top sirloin steak, thinly sliced**
- **½ pound sliced fresh mushrooms**
- **1 medium onion, cut into thin wedges**
- **½ pound fresh snow peas**
- **Hot cooked rice**

1. In a small bowl, whisk soy sauce, sherry, cornstarch and sugar. Transfer 1/4 cup mixture to a large bowl; stir in 1 tablespoon oil and garlic. Add beef; toss to coat. Let stand 15 minutes.

2. Heat a large skillet over medium-high heat. Add half of the beef mixture; stir-fry 1-2 minutes or until no longer pink. Remove from pan; repeat with remaining beef.

3. In same pan, heat remaining oil over medium-high heat until hot. Add mushrooms and onion; cook and stir until mushrooms are tender. Add snow peas; cook 2-3 minutes longer or until crisp-tender.

4. Stir remaining soy sauce mixture and add to pan. Bring to a boil; cook and stir 1-2 minutes or until sauce is thickened. Return beef to pan; heat through. Serve with rice.

Cranberry Pot Roast

A local restaurant had pot roast with cranberry gravy on the menu, which sounded so good. One day, I added some leftover cranberry barbecue sauce to my pot roast. The tender and flavorful results were the basis for this recipe.

—JIM ULBERG ELK RAPIDS, MI

PREP: 20 MIN. • **COOK:** 2¾ HOURS
MAKES: 10-12 SERVINGS

- **2 tablespoons all-purpose flour**
- **1 teaspoon salt**
- **½ teaspoon pepper**
- **1 beef chuck roast (4 to 5 pounds)**
- **2 tablespoons canola oil**
- **1 medium onion**
- **6 whole cloves**
- **1 cup water**
- **1 medium carrot, shredded**
- **2 cinnamon sticks (3 inches)**
- **1 can (14 ounces) whole-berry cranberry sauce**
- **2 tablespoons cider vinegar**

1. Combine flour, salt and pepper; rub over roast. In a Dutch oven, brown roast in oil. Cut onion in half and stick the cloves into it. Add onion, water, carrot and cinnamon to pan. Bring to a boil. Reduce heat; cover and simmer for 2 hours, adding water if needed.

2. Skim fat. Combine cranberry sauce and vinegar; pour over the roast. Cover and simmer 30-45 minutes longer or until meat is tender. Discard onion, cloves and cinnamon.

TRADITIONAL BOILED DINNER

EAT SMART
Ginger Steak Fried Rice

START TO FINISH: 30 MIN.
MAKES: 4 SERVINGS

- **2 eggs, lightly beaten**
- **2 teaspoons olive oil**
- **¾ pound beef top sirloin steak, cut into thin strips**
- **4 tablespoons reduced-sodium soy sauce, divided**
- **1 package (12 ounces) broccoli coleslaw mix**
- **1 cup frozen peas**
- **2 tablespoons grated fresh gingerroot**
- **3 garlic cloves, minced**
- **2 cups cooked brown rice**
- **4 green onions, sliced**

1. In a large nonstick skillet coated with cooking spray, cook and stir eggs over medium heat until no liquid egg remains, breaking up eggs into small pieces. Remove from pan; wipe skillet clean if necessary.
2. In same pan, heat oil over medium-high heat. Add beef; stir-fry 1-2 minutes or until no longer pink. Stir in 1 tablespoon soy sauce; remove beef from pan.
3. Add coleslaw mix, peas, ginger and garlic to the pan; cook and stir until coleslaw mix is crisp-tender. Add rice and remaining soy sauce, tossing to combine rice with vegetable mixture and heat through. Stir in cooked eggs, beef and green onions; heat through.

PER SERVING *346 cal., 9 g fat (3 g sat. fat), 140 mg chol., 732 mg sodium, 36 g carb., 6 g fiber, 29 g pro.* ***Diabetic Exchanges:*** *3 lean meat, 2 starch, 1 vegetable, ½ fat.*

Traditional Boiled Dinner

Corned beef is a frequent treat in our family. We love the savory flavor the vegetables pick up from simmering with the pickling spices.
—**JOY STRASSER** MUKWONAGO, WI

PREP: 10 MIN. • **COOK:** 2½ HOURS
MAKES: 6 SERVINGS

- **1 corned beef brisket with spice packet (3 pounds)**
- **1 teaspoon whole black peppercorns**
- **2 bay leaves**
- **2 medium potatoes, peeled and quartered**
- **3 medium carrots, quartered**
- **1 medium onion, cut into 6 wedges**
- **1 small head green cabbage, cut into 6 wedges**
- **Prepared horseradish or mustard, optional**

1. Place the brisket and contents of spice packet in a Dutch oven. Add the peppercorns, bay leaves and enough water to cover; bring to a boil. Reduce heat; cover and simmer for 2 hours or until meat is almost tender.
2. Add potatoes, carrots and onion; bring to a boil. Reduce heat; cover and simmer for 10 minutes. Add cabbage, cover and simmer for 15-20 minutes or until tender. Discard bay leaves and peppercorns. Thinly slice meat; serve with vegetables and horseradish or mustard if desired.

Popular in **New England**, the thrifty **boiled dinner** may contain a **variety of foods** that the cook has **on hand**. Ham, chicken, parsnips or turnips may be used.

GINGER STEAK FRIED RICE

SECOND-CHANCE REUBENS

Second-Chance Reubens

If you have lots of tasty meat loaf recipes, you've probably wondered how to liven up the leftovers. This great recipe is the answer! If you like Rueben sandwiches, you'll love this new take on an old favorite.
—**KIMBERLEY JOHNSON** ENGLEWOOD, CO

START TO FINISH: 20 MIN.
MAKES: 4 SERVINGS

- **8 slices rye bread**
- **4 tablespoons Thousand Island salad dressing, divided**
- **4 slices cooked meat loaf, warmed**
- **1 cup sauerkraut, rinsed and well drained**
- **4 slices Swiss cheese**
- **2 tablespoons butter, softened**

1. Spread four bread slices with half of salad dressing. Layer each with meat loaf, sauerkraut and cheese. Spread remaining bread with remaining salad dressing; place over cheese. Butter outsides of sandwiches.
2. In a large skillet over medium heat, toast sandwiches for 2-3 minutes on each side or until bread is lightly browned and cheese is melted.

German Meatballs with Gingersnap Gravy

This recipe was one of Mom's favorites, and now my family enjoys it as well. The beauty of the recipe is that you don't have to brown the meatballs. The gingersnaps give the gravy its rich taste. I have, at times, substituted ground turkey for the beef, and it works just as well.
—**EVELYN KAY** BANNING, CA

PREP: 20 MIN. • **COOK:** 25 MIN.
MAKES: 4 SERVINGS

- **1 egg, beaten**
- **¾ cup soft bread crumbs**
- **1¾ cups water, divided**
- **¼ cup chopped onion**
- **½ teaspoon salt**
- **Dash pepper**
- **1 pound lean ground beef (90% lean)**
- **2 beef bouillon cubes**
- **⅓ cup packed brown sugar**
- **¼ cup raisins**
- **2½ teaspoons lemon juice**
- **½ cup coarsely crushed gingersnaps (about 10 cookies)**
- **Cooked noodles**

1. Combine egg, bread crumbs, 1/4 cup water, onion, salt and pepper; crumble beef over mixture and mix well. Shape into 2½-in. balls.
2. In a large skillet, bring remaining water to a boil. Add bouillon, brown sugar, raisins, lemon juice and gingersnaps. Stir until thoroughly combined. Add meatballs to skillet. Simmer, uncovered, for 20 minutes or until meat is no longer pink. Stir occasionally. Serve with noodles.

BBQ Hoedown Tacos

PREP: 20 MIN. • **COOK:** 15 MIN.
MAKES: 4 SERVINGS

- **1 pound ground beef**
- **1 small onion, chopped**
- **¾ cup barbecue sauce**
- **1 can (4 ounces) chopped green chilies**
- **1 teaspoon ground coriander**
- **1 teaspoon ground cumin**
- **½ teaspoon salt**
- **2 cups angel hair coleslaw mix**
- **¼ cup green goddess salad dressing**
- **8 flour tortillas (6 inches), warmed**
- **8 slices pepper jack cheese**

1. In a large nonstick skillet, cook beef and onion over medium heat until meat is no longer pink; drain. Stir in the barbecue sauce, chilies, coriander, cumin and salt. Bring to a boil. Reduce the heat and simmer, uncovered, for 5-7 minutes to allow flavors to blend.

2. In a small bowl, combine coleslaw mix and salad dressing; toss to coat. On each tortilla, layer cheese, beef mixture and coleslaw; fold to close.

"Here's a twist on traditional tacos that the whole family will love. It's easy to make after a long day at work."
—**DENISE POUNDS** HUTCHINSON, KS

BBQ HOEDOWN TACOS

EAT SMART

Summer Salad with Citrus Vinaigrette

I live in Orange County, which is so named for its beautiful orange groves. This salad is one of my favorite ways to use fresh oranges. It makes a nice light supper on a hot day.

—**CAROLYN WILLIAMS** COSTA MESA, CA

START TO FINISH: 20 MIN.
MAKES: 4 SERVINGS

VINAIGRETTE

- **3 tablespoons orange juice**
- **3 tablespoons red wine vinegar**
- **2 teaspoons honey**
- **1½ teaspoons Dijon mustard**
- **1 teaspoon olive oil**

SALAD

- **1 pound beef top sirloin steak, cut into thin strips**
- **1 tablespoon canola oil**
- **½ teaspoon salt, optional**
- **4 cups torn romaine**
- **2 large oranges, peeled and sectioned**
- **½ cup sliced fresh strawberries**
- **¼ cup chopped walnuts, toasted, optional**

1. Whisk the vinaigrette ingredients; set aside. In a large skillet, stir-fry steak in oil for 1-2 minutes. Sprinkle with salt if desired.

2. In a large bowl, toss romaine, oranges, strawberries and steak. Add vinaigrette and toss to coat. Top with walnuts if desired.

PER SERVING *265 cal., 10 g fat (2 g sat. fat), 46 mg chol., 101 mg sodium, 19 g carb., 4 g fiber, 28 g pro.* ***Diabetic Exchanges:*** *3 lean meat, 1 vegetable, 1 fat, 1/2 starch, 1/2 fruit.*

MAKEOVER COUNTRY-FRIED STEAKS

EAT SMART

Makeover Country-Fried Steak

A healthier country-fried steak? Sounds like an oxymoron, but it's not. This dish keeps its classic comfort-food flavor while dropping over half the fat.

—TASTE OF HOME TEST KITCHEN

PREP: 20 MIN. • **COOK:** 15 MIN.
MAKES: 4 SERVINGS

- **1 beef top round steak (1 pound)**
- **½ teaspoon salt**
- **½ teaspoon garlic powder, divided**
- **½ teaspoon pepper, divided**
- **¼ teaspoon onion powder**
- **½ cup buttermilk**
- **¾ cup plus 4½ teaspoons all-purpose flour, divided**
- **1 tablespoon canola oil**
- **4½ teaspoons butter**
- **1 cup 2% milk**

1. Cut steak into four serving-size pieces; pound to 1/4-in. thickness. Combine the salt, 1/4 teaspoon garlic powder, 1/4 teaspoon pepper and onion powder; sprinkle over steaks.
2. Place buttermilk and 3/4 cup flour in separate shallow bowls. Dip steaks in buttermilk, then flour.
3. In a large skillet, cook steaks in oil over medium heat for 3-4 minutes on each side or until no longer pink. Remove and keep warm.
4. In a small saucepan, melt butter. Stir in remaining flour until smooth; gradually add milk. Bring to a boil; cook and stir for 1 minute or until thickened. Stir in remaining garlic powder and pepper. Serve with steak.

PER SERVING *318 cal., 13 g fat (5 g sat. fat), 80 mg chol., 410 mg sodium, 19 g carb., 1 g fiber, 30 g pro.*

FREEZE IT

Hamburger Stroganoff

I've been making this simple and satisfying dish for many years. Just last year, I tried freezing the ground beef mixture so I'd have a head start on a future dinner. It worked great!

—ALINE CHRISTENOT CHESTER, MT

START TO FINISH: 15 MIN.
MAKES: 2 MAIN DISHES (2 SERVINGS EACH)

- **1 pound ground beef**
- **¼ cup chopped onion**
- **1 garlic clove, minced**
- **1 can (10½ ounces) condensed beef consomme, undiluted**
- **1 can (4 ounces) mushroom stems and pieces, undrained**
- **3 tablespoons lemon juice**
- **¼ teaspoon pepper**

ADDITIONAL INGREDIENTS (FOR EACH DISH)

- **2 cups cooked spiral pasta**
- **½ cup sour cream**
- **2 tablespoons water**

1. In a large skillet over medium heat, cook beef, onion and garlic until meat is no longer pink; drain. Stir in the consomme, mushrooms, lemon juice and pepper.
2. For each main dish, stir pasta, sour cream and water into half of the meat mixture; heat through (do not boil).

FREEZE OPTION *Place half of the mixture in a freezer container; cover and freeze for up to 3 months. Thaw in the refrigerator. Place in a small saucepan and proceed as directed.*

It's smart to double up on **prep** and **freeze half** of the recipe for future meals. Many **meatballs**, meat loaves and **taco fillings freeze very well**.

FREEZE IT

Italian-Style Salisbury Steaks

This is my husband's favorite. He loves it! If you like, you can top each serving with mozzarella or Parmesan cheese.

—HEATHER NALLEY EASLEY, SC

START TO FINISH: 25 MIN.
MAKES: 4 SERVINGS

- **1 egg, beaten**
- **1 teaspoon Worcestershire sauce**
- **½ cup seasoned bread crumbs**
- **½ teaspoon garlic powder**
- **½ teaspoon pepper**
- **1 pound ground beef**
- **1 tablespoon canola oil**
- **1 can (14½ ounces) diced tomatoes with basil, oregano and garlic, undrained**
- **1 can (8 ounces) Italian tomato sauce**

1. In a large bowl, combine the first five ingredients. Crumble beef over mixture and mix well. Shape into four oval patties. In a large skillet, brown patties in oil on both sides. Drain.

2. In a small bowl, combine diced tomatoes and tomato sauce. Pour over patties. Bring to a boil. Reduce heat; cover and simmer for 10-15 minutes or until meat is no longer pink.

FREEZE OPTION *Freeze individual cooled steaks with some tomato mixture in resealable freezer bags. To use, partially thaw in refrigerator overnight. Microwave, covered, on high in a microwave-safe dish until heated through, gently stirring and adding a little water if necessary.*

ITALIAN-STYLE SALISBURY STEAKS

"Top this hearty stew with crumbled blue cheese just before serving to add a burst of flavor. Serve some now and store the rest in the freezer for another meal."

—**NANCY LATULIPPE** SIMCOE, ON

MUSHROOM BEEF STEW

FREEZE IT

Mushroom Beef Stew

PREP: 45 MIN. • **COOK:** 1½ HOURS
MAKES: 9 SERVINGS

- **1 carton (32 ounces) beef broth**
- **1 ounce dried mixed mushrooms**
- **¼ cup all-purpose flour**
- **1 teaspoon salt**
- **1 teaspoon pepper**
- **1 boneless beef chuck roast (2 pounds), cubed**
- **3 tablespoons canola oil**
- **1 pound whole baby portobello mushrooms**
- **5 medium carrots, chopped**
- **1 large onion, chopped**
- **3 garlic cloves, minced**
- **3 teaspoons minced fresh rosemary or 1 teaspoon dried rosemary, crushed**

ADDITIONAL INGREDIENTS

- **2 tablespoons cornstarch**
- **2 tablespoons cold water**
- **Hot cooked egg noodles, optional**
- **¼ cup crumbled blue cheese**

1. Bring broth and dried mushrooms to a boil in a large saucepan. Remove from heat; let stand 15-20 minutes or until mushrooms are softened. Drain mushrooms, reserving liquid; finely chop mushrooms. Set aside.

2. Combine flour, salt and pepper in a large resealable plastic bag; set aside 1 tablespoon for sauce. Add beef, a few pieces at a time, to the remaining flour mixture and shake to coat.

3. Brown beef in oil in batches in a Dutch oven. Add portobello mushrooms, carrots and onion; saute until onion is tender. Add garlic, rosemary and rehydrated mushrooms; cook 1 minute. Stir in reserved flour mixture until blended; gradually add mushroom broth.

4. Bring to a boil. Reduce heat; cover and simmer 1½ to 2 hours or until beef is tender.

5. Bring stew to a boil. Combine cornstarch and water until smooth; gradually stir into pan. Return to a boil; cook and stir 2 minutes or until thickened. Serve with egg noodles if desired; top with blue cheese.

FREEZE OPTION *Freeze cooled stew in freezer containers up to 6 months. To use, thaw in the refrigerator overnight. Place in a Dutch oven; reheat. Serve with egg noodles if desired; top with blue cheese.*

EAT SMART

Black Bean and Beef Tostadas

Just a handful of ingredients add up to one of our family's favorites. Also easy to double for company!

—**SUSAN BROWN** KANSAS CITY, KS

START TO FINISH: 30 MIN.
MAKES: 4 SERVINGS

- **½ pound lean ground beef (90% lean)**
- **1 can (10 ounces) diced tomatoes and green chilies, undrained**
- **1 can (15 ounces) black beans, rinsed and drained**
- **1 can (16 ounces) refried beans, warmed**
- **8 tostada shells**
- **Optional toppings: shredded lettuce, shredded reduced-fat Mexican cheese blend, sour cream and/or salsa**

1. In a large skillet, cook beef over medium heat until no longer pink; drain. Stir in tomatoes. Bring to a boil. Reduce heat; simmer, uncovered, for 6-8 minutes or until most of the liquid is evaporated. Stir in the black beans; heat through.

2. Spread refried beans over tostada shells. Top with beef mixture. Serve with toppings of your choice.

PER SERVING *390 cal., 11 g fat (3 g sat. fat), 44 mg chol., 944 mg sodium, 49 g carb., 12 g fiber, 24 g pro.* ***Diabetic Exchanges:*** *3 starch, 3 lean meat.*

BLACK BEAN AND BEEF TOSTADAS

Greek Ravioli Skillet

Looking to please picky palates? One tester loved this simple skillet entree so much that she made it at home for her 2-year-old daughter. Her daughter said "Mmmmm!" after every bite.

—TASTE OF HOME TEST KITCHEN

START TO FINISH: 30 MIN.
MAKES: 6 SERVINGS

- **1 package (20 ounces) refrigerated cheese ravioli**
- **1 pound ground beef**
- **1 medium zucchini, sliced**
- **1 small red onion, chopped**
- **3 cups marinara or spaghetti sauce**
- **½ cup water**
- **¼ teaspoon pepper**
- **2 medium tomatoes, chopped**
- **½ cup cubed feta cheese**
- **½ cup pitted Greek olives, halved**
- **2 tablespoons minced fresh basil, divided**

1. Cook ravioli according to package directions. Meanwhile, in a large skillet, cook the beef, zucchini and onion over medium heat until meat is no longer pink; drain.

2. Drain ravioli; add to skillet. Stir in the marinara sauce, water and pepper. Bring to a boil. Reduce heat; simmer, uncovered, for 5 minutes.

3. Add the tomatoes, cheese, olives and 1 tablespoon basil. Sprinkle with remaining basil.

GREEK RAVIOLI SKILLET

Freezer Burritos

I love burritos, but the frozen ones are so high in salt and chemicals. So I created these. They're great to have on hand for quick dinners or late-night snacks—I've even had them for breakfast!

—LAURA WINEMILLER DELTA, PA

PREP: 35 MIN. • **COOK:** 15 MIN.
MAKES: 12 SERVINGS

- **1¼ pounds lean ground beef (90% lean)**
- **¼ cup finely chopped onion**
- **1¼ cups salsa**
- **2 tablespoons reduced-sodium taco seasoning**
- **2 cans (15 ounces each) pinto beans, rinsed and drained**
- **½ cup water**
- **2 cups (8 ounces) shredded reduced-fat cheddar cheese**
- **12 flour tortillas (8 inches), warmed**

1. In a large skillet, cook beef and onion over medium heat until meat is no longer pink; drain. Stir in salsa and taco seasoning. Bring to a boil. Reduce heat; simmer, uncovered, for 2-3 minutes. Transfer to a large bowl; set aside.

2. In a food processor, combine pinto beans and water. Cover and process until almost smooth. Add to beef mixture. Stir in cheese.

3. Spoon 1/2 cup beef mixture down the center of each tortilla. Fold ends and sides over filling; roll up. Wrap each burrito in waxed paper and foil. Freeze for up to 1 month.

TO USE FROZEN BURRITOS *Remove foil and waxed paper. Place one burrito on a microwave-safe plate. Microwave on high for 2½ to 2¾ minutes or until a thermometer reads 165°, turning burrito over once. Let stand for 20 seconds.*

NOTE *This recipe was tested in a 1,100-watt microwave.*

PER SERVING *345 cal., 11 g fat (4 g sat. fat), 36 mg chol., 677 mg sodium, 40 g carb., 3 g fiber, 22 g pro.* ***Diabetic Exchanges:*** *2½ starch, 2 lean meat, ½ fat.*

Steak au Poivre

Steak served with mushrooms, cream and brandy: What could be better? This elegant entree can be prepared in just 20 minutes. I like to serve it with thinly sliced French bread baguette to soak up the rich sauce.

—**BARBARA PLETZKE** HERNDON, VA

START TO FINISH: 20 MIN.
MAKES: 4 SERVINGS

- **4 beef tenderloin steaks (6 ounces each)**
- **1 tablespoon coarsely ground pepper**
- **½ teaspoon salt**
- **1 tablespoon plus 2 teaspoons olive oil, divided**
- **2 cups sliced fresh shiitake mushrooms**
- **1 tablespoon minced fresh thyme**
- **2 tablespoons brandy**
- **2 tablespoons heavy whipping cream**

1. Sprinkle steaks with pepper and salt. In a large skillet over medium heat, cook steaks in 1 tablespoon oil for 4-5 minutes on each side or until meat reaches desired doneness (for medium-rare, a thermometer should read 145°; medium, 160°; well-done, 170°). Remove and keep warm.

2. In the same skillet, saute mushroom in remaining oil. Add thyme; cook 1 minute longer. Remove from the heat. Add brandy; cook over medium heat until liquid is evaporated. Stir in cream. Serve sauce with steaks.

Ragu Bolognese

My family loves homemade spaghetti sauce and they always go crazy for this one. I make sure to serve it with plenty of garlic bread.

—**KATE GAUL** DUBUQUE, IA

PREP: 25 MIN. • **COOK:** 2 HOURS
MAKES: 10 SERVINGS (7½ CUPS)

- **1 pound ground beef**
- **½ pound ground pork**
- **¼ pound bacon strips, diced**
- **2 medium onions, chopped**
- **2 celery ribs, chopped**
- **2 small carrots, chopped**
- **4 garlic cloves, minced**
- **1 cup dry red wine or beef broth**
- **1 can (28 ounces) crushed tomatoes**
- **1 can (15 ounces) tomato sauce**
- **2 tablespoons tomato paste**
- **2 bay leaves**
- **2 teaspoons sugar**
- **1 teaspoon salt**
- **½ teaspoon dried thyme**
- **½ teaspoon dried oregano**
- **½ teaspoon each ground cumin, nutmeg and pepper**
- **½ cup heavy whipping cream**
- **2 tablespoons butter**
- **2 tablespoons minced fresh parsley**
- **½ cup grated Parmesan cheese**
- **Hot cooked pasta**

1. In a Dutch oven, cook the beef, pork, bacon, onions, celery and carrots over medium heat until beef is no longer pink; drain. Add garlic; cook 2 minutes longer. Add wine; cook for 4-5 minutes or until liquid is reduced by half.

2. Stir in the tomatoes, tomato sauce, tomato paste, bay leaves, sugar and seasonings. Bring to a boil. Reduce heat; simmer sauce, uncovered, for 1½ to 2 hours or until thickened, stirring occasionally.

3. Discard bay leaves. Add the cream, butter and parsley; cook 2 minutes longer. Stir in cheese. Serve with pasta.

Bolognese refers to a **hearty style** of sauce that contains **wine**, milk or **cream**, and **lots of meat**–usually pork.

RAGU BOLOGNESE

PIZZA JOES

Pizza Joes

These Italian-style sloppy joes are just great. They can be prepared and held until everyone's settled and all set to eat.

—JOANNE SCHLABACH SHREVE, OH

START TO FINISH: 30 MIN.
MAKES: 6 SERVINGS

- **1 pound lean ground beef (90% lean)**
- **1 can (15 ounces) pizza sauce**
- **1 teaspoon dried oregano**
- **½ medium onion**
- **½ medium green pepper**
- **1 ounce sliced pepperoni**
- **6 hamburger buns, split**
- **½ cup shredded mozzarella cheese**
- **½ cup sliced fresh mushrooms**

1. In a large skillet over medium heat, cook beef until no longer pink; drain. Stir in pizza sauce and oregano.

2. In a food processor, combine the onion, pepper and pepperoni; cover and process until chopped. Add to beef mixture. Simmer 20-25 minutes or until vegetables are tender. Spoon mixture onto buns. Top with cheese and mushrooms.

Sweet-and-Sour Beef

This healthful stir-fry recipe is a family favorite. I've used a variety of meats and apples and sometimes replace the green onion with yellow onion. It always tastes great!

—BRITTANY MCCLOUD KENYON, MN

START TO FINISH: 30 MIN.
MAKES: 4 SERVINGS

- **1 tablespoon cornstarch**
- **2 tablespoons cold water**
- **1 pound beef top sirloin steak, cut into ½-inch cubes**
- **1 teaspoon salt**
- **½ teaspoon pepper**
- **3 teaspoons canola oil, divided**
- **1 large green pepper, cut into ½-inch pieces**
- **1 large sweet red pepper, cut into ½-inch pieces**
- **2 medium tart apples, chopped**
- **½ cup plus 2 tablespoons thinly sliced green onions, divided**
- **⅔ cup packed brown sugar**
- **½ cup cider vinegar**
- **Hot cooked rice, optional**

1. In a small bowl, mix cornstarch and water until smooth. Sprinkle beef with salt and pepper. In a large nonstick skillet or wok coated with cooking spray, heat 2 teaspoons oil over medium-high heat. Add beef; stir-fry 2-3 minutes or until no longer pink. Remove from pan.

2. In same skillet, stir-fry peppers and apples in remaining oil for 2 minutes. Stir in 1/2 cup green onions; stir-fry 1-3 minutes longer or until peppers are crisp-tender. Remove from pan.

3. Add brown sugar and vinegar to skillet; bring to a boil, stirring to dissolve sugar. Stir cornstarch mixture and add to pan. Return to a boil; cook and stir 1-2 minutes longer or until thickened.

4. Return beef and pepper mixture to pan; heat through. If desired, serve with rice. Sprinkle with remaining green onion.

SWEET-AND-SOUR BEEF

EAT SMART

Chili Beef Pasta

START TO FINISH: 30 MIN.
MAKES: 6 SERVINGS

- **1 pound lean ground beef (90% lean)**
- **2 tablespoons dried minced onion**
- **2 teaspoons dried oregano**
- **2 teaspoons chili powder**
- **½ teaspoon garlic powder**
- **⅛ teaspoon salt**
- **3 cups tomato juice**
- **2 cups water**
- **1 can (6 ounces) tomato paste**
- **1 teaspoon sugar**
- **8 ounces uncooked whole wheat spiral pasta**
- **Chopped tomatoes and minced fresh oregano, optional**

1. In a Dutch oven, cook beef over medium heat 6-8 minutes or until no longer pink, breaking into crumbles; drain. Stir in seasonings.

2. Add tomato juice, water, tomato paste and sugar to pan; bring to a boil. Stir in pasta. Reduce heat; simmer, covered, 20-22 minutes or until pasta is tender, stirring occasionally. If desired, top each serving with tomatoes and oregano.

PER SERVING *319 cal., 7 g fat (2 g sat. fat), 47 mg chol., 442 mg sodium, 41 g carb., 6 g fiber, 24 g pro.* ***Diabetic Exchanges:*** *3 lean meat, 2 starch, 1 vegetable.*

Don't like **whole wheat** pasta? Try **multigrain**. It looks and tastes like **white,** but is **better for you.**

"When I got married, my aunt gave me her cherished recipe for skillet spaghetti. Over the years, I've tinkered with the ingredients and seasonings to create a healthier dish that my family truly loves."
—**KRISTEN KILLIAN** DEPEW, NY

CHILI BEEF PASTA

SPANISH BEEF HASH

FREEZE IT

Spanish Beef Hash

This tasty blend smells so good as it cooks that it lures people into the kitchen from all over the house.

—**THOMAS REYNOLDS** TAMPA, FL

PREP: 40 MIN. **COOK:** 30 MIN.
MAKES: 6 SERVINGS

- **1 pound ground beef**
- **2 cups chopped sweet yellow, red and/or green peppers**
- **1 small onion, chopped**
- **3 garlic cloves, minced**
- **2 small potatoes, peeled and cut into ¾-inch cubes**
- **2 medium tomatoes, chopped**
- **1 can (8 ounces) tomato sauce**
- **⅔ cup chopped pitted green olives**
- **½ cup sliced fresh mushrooms**
- **½ cup dry red wine or beef broth**
- **1 tablespoon Louisiana-style hot sauce**
- **1 tablespoon Worcestershire sauce**
- **1½ teaspoons reduced-sodium soy sauce**
- **1 teaspoon pepper**
- **½ teaspoon salt**
- **½ teaspoon dried oregano**
- **¼ teaspoon Cajun seasoning**
- **Hot cooked rice**

1. In a Dutch oven, cook the beef, peppers, onion and garlic over medium heat until meat is no longer pink; drain. Add the potatoes, tomatoes, tomato sauce, olives, mushrooms, red wine and seasonings.

2. Bring to a boil. Reduce heat; simmer, uncovered, for 30-35 minutes or until potatoes are tender. Serve with rice.

FREEZE OPTION *Freeze cooled beef mixture in freezer containers. To use, partially thaw in refrigerator overnight. Heat through in a saucepan, stirring occasionally and adding a little broth or water if necessary.*

FREEZE IT

Hearty Penne Beef

This is comfort food at its finest! The best of everything is found here—it's tasty, easy and a great way to sneak in some spinach for extra nutrition.

—**TASTE OF HOME TEST KITCHEN**

START TO FINISH: 30 MIN.
MAKES: 4 SERVINGS

- **1¾ cups uncooked penne pasta**
- **1 pound ground beef**
- **1 teaspoon minced garlic**
- **1 can (15 ounces) tomato puree**
- **1 can (14½ ounces) beef broth**
- **1½ teaspoons Italian seasoning**
- **1 teaspoon Worcestershire sauce**
- **¼ teaspoon salt**
- **¼ teaspoon pepper**
- **2 cups chopped fresh spinach**
- **2 cups (8 ounces) shredded part-skim mozzarella cheese**

1. Cook pasta according to package directions. Meanwhile, in a Dutch oven, cook beef over medium heat until no longer pink. Add garlic; cook 1 minute longer. Drain. Stir in the tomato puree, broth, Italian seasoning, Worcestershire sauce, salt and pepper.

2. Bring to a boil. Reduce heat; simmer, uncovered, for 10-15 minutes or until mixture is slightly thickened. Add spinach; cook for 1-2 minutes or until wilted.

3. Drain pasta; stir into beef mixture. Sprinkle with cheese; cover and cook for 3-4 minutes or until the cheese is melted.

FREEZE OPTION *Freeze cooled pasta mixture in freezer containers. To use, partially thaw in refrigerator overnight. Heat through in a saucepan, stirring occasionally and adding a little broth or water if necessary.*

Creole Steaks

Here's a nice way to serve convenient cubed steaks. I created the recipe as a variation on Swiss steak. Team it up with rice to catch all the flavorful sauce.

—NICOLE FILIZETTI JACKSONVILLE, FL

PREP: 15 MIN. **COOK:** 35 MIN.
MAKES: 4 SERVINGS

- **1 large onion, chopped**
- **¼ cup chopped green pepper**
- **¼ cup chopped celery**
- **4 tablespoons canola oil, divided**
- **3 garlic cloves, minced**
- **1 tablespoon all-purpose flour**
- **½ teaspoon salt**
- **½ teaspoon dried thyme**
- **½ teaspoon cayenne pepper**
- **½ teaspoon pepper**
- **2 cans (14½ ounces each) fire-roasted diced tomatoes, undrained**
- **¼ teaspoon hot pepper sauce**
- **1 tablespoon lemon juice**
- **4 beef cubed steaks (4 ounces each)**
- **Additional salt and pepper**

1. In a large skillet, saute onion, green pepper and celery in 2 tablespoons oil until crisp-tender. Add garlic; cook 1 minute longer. Stir in flour, salt, thyme, cayenne and pepper.
2. Add tomatoes and pepper sauce; bring to a boil. Reduce heat; simmer, uncovered, for 20-25 minutes or until thickened, stirring occasionally. Remove from the heat; stir in lemon juice and keep warm.
3. Sprinkle steaks with salt and pepper to taste. In another large skillet, cook steaks in remaining oil over medium heat for 3-4 minutes on each side or until no longer pink. Serve with sauce.

Cubed steak is from the round, an **economical** but tough cut of **beef**. The steaks are **tenderized** at the butcher.

EAT SMART

Mexican Fiesta Steak Stir-Fry

The best part of throwing a party is being able to enjoy time with your company. With this flavorful stir-fry on the menu, you'll be out of the kitchen with time to spare!

—PATRICIA SWART GALLOWAY, NJ

START TO FINISH: 30 MIN.
MAKES: 4 SERVINGS

- **1 pound boneless beef top loin steak, trimmed and cut into thin strips**
- **3 garlic cloves, minced**
- **1 to 2 tablespoons canola oil**
- **1 package (14 ounces) frozen pepper strips, thawed**
- **1⅓ cups chopped sweet onion**
- **2 plum tomatoes, chopped**
- **1 can (4 ounces) chopped green chilies**
- **½ teaspoon salt**
- **½ teaspoon dried oregano**
- **¼ teaspoon pepper**
- **Hot cooked rice**

1. In a large skillet or wok, stir-fry beef and garlic in oil until meat is no longer pink. Remove and keep warm.
2. Add peppers and onion to pan; stir-fry until tender. Stir in the tomatoes, chilies, salt, oregano, pepper and beef; heat through. Serve with rice.

PER SERVING *247 cal., 9 g fat (2 g sat. fat), 50 mg chol., 473 mg sodium, 13 g carb., 3 g fiber, 26 g pro.* ***Diabetic Exchanges:*** *3 lean meat, 2 vegetable, 1 fat.*

MEXICAN FIESTA STEAK STIR-FRY

Poultry

Healthy, versatile, quick and delicious...**turkey** and **chicken** dishes off the stovetop really seem to have it all. From zesty **lettuce wraps** and **chicken gyros** to exciting **salads** and company-special **dinners**, you're sure to discover dozens of **instant classics** in these pages.

EAT SMART

Crispy Asian Chicken Salad

Asian flavor, crunchy almonds and crispy breaded chicken make this hearty salad something special.

—**BETH DAUENHAUER** PUEBLO, CO

START TO FINISH: 30 MIN.
MAKES: 2 SERVINGS

- **2 boneless skinless chicken breast halves (4 ounces each)**
- **2 teaspoons hoisin sauce**
- **1 teaspoon sesame oil**
- **½ cup panko (Japanese) bread crumbs**
- **4 teaspoons sesame seeds**
- **2 teaspoons canola oil**
- **4 cups spring mix salad greens**
- **1 small green pepper, julienned**
- **1 small sweet red pepper, julienned**
- **1 medium carrot, julienned**
- **½ cup sliced fresh mushrooms**

- **2 tablespoons thinly sliced onion**
- **2 tablespoons sliced almonds, toasted**
- **¼ cup reduced-fat sesame ginger salad dressing**

1. Flatten chicken breasts to ½-in. thickness. Combine hoisin sauce and sesame oil; brush over chicken. In a shallow bowl, combine panko and sesame seeds; dip chicken in mixture.
2. In a large nonstick skillet coated with cooking spray, cook chicken in oil for 5-6 minutes on each side or until no longer pink.
3. Meanwhile, divide salad greens between two plates. Top with peppers, carrot, mushrooms and onion. Slice chicken; place on top. Sprinkle with almonds and drizzle with dressing.

PER SERVING *386 cal., 17 g fat (2 g sat. fat), 63 mg chol., 620 mg sodium, 29 g carb., 6 g fiber, 30 g pro.* ***Diabetic Exchanges:*** *3 lean meat, 2 vegetable, 2 fat, 1 starch.*

CRISPY ASIAN CHICKEN SALAD

White Wine Coq au Vin

Coq au vin is a chicken dish typically made with red wine. This wonderful version calls for white wine instead.

—**TASTE OF HOME TEST KITCHEN**

PREP: 25 MIN. • **COOK:** 40 MIN.
MAKES: 2 SERVINGS

- **4 cups water**
- **1 cup pearl onions**
- **4 bacon strips, cut into 1-inch pieces**
- **2 bone-in chicken breast halves (8 ounces each)**
- **¼ teaspoon salt**
- **⅛ teaspoon pepper**
- **¾ cup sliced fresh mushrooms**
- **2 garlic cloves, minced**
- **4½ teaspoons all-purpose flour**
- **¾ cup chicken broth**
- **¾ cup white wine or additional chicken broth**
- **1 bay leaf**
- **½ teaspoon dried thyme**
- **Hot cooked noodles**

1. In a large saucepan, bring water to a boil. Add onions; boil for 3 minutes. Drain and rinse in cold water; peel and set aside.
2. In a large skillet, cook bacon over medium heat until crisp. Using a slotted spoon, remove to paper towels.
3. Sprinkle chicken with salt and pepper. Brown chicken in the drippings; remove and keep warm. Add onions and mushrooms to drippings; saute until crisp-tender. Add garlic; cook 1 minute longer.
4. Combine flour and broth; stir into onion mixture. Add the wine, bay leaf and thyme; bring to a boil. Return chicken and bacon to the pan. Reduce heat; cover and simmer for 25-30 minutes or until a thermometer reads 170°.
5. Remove chicken and keep warm. Cook sauce over medium heat until slightly thickened. Discard bay leaf. Serve chicken and sauce with noodles.

"Here's one of my most-requested recipes, thanks to the special white wine and mustard sauce. It makes an ordinary weeknight dinner feel like a little party."
—**SUSAN WARREN** NORTH MANCHESTER, IN

TURKEY SCALLOPINE

EAT SMART

Turkey Scallopine

START TO FINISH: 25 MIN.
MAKES: 4 SERVINGS

- **⅓ cup all-purpose flour**
- **¼ teaspoon dried rosemary, crushed**
- **¼ teaspoon dried thyme**
- **⅛ teaspoon white pepper**
- **1 package (17.6 ounces) turkey breast cutlets**
- **4 teaspoons canola oil**
- **¼ cup white wine or reduced-sodium chicken broth**
- **½ teaspoon cornstarch**
- **⅓ cup reduced-sodium chicken broth**
- **½ cup reduced-fat sour cream**
- **1 teaspoon spicy brown mustard Paprika, optional**

1. In a shallow bowl, mix flour and seasonings. Dip cutlets in flour mixture to coat both sides; shake off excess. In a large nonstick skillet coated with cooking spray, heat oil over medium heat. Add turkey in batches and cook 2-4 minutes on each side or until no longer pink. Remove to a serving plate; keep warm.

2. Add wine to pan; increase heat to medium-high. Cook 30 seconds, stirring to loosen browned bits from pan. In a small bowl, mix cornstarch and broth until smooth; stir into skillet. Bring to a boil; cook and stir 1-2 minutes or until slightly thickened.

3. Stir in sour cream and mustard; heat through. Pour over turkey. If desired, sprinkle with paprika.

PER SERVING *263 cal., 8 g fat (2 g sat. fat), 88 mg chol., 194 mg sodium, 11 g carb., trace fiber, 34 g pro.* ***Diabetic Exchanges:*** *4 lean meat, 1 starch, 1 fat.*

Scallopine are thin cutlets of meat that are **breaded** and fried, then served with a **pan sauce**. **Scallopini** is an alternate spelling.

Pecan-Crusted Chicken Waffle Sandwiches

Chicken and waffles is a Southern tradition. I turned it into a sandwich with crunchy pecans and a sweet, spicy mustard sauce to give it a kick.
—**ELIZABETH DUMONT** BOULDER, CO

START TO FINISH: 30 MIN.
MAKES: 4 SERVINGS

- **4 boneless skinless chicken breast halves (5 ounces each)**
- **1 egg**
- **½ cup plus ⅓ cup maple syrup, divided**
- **1 cup finely chopped pecans**
- **⅔ cup dry bread crumbs**
- **¾ teaspoon plus ⅛ teaspoon salt, divided**
- **½ teaspoon plus ⅛ teaspoon pepper, divided**
- **¼ cup canola oil**
- **¼ cup spicy brown mustard**
- **1 tablespoon white wine vinegar**
- **8 frozen waffles, toasted**

1. Flatten chicken to ½-in. thickness. In a shallow bowl, whisk egg and ½ cup syrup. In another shallow bowl, combine the pecans, bread crumbs, ¾ teaspoon salt and ½ teaspoon pepper. Dip chicken in egg mixture, then coat with pecan mixture.

2. In a large skillet over medium heat, cook chicken in oil in batches for 5-6 minutes on each side or until no longer pink. Meanwhile, combine the mustard, vinegar and remaining syrup, salt and pepper.

3. Drizzle 1 tablespoon sauce mixture over each of four waffles; top with chicken and drizzle with remaining sauce mixture. Top with remaining waffles.

PECAN-CRUSTED CHICKEN WAFFLE SANDWICHES

EAT SMART

Open-Faced Meatball Sandwiches

My husband and I love meatball subs, so I tried to come up with a slimmed-down version that's easy to make after a long day. The meatballs freeze well, too.

—**KAREN BARTHEL** NORTH CANTON, OH

PREP: 30 MIN. • **COOK:** 10 MIN.
MAKES: 8 SERVINGS

- **¼ cup egg substitute**
- **½ cup soft bread crumbs**
- **¼ cup finely chopped onion**
- **2 garlic cloves, minced**
- **½ teaspoon onion powder**
- **½ teaspoon dried oregano**
- **½ teaspoon dried basil**
- **¼ teaspoon pepper**
- **Dash salt**
- **1¼ pounds lean ground turkey**
- **2 cups garden-style pasta sauce**
- **4 hoagie buns, split**
- **2 tablespoons shredded part-skim mozzarella cheese**
- **Shredded Parmesan cheese, optional**

1. In a large bowl, combine the first nine ingredients. Crumble turkey over mixture and mix well. Shape into 1-in. meatballs.

2. In a large skillet coated with cooking spray, brown meatballs in batches; drain.

3. Place meatballs in a large saucepan. Add the pasta sauce; bring to a boil. Reduce heat; cover and simmer for 10-15 minutes or until meat is no longer pink.

4. Spoon meatballs and sauce onto bun halves; sprinkle with mozzarella cheese and, if desired, Parmesan cheese.

PER SERVING *231 cal., 9 g fat (2 g sat. fat), 60 mg chol., 488 mg sodium, 21 g carb., 2 g fiber, 17 g pro.* ***Diabetic Exchanges:*** *2 lean meat, 1 starch, 1 vegetable.*

"These Buffalo chicken wraps are excellent. Honey and lime juice help tone down the hot wing sauce for a refreshing zip. They're perfect for lunch or a light summer meal. For quicker preparation, use bottled blue cheese dressing instead of homemade."

—**PRISCILLA GILBERT** INDIAN HARBOUR BEACH, FL

Buffalo Chicken Lettuce Wraps

START TO FINISH: 25 MIN.
MAKES: 8 SERVINGS

- **⅓ cup crumbled blue cheese**
- **¼ cup mayonnaise**
- **2 tablespoons milk**
- **4½ teaspoons lemon juice**
- **1 tablespoon minced fresh parsley**
- **1 teaspoon Worcestershire sauce**
- **1 pound boneless skinless chicken breasts, cubed**
- **1 teaspoon salt**
- **1 tablespoon canola oil**
- **¼ cup lime juice**
- **¼ cup Louisiana-style hot sauce**
- **¼ cup honey**
- **1 small cucumber, halved lengthwise, seeded and thinly sliced**
- **1 celery rib, thinly sliced**
- **¾ cup julienned carrots**
- **8 Bibb or Boston lettuce leaves**

1. For dressing, in a small bowl, combine the first six ingredients. Cover and refrigerate until serving.

2. Sprinkle chicken with salt. In a large skillet, cook chicken in oil until no longer pink. Combine the lime juice, hot sauce and honey; pour over chicken. Bring to a boil. Reduce heat; simmer, uncovered, for 2-3 minutes or until slightly thickened. Remove from the heat; stir in the cucumber, celery and carrots.

3. Spoon ½ cup chicken mixture onto each lettuce leaf; fold sides over filling and secure with a toothpick. Serve with blue cheese dressing.

BUFFALO CHICKEN LETTUCE WRAPS

Crumb-Coated Chicken & Blackberry Salsa

Maple lends a sweet touch to fresh blackberry salsa. Besides chicken, it's also great with fried fish.

—**TAMMY THOMAS** MORRISVILLE, VT

START TO FINISH: 25 MIN.
MAKES: 2 SERVINGS

- **½ cup fresh blackberries**
- **1 jalapeno pepper, seeded and minced**
- **2 tablespoons minced fresh cilantro**
- **2 tablespoons chopped red onion**
- **2 tablespoons maple syrup**
- **2 tablespoons balsamic vinegar**
- **2 boneless skinless chicken breast halves (5 ounces each)**
- **⅛ teaspoon salt**
- **⅛ teaspoon pepper**
- **¼ cup all-purpose flour**
- **1 egg, beaten**
- **½ cup panko (Japanese) bread crumbs**
- **1 tablespoon olive oil**

1. In a small bowl, combine the first six ingredients. Cover and refrigerate until serving.
2. Flatten chicken to ¼-in. thickness; sprinkle with salt and pepper. Place the flour, egg and bread crumbs in separate shallow bowls. Coat chicken with flour, dip in egg, then coat with crumbs.
3. In a large skillet, cook chicken in oil over medium heat for 4-6 minutes on each side or until no longer pink. Serve with salsa.

NOTE *Wear disposable gloves when cutting hot peppers; the oils can burn skin. Avoid touching your face.*

QUICK TURKEY SPAGHETTI

EAT SMART

Quick Turkey Spaghetti

My family never tires of this versatile entree. We can have it once a week, and it's different each time! I sometimes omit the turkey for a meatless meal, change up the veggies or use my own tomato sauce.

—**MARY LOU MOELLER** WOOSTER, OH

PREP: 15 MIN. • **COOK:** 25 MIN.
MAKES: 4 SERVINGS

- **1 pound lean ground turkey**
- **1 small green pepper, chopped**
- **½ cup sliced fresh mushrooms**
- **¼ cup chopped onion**
- **1 can (15 ounces) tomato sauce**
- **6 ounces uncooked multigrain spaghetti, broken into 2-inch pieces**
- **¾ cup water**
- **¼ teaspoon garlic salt**
- **Grated Parmesan cheese, optional**

1. In a large nonstick skillet coated with cooking spray, cook the turkey, pepper, mushrooms and onion over medium heat until meat is no longer pink and vegetables are crisp-tender.
2. Stir in the tomato sauce, spaghetti, water and garlic salt. Bring to a boil. Reduce heat; cover and simmer for 15-20 minutes or until spaghetti and vegetables are tender. Garnish with cheese if desired.

PER SERVING *357 cal., 10 g fat (3 g sat. fat), 90 mg chol., 728 mg sodium, 36 g carb., 4 g fiber, 30 g pro.* ***Diabetic Exchanges:*** *3 lean meat, 2 starch, 1 vegetable.*

MEDITERRANEAN ONE-DISH MEAL

EAT SMART

Mediterranean One-Dish Meal

I came up with this recipe one night when I was improvising with what I had on hand. I love to make simple, healthy one-dish dinners with lots of vegetables. Feta and Greek olives give this meal a flavor that people seem to love!

—**DONNA JESSER** EVERETT, WA

PREP: 15 MIN. • **COOK:** 25 MIN.
MAKES: 4 SERVINGS

- **¾ pound Italian turkey sausage links, cut into 1-inch pieces**
- **1 medium onion, chopped**
- **2 garlic cloves, minced**
- **1 can (14½ ounces) no-salt-added diced tomatoes, undrained**
- **¼ cup Greek olives**
- **1 teaspoon dried oregano**
- **½ cup quinoa, rinsed**
- **3 cups fresh baby spinach**
- **½ cup crumbled feta cheese**

1. In a large nonstick skillet coated with cooking spray, cook sausage and onion over medium heat until sausage is browned and onion is tender. Add garlic; cook 1 minute longer. Stir in the tomatoes, olives and oregano; bring to a boil.

2. Stir in quinoa. Top with spinach. Reduce heat; cover and simmer for 12-15 minutes or until liquid is absorbed. Remove from the heat; fluff with a fork. Sprinkle with cheese.

NOTE *Look for quinoa in the cereal, rice or organic food aisle.*

PER SERVING *307 cal., 14 g fat (3 g sat. fat), 58 mg chol., 845 mg sodium, 26 g carb., 5 g fiber, 21 g pro.*

EAT SMART

Chicken Gyros

These yummy Greek specialties are a cinch to prepare at home. Tender chicken and a creamy cucumber sauce are tucked into pitas.

—**TASTE OF HOME TEST KITCHEN**

PREP: 20 MIN. + MARINATING
COOK: 10 MIN. • **MAKES:** 2 SERVINGS

- **¼ cup lemon juice**
- **2 tablespoons olive oil**
- **¾ teaspoon minced garlic, divided**
- **½ teaspoon ground mustard**
- **½ teaspoon dried oregano**
- **½ pound boneless skinless chicken breasts, cut into ½-inch strips**
- **½ cup chopped peeled cucumber**
- **⅓ cup plain yogurt**
- **¼ teaspoon dill weed**
- **2 whole pita breads**
- **½ small red onion, thinly sliced**

1. In a large resealable plastic bag, combine the lemon juice, oil, 1/2 teaspoon garlic, mustard and oregano; add chicken. Seal bag and turn to coat; refrigerate for at least 1 hour. Combine cucumber, yogurt, dill and remaining garlic; chill until serving.

2. Drain and discard marinade. In a large nonstick skillet, cook and stir the chicken for 7-8 minutes or until no longer pink. Spoon onto pita breads. Top with yogurt mixture and onion; fold in half.

PER SERVING *1 gyro equals 367 cal., 9 g fat (2 g sat. fat), 68 mg chol., 397 mg sodium, 39 g carb., 2 g fiber, 30 g pro.* ***Diabetic Exchanges:*** *3 lean meat, 2½ starch, 1 fat.*

Oregano lends an herby, earthy flavor to Greek dishes. **Mexican oregano** has a more **robust** flavor and is **not as sweet** as the **Mediterranean** variety.

CHICKEN GYROS

EAT SMART

Family-Favorite Taco Salad

This lighter, healthier version of classic Southwestern fare is a favorite with my family. I love the fact that besides being delicious, it's quick to prepare on busy weeknights.

—LYNNE GRAVES PALISADE, MN

START TO FINISH: 20 MIN.
MAKES: 6 SERVINGS

- **1½ pounds lean ground turkey**
- **1 can (14½ ounces) diced tomatoes, undrained**
- **2 teaspoons dried minced onion**
- **2 teaspoons chili powder**
- **1 teaspoon garlic powder**
- **1 teaspoon seasoned salt**
- **½ teaspoon ground cumin**
- **¼ teaspoon pepper**
- **6 cups shredded lettuce**
- **½ cup shredded reduced-fat Mexican cheese blend**
- **6 tablespoons fat-free sour cream, optional**

1. In a large nonstick skillet, cook turkey over medium heat until no longer pink; drain. Stir in tomatoes and seasonings; heat through.

2. Divide lettuce among six plates; top each with 2/3 cup turkey mixture, 4 teaspoons cheese and, if desired, 1 tablespoon sour cream.

PER SERVING *239 cal., 12 g fat (4 g sat. fat), 99 mg chol., 551 mg sodium, 9 g carb., 2 g fiber, 25 g pro.* ***Diabetic Exchanges:*** *3 lean meat, 1 vegetable, 1 fat.*

Sweet-and-Sour Popcorn Chicken

Yummy popcorn chicken simmered in homemade sweet and sour sauce is the secret shortcut in this fabulous entree. It's one easy recipe that you'll find yourself returning to again and again.

—AMY CORLEW-SHERLOCK LAPEER, MI

START TO FINISH: 25 MIN.
MAKES: 4 SERVINGS

- **1 medium green pepper, cut into 1-inch pieces**
- **1 small onion, thinly sliced**
- **1 tablespoon canola oil**
- **1 can (20 ounces) unsweetened pineapple chunks**
- **3 tablespoons white vinegar**
- **2 tablespoons soy sauce**
- **2 tablespoons ketchup**
- **⅓ cup packed brown sugar**
- **2 tablespoons cornstarch**
- **1 package (12 ounces) frozen popcorn chicken**

1. In a large skillet or wok, stir-fry green pepper and onion in oil for 3-4 minutes or until crisp-tender. Drain pineapple, reserving the juice in a 2-cup measuring cup; set pineapple aside. Add enough water to the juice to measure 1⅓ cups; stir in the vinegar, soy sauce and ketchup.

2. In a large bowl, combine brown sugar and cornstarch. Stir in pineapple juice mixture until smooth. Gradually add to the skillet. Bring to a boil; cook and stir for 2 minutes or until thickened. Stir in pineapple and heat through.

3. Meanwhile, microwave chicken according to package directions. Stir into pineapple mixture. Serve immediately.

FAMILY-FAVORITE TACO SALAD

"If you want to put something on the table that'll give you time to spare on busy nights, give this delicious dish a try. From start to finish, you're only 20 minutes away from a vibrantly colored meal."
—**MARGARET WILSON** SUN CITY, CA

Angel Hair Pasta with Chicken

START TO FINISH: 20 MIN.
MAKES: 4 SERVINGS

- **8 ounces uncooked angel hair pasta**
- **1 pound boneless skinless chicken breasts, cut into 1-inch pieces**
- **2 tablespoons olive oil, divided**
- **2 medium carrots, sliced diagonally**
- **1½ cups fresh broccoli florets**
- **2 to 3 teaspoons minced garlic**
- **1⅓ cups chicken broth**
- **½ cup grated Parmesan cheese**
- **2 teaspoons dried basil**
- **½ teaspoon salt**
- **Additional grated Parmesan cheese**

1. Cook pasta according to package directions. Meanwhile, in a large skillet, saute chicken in 1 tablespoon oil for 4-5 minutes or until no longer pink; drain. Remove and keep warm.
2. In the same skillet over medium heat, cook carrots in remaining oil for 3 minutes, stirring occasionally. Add broccoli and garlic; cook 2 minutes longer. Stir in the chicken, broth, cheese, basil and salt. Bring to a boil. Reduce heat; simmer, uncovered, for 4-6 minutes or until vegetables are tender.
3. Drain pasta; serve with chicken mixture. Sprinkle with additional cheese.

EAT SMART

Chicken Sausages with Peppers

Chicken sausage is a lower-calorie alternative to its pork counterpart, but it doesn't skimp on the bold, savory flavors you love. Try it with sweet, crunchy bell peppers for a fast and healthy dinner.
—**DEBORAH SCHAEFER** DURAND, MI

START TO FINISH: 30 MIN.
MAKES: 4 SERVINGS

- **1 small onion, halved and sliced**
- **1 small sweet orange pepper, julienned**
- **1 small sweet red pepper, julienned**
- **1 tablespoon olive oil**
- **1 garlic clove, minced**
- **1 package (12 ounces) fully cooked apple chicken sausage links or flavor of your choice, cut into 1-inch pieces**

In a large nonstick skillet, saute onion and peppers in oil until crisp-tender. Add garlic; cook 1 minute longer. Stir in sausages; heat through.

PER SERVING *208 cal., 11 g fat (2 g sat. fat), 60 mg chol., 483 mg sodium, 14 g carb., 1 g fiber, 15 g pro.* ***Diabetic Exchanges:*** *2 lean meat, 1 vegetable, ½ starch, ½ fat.*

CHICKEN SAUSAGES WITH PEPPERS

TURKEY SAUSAGE & SPINACH ORECCHIETTE

Turkey Sausage & Spinach Orecchiette

It was fun to come up with a recipe on my own and have my picky husband love it! Little ear-shaped orecchiette pasta is delicious with spicy turkey sausage.

—ANDREA PHILLIPS LAKEVILLE, MN

START TO FINISH: 30 MIN.
MAKES: 4 SERVINGS

- **½ pound uncooked orecchiette or small tube pasta**
- **3 hot Italian turkey sausage links, casings removed**
- **¼ cup chopped onion**
- **2 garlic cloves, minced**
- **¼ teaspoon crushed red pepper flakes**
- **3 cups fresh spinach**
- **½ cup shredded Asiago cheese**
- **¼ cup grated Parmesan cheese**
- **¼ cup rinsed and drained white kidney or cannellini beans**
- **¼ cup chopped roasted sweet red pepper**
- **½ teaspoon Italian seasoning**
- **Additional shredded Asiago cheese, optional**

1. Cook orecchiette according to package directions.

2. In a large skillet, cook and stir the sausage, onion, garlic and pepper flakes over medium heat for 6-8 minutes or until sausage is no longer pink; drain. Add the spinach, Asiago cheese, Parmesan cheese, beans, peppers and Italian seasoning; cook just until spinach is wilted, stirring occasionally.

3. Drain the orecchiette; add to sausage mixture and toss to combine. Sprinkle with additional Asiago cheese if desired.

Chutney has **sweet, sour, spicy and savory** flavors. It's often fruit-flavored, with **mango** being the most popular. Chutney **enhances** savory dishes.

Curried Chicken Rice Salad

Since I usually make and serve this salad while my teacher friends and I are on summer break, I always associate the recipe with relaxed good times! It's best to make ahead so that the flavors can mingle.

—PAMELA HESSELBART SYLVANIA, OH

PREP: 50 MIN. + CHILLING
MAKES: 6 SERVINGS

- **1 package (6.6 ounces) toasted almond rice pilaf**
- **2 cups cubed cooked chicken**
- **¾ cup diced celery**
- **½ cup dried cranberries**
- **½ cup golden raisins**
- **½ cup mayonnaise**
- **⅓ cup chutney**
- **3 tablespoons sour cream**
- **2 tablespoons lemon juice**
- **1 teaspoon curry powder**
- **2 medium apples, cubed**
- **6 lettuce leaves**
- **¼ cup sliced almonds, toasted**

1. Cook rice pilaf according to package directions; cool. In a large bowl, combine the chicken, celery, cranberries, raisins and rice.

2. In a small bowl, combine the mayonnaise, chutney, sour cream, lemon juice and curry powder; stir in apples. Add to rice mixture; toss to coat. Cover and refrigerate for at least 2 hours.

3. Serve on lettuce; garnish with almonds.

Pretzel-Crusted Chicken with Mixed Greens

The secret to crunchy success is grinding up the sourdough pretzel nuggets until they're finely crushed. Change up the flavor and use hot wing or buttermilk ranch pretzel nuggets.

—**KERRI BALLIET** SHOREWOOD, WI

START TO FINISH: 30 MIN.
MAKES: 4 SERVINGS (⅔ CUP SAUCE)

- **2 cups sourdough pretzel nuggets**
- **½ cup all-purpose flour**
- **2 eggs**
- **¼ cup buttermilk**
- **2 garlic cloves, minced**
- **⅛ teaspoon pepper**
- **5 tablespoons olive oil, divided**
- **4 boneless skinless chicken breast halves (5 ounces each)**
- **⅔ cup mayonnaise**
- **2 tablespoons Dijon mustard**
- **2 teaspoons cider vinegar**
- **⅛ teaspoon salt**
- **⅛ teaspoon pepper**
- **1 package (5 ounces) spring mix salad greens**

1. Place pretzels in a food processor; process until finely crushed. Place pretzels and flour in separate shallow bowls. In another shallow bowl, whisk the eggs, buttermilk, garlic and pepper. Pound chicken to 1/4-in. thickness. Dip both sides of chicken in flour, egg mixture, and then in the pretzel crumbs.

2. In a large skillet, heat 3 tablespoons oil over medium heat. Add chicken; cook for 4-6 minutes on each side or until no longer pink.

3. Meanwhile, in a small bowl, mix mayonnaise and mustard. Remove 2 tablespoons to another bowl for dressing; whisk in remaining oil, vinegar, salt and pepper.

4. Place salad greens in a large bowl. Drizzle with dressing; toss to coat. Serve with chicken and remaining mayonnaise mixture.

CHICKEN MARSALA WITH GORGONZOLA

Chicken Marsala with Gorgonzola

Chicken topped with creamy Gorgonzola is quick enough for weeknight cooking but also elegant enough for a dinner party. We live near the Faribault, Minnesota, caves that are used to age the lovely Amableu Gorgonzola cheese, so this is a favorite for us.

—**JILL ANDERSON** SLEEPY EYE, MN

PREP: 10 MIN. • **COOK:** 30 MIN.
MAKES: 4 SERVINGS

- **4 boneless skinless chicken breast halves (6 ounces each)**
- **¼ teaspoon plus ⅛ teaspoon salt, divided**
- **¼ teaspoon pepper**
- **3 tablespoons olive oil, divided**
- **½ pound sliced baby portobello mushrooms**
- **2 garlic cloves, minced**
- **1 cup Marsala wine**
- **⅔ cup heavy whipping cream**
- **½ cup crumbled Gorgonzola cheese, divided**
- **2 tablespoons minced fresh parsley**

1. Sprinkle chicken with 1/4 teaspoon salt and pepper. In a large skillet, cook chicken in 2 tablespoons oil over medium heat 6-8 minutes on each side or until a thermometer reads 165°. Remove and keep warm.

2. In same skillet, saute mushrooms in remaining oil until tender. Add garlic; cook 1 minute.

3. Add wine, stirring to loosen browned bits from pan. Bring to a boil; cook until liquid is reduced by a third. Stir in cream and remaining salt. Return to a boil; cook until slightly thickened.

4. Return chicken to pan; add 1/3 cup cheese. Cook until cheese is melted. Sprinkle with remaining cheese; garnish with parsley.

EAT SMART

Summertime Orzo & Chicken

For lunch or dinner, this easy-as-can-be dish is likely to become a summer staple in your house. It's that good. If you prefer, grill the chicken breasts instead of cooking in a skillet.

—**FRAN MACMILLAN** WEST MELBOURNE, FL

START TO FINISH: 30 MIN.
MAKES: 4 SERVINGS

- **¾ cup uncooked orzo pasta**
- **1 pound boneless skinless chicken breasts, cut into 1-inch pieces**
- **1 medium cucumber, chopped**
- **1 small red onion, chopped**
- **¼ cup minced fresh parsley**
- **2 tablespoons lemon juice**
- **1 tablespoon olive oil**
- **1 teaspoon salt**
- **¼ teaspoon pepper**
- **¼ cup crumbled reduced-fat feta cheese**

1. Cook pasta according to package directions. Meanwhile, in a large skillet coated with cooking spray, cook chicken over medium heat for 6-8 minutes or until no longer pink.
2. In a large bowl, combine the cucumber, onion, parsley and chicken. Drain pasta; stir into chicken mixture. In a small bowl, whisk the lemon juice, oil, salt and pepper. Pour over chicken mixture; toss to coat.
3. Serve warm or cold. Just before serving, sprinkle with cheese.

PER SERVING *323 cal., 7 g fat (2 g sat. fat), 65 mg chol., 742 mg sodium, 33 g carb., 2 g fiber, 30 g pro.* ***Diabetic Exchanges:*** *3 lean meat, 2 starch, 1 vegetable, 1 fat.*

SUMMERTIME ORZO & CHICKEN

EAT SMART FREEZE IT

Chicken and Bows

I first made this recipe when I was a professional nanny. It comes together quickly at dinner time when the kids are hungry and you're strapped for time.

—**DANETTE FORBES** OVERLAND PARK, KS

START TO FINISH: 25 MIN.
MAKES: 12 SERVINGS

- **1 package (16 ounces) bow tie pasta**
- **2 pounds boneless skinless chicken breasts, cut into strips**
- **1 cup chopped sweet red pepper**
- **¼ cup butter, cubed**
- **2 cans (10¾ ounces each) condensed cream of chicken soup, undiluted**
- **2 cups frozen peas**
- **1½ cups 2% milk**
- **1 teaspoon garlic powder**
- **¼ to ½ teaspoon salt**
- **¼ teaspoon pepper**
- **⅔ cup grated Parmesan cheese**

1. Cook pasta according to package directions. Meanwhile, in a Dutch oven, cook chicken and red pepper in butter over medium heat for 5-6 minutes or until the chicken is no longer pink.
2. Stir in the soup, peas, milk, garlic powder, salt and pepper; heat through. Stir in cheese.
3. Drain pasta; add to the chicken mixture and toss to coat.

FREEZE OPTION *Transfer individual portions of cooled mixture to freezer containers. Freeze up to 3 months. To use, thaw in the refrigerator overnight. Transfer to an ungreased shallow microwave-safe dish. Cover and microwave on high until heated through, stirring occasionally.*

PER SERVING *357 cal., 12 g fat (5 g sat. fat), 64 mg chol., 636 mg sodium, 37 g carb., 3 g fiber, 26 g pro.* ***Diabetic Exchanges:*** *3 lean meat, 2 starch, 2 fat.*

THAI CHICKEN PASTA

Thai Chicken Pasta

I try to buy fresh chicken when it's on sale. I cook a big batch in the slow cooker, then cut it up and package it in small amounts suitable for recipes like this. When I want it, I just need to be pull it out of the freezer and let it thaw.

—JENI PITTARD COMMERCE, GA

START TO FINISH: 25 MIN.
MAKES: 2 SERVINGS

- **3 ounces uncooked whole wheat linguine**
- **½ cup salsa**
- **2 tablespoons reduced-fat creamy peanut butter**
- **1 tablespoon orange juice**
- **1½ teaspoons honey**
- **1 teaspoon reduced-sodium soy sauce**
- **1 cup cubed cooked chicken breast**
- **1 tablespoon chopped unsalted peanuts**
- **1 tablespoon minced fresh cilantro**

1. Cook linguine according to package directions.

2. Meanwhile, in a microwave-safe dish, combine the salsa, peanut butter, orange juice, honey and soy sauce. Cover and microwave on high for 1 minute; stir. Add the chicken; heat through.

3. Drain linguine. Serve with chicken mixture. Garnish with peanuts and cilantro.

NOTE *This recipe was tested in a 1,100-watt microwave.*

To **keep cilantro fresh**, trim the stems and place the bunch **in a tumbler** containing an inch or two **of water**. Remove any loose leaves so only the **stems** are in the water. Cover with a produce bag to trap the **humidity**.

"We just love this dinner, especially when we want a yummy meal—and fast. The turkey is also excellent on tortilla chips, which we usually have on the side."

—JOAN HALLFORD
NORTH RICHLAND HILLS, TX

HEARTY TURKEY & RICE

EAT SMART FREEZE IT

Hearty Turkey & Rice

START TO FINISH: 25 MIN.
MAKES: 4 SERVINGS

- **1½ cups instant brown rice**
- **1 pound extra-lean ground turkey**
- **1 medium onion, chopped**
- **1½ cups salsa**
- **1 can (8 ounces) no-salt-added tomato sauce**
- **1 teaspoon reduced-sodium chicken bouillon granules**
- **¼ teaspoon salt**
- **¼ cup shredded reduced-fat cheddar cheese**
- **¼ cup reduced-fat sour cream**
- **Chopped tomatoes, baked tortilla chips and sliced ripe olives, optional**

1. Cook rice according to package directions.
2. Meanwhile, in a large nonstick skillet coated with cooking spray, cook turkey and onion over medium heat until meat is no longer pink. Add the salsa, tomato sauce, bouillon and salt; heat through.
3. Serve with rice; top with cheese and sour cream. Garnish with tomatoes, chips and olives if desired.

FREEZE OPTION *Transfer individual portions of cooled meat mixture to freezer containers. To use, partially thaw in refrigerator overnight. Heat through in a saucepan, stirring occasionally and adding a little water if necessary. Serve with rice.*

PER SERVING *354 cal., 5 g fat (2 g sat. fat), 55 mg chol., 732 mg sodium, 40 g carb., 3 g fiber, 34 g pro.* ***Diabetic Exchanges:*** *4 lean meat, 2 starch, 2 vegetable, ½ fat.*

Extra-lean **ground turkey** works fine for **crumbled** meat dishes. For **burgers** or meat loaf, use meat with a **higher fat** content.

CLASSIC TURKEY BURGERS

EAT SMART

Classic Turkey Burgers

Although I've tried a number of turkey burgers, I always thought they were too dry. Cooking the onion first before adding it to the patties makes these burgers moist and flavorful.

—SHIRLEA ANN ROMAN JAMESTOWN, NY

PREP: 20 MIN. + CHILLING • **COOK:** 10 MIN.
MAKES: 2 SERVINGS

- **⅓ cup finely chopped onion**
- **½ teaspoon canola oil**
- **½ cup soft bread crumbs**
- **½ teaspoon reduced-sodium soy sauce**
- **½ teaspoon Worcestershire sauce**
- **¼ teaspoon garlic powder**
- **¼ teaspoon poultry seasoning**
- **⅛ teaspoon ground mustard**
- **⅛ teaspoon pepper**
- **Dash salt**
- **½ pound lean ground turkey**
- **2 hamburger buns, split**
- **2 lettuce leaves**
- **2 slices tomato**

1. Place onion and oil in a small skillet; cover and cook for 3-4 minutes or until very soft, stirring occasionally. Cool.
2. In a large bowl, combine the bread crumbs, soy sauce, Worcestershire sauce, garlic powder, poultry seasoning, mustard, pepper, salt and onion. Crumble turkey over mixture and mix just until combined. Shape into two patties. Wrap in plastic wrap and refrigerate for at least 20 minutes.
3. In a nonstick skillet coated with cooking spray, cook patties over medium heat for 4-5 minutes on each side or until a thermometer reads 165°. Serve on buns with lettuce and tomato.

PER SERVING *353 cal., 13 g fat (3 g sat. fat), 90 mg chol., 549 mg sodium, 32 g carb., 2 g fiber, 25 g pro.* ***Diabetic Exchanges:*** *3 lean meat, 2 starch, ½ fat.*

Pineapple Chicken Fajitas

PREP: 25 MIN. • **COOK:** 15 MIN.
MAKES: 8 SERVINGS

- **2 pounds boneless skinless chicken breasts, cut into strips**
- **1 tablespoon olive oil**
- **1 each medium green, sweet red and yellow peppers, julienned**
- **1 medium onion, cut into thin wedges**
- **2 tablespoons fajita seasoning mix**
- **¼ cup water**
- **2 tablespoons honey**
- **1 tablespoon dried parsley flakes**
- **1 teaspoon garlic powder**
- **½ teaspoon salt**
- **½ cup unsweetened pineapple chunks, drained**
- **8 flour tortillas (10 inches), warmed**

1. In a large nonstick skillet, cook chicken in oil for 4-5 minutes. Add peppers and onion; cook and stir 4-5 minutes longer.

2. In a small bowl, combine seasoning mix and water; stir in the honey, parsley, garlic powder and salt. Stir into skillet. Add pineapple. Cook and stir for 1-2 minutes or until chicken is no longer pink and vegetables are tender.

3. Place chicken mixture on one side of each tortilla; fold tortillas over filling.

"Honey and pineapple add a sweet twist to these fajitas that my family loves. I like to serve them with coleslaw and baked or fried potatoes."
—**RAYMONDE BOURGEOIS** SWASTIKA, ON

PINEAPPLE CHICKEN FAJITAS

EAT SMART

Turkey a la King

I like to make this dish with our leftover turkey. It's a nice change from casseroles and so simple. Serve over rice, noodles, biscuits or toast.
—**PAT LEMKE** BRANDON, WI

START TO FINISH: 30 MIN.
MAKES: 4 SERVINGS

- **1¾ cups sliced fresh mushrooms**
- **1 celery rib, chopped**
- **¼ cup chopped onion**
- **¼ cup chopped green pepper**
- **2 tablespoons butter**
- **¼ cup all-purpose flour**
- **1 cup reduced-sodium chicken broth**
- **1 cup fat-free milk**
- **2 cups cubed cooked turkey breast**
- **1 cup frozen peas**
- **½ teaspoon salt**
- **2 cups hot cooked rice**

1. In a large nonstick skillet, saute the mushrooms, celery, onion and pepper in butter until tender.

2. Combine flour and broth until smooth; stir into vegetable mixture. Stir in milk. Bring to a boil. Cook and stir for 2 minutes or until thickened. Add the turkey, peas and salt; heat through. Serve with rice.

PER SERVING *350 cal., 7 g fat (4 g sat. fat), 76 mg chol., 594 mg sodium, 40 g carb., 3 g fiber, 30 g pro.* ***Diabetic Exchanges:*** *3 lean meat, 2 starch, 1½ fat, 1 vegetable.*

FRUITED CHICKEN PASTA SALAD

Fruited Chicken Pasta Salad

This fresh five-ingredient salad is ideal for summertime. It travels great as a lunch box entree, too. You will love the combination of sweet fruit with savory chicken and pasta.

—**BRIDGET FRANCOEUR** ADRIAN, MI

PREP: 25 MIN. + CHILLING
MAKES: 6 SERVINGS

- **2 cups uncooked bow tie pasta**
- **2 cups cubed cooked chicken**
- **1 can (11 ounces) mandarin oranges, drained**
- **1 cup halved green grapes**
- **½ cup ranch salad dressing**

1. Cook pasta according to the package directions. Meanwhile, in a large bowl, combine the chicken, oranges and grapes. Drain and rinse pasta with cold water; add to chicken mixture. Drizzle with dressing and toss to coat.

2. Cover and refrigerate the salad for at least 1 hour before serving.

To make the salad more **hearty**, stir in some cubed **cheddar** cheese. Substitute **red grapes** for a burst of color. It would also be tasty with **poppy seed** vinaigrette instead of ranch.

Pork

Why not shake up dinner tonight with **pork**? Discover zesty **ham steaks**, rich **sausage pastas**, decadent chili dogs and more in this **taste-tempting chapter**. With dozens of delicious recipes right at your fingertips, **delectable pork chops** are just the beginning!

Saucy Bratwurst Supper

For a change-of-pace dinner, I pull out this sensational bratwurst recipe. The caraway and other seasonings give the meat wonderful Old World flair. My husband thinks it's terrific.

—ROBIN HUBER CALGARY, AB

PREP: 25 MIN. • **COOK:** 20 MIN.
MAKES: 4-6 SERVINGS

- **4 to 6 fresh bratwurst links**
- **1 medium onion, chopped**
- **3 garlic cloves, minced**
- **1 tablespoon canola oil**
- **2 cups sliced fresh mushrooms**
- **2 medium tomatoes, chopped**
- **2 tablespoons cider vinegar**
- **1 bay leaf**
- **1 teaspoon caraway seeds**
- **½ teaspoon salt**
- **½ teaspoon pepper**
- **1 cup apple juice**
- **2 tablespoons cornstarch**
- **¼ cup water**

1. In a large skillet, brown bratwurst; remove and set aside. In the same pan, saute onion and garlic in oil until tender. Add mushrooms, tomatoes, vinegar, bay leaf, caraway, salt and pepper. Cook and stir for 2-3 minutes.
2. Return bratwurst to skillet. Add apple juice; bring to a boil. Reduce heat; cover and simmer for 18-22 minutes or until a thermometer reads 160°.
3. Discard bay leaf. Remove bratwurst; keep warm. Combine cornstarch and water until smooth. Gradually add to sauce mixture; bring to a boil. Cook and stir for 2 minutes. Serve with the bratwurst.

Serve the **bratwurst** with mashed **potatoes,** sweet potato fries or **hot buttered noodles** to catch the zesty vegetable **sauce.**

Pork Fried Rice

I have been making this recipe for my husband ever since he discovered fried rice while in the Navy. He even loves to eat the leftovers!

—JUDY LAMMERS COLUMBIA, MO

START TO FINISH: 15 MIN.
MAKES: 4 SERVINGS

- **1 teaspoon canola oil**
- **2 eggs, beaten**
- **3 cups cooked rice**
- **2 cups cubed cooked pork**
- **½ cup frozen peas, thawed**
- **¼ cup reduced-sodium soy sauce**
- **½ teaspoon garlic powder**
- **2 cups shredded lettuce**
- **2 green onions, thinly sliced**

1. In a large skillet, heat oil over medium-high heat. Pour eggs into skillet. As eggs set, lift edges, letting uncooked portion flow underneath. When eggs are completely cooked, remove to plate. Set aside.
2. In the same skillet, combine the rice, pork, peas, soy sauce and garlic powder; heat through. Chop egg into small pieces; add to skillet. Remove from the heat; stir in lettuce and onions. Serve immediately.

PLUM-GOOD PORK CHOPS

EAT SMART

Plum-Good Pork Chops

Ginger and plum sauce add Asian flavor to make this dish a standout. A side of crisp broccoli coleslaw is the perfect partner.

—TASTE OF HOME TEST KITCHEN

START TO FINISH: 30 MIN.
MAKES: 4 SERVINGS

- **4 bone-in pork loin chops (7 ounces each)**
- **2 teaspoons canola oil**
- **¾ cup plum sauce**
- **¼ cup orange juice**
- **5 teaspoons reduced-sodium soy sauce**
- **2 garlic cloves, minced**
- **2 teaspoons Dijon mustard**
- **1 teaspoon minced fresh gingerroot**
- **¼ teaspoon pepper**
- **1 package (12 ounces) broccoli coleslaw mix**
- **1 medium carrot, grated**
- **2 green onions, chopped**
- **2 teaspoons sesame seeds, toasted**

1. In a large skillet, brown chops in oil. Combine the plum sauce, orange juice, soy sauce, garlic, mustard, ginger and pepper; pour over chops. Bring to a boil. Reduce heat; cover and simmer for 15-20 minutes or until tender. Remove pork chops and keep warm. Set aside ½ cup sauce mixture.

2. In the same skillet, cook the coleslaw mix, carrot and onions over medium heat until crisp-tender. Serve with pork chops; drizzle with reserved sauce and sprinkle with sesame seeds.

PER SERVING *373 cal., 11 g fat (3 g sat. fat), 86 mg chol., 685 mg sodium, 30 g carb., 3 g fiber, 33 g pro.* ***Diabetic Exchanges:*** *4 lean meat, 1½ starch, 1 vegetable, ½ fat.*

Tortellini Carbonara

Bacon, cream and Parmesan make a heavenly classic sauce for pasta. Add more cheese, bacon or parsley to suit your family's tastes. Great for company!

—CATHY CROYLE DAVIDSVILLE, PA

START TO FINISH: 20 MIN.
MAKES: 4 SERVINGS

- **1 package (9 ounces) refrigerated cheese tortellini**
- **8 bacon strips, cooked and crumbled**
- **1 cup heavy whipping cream**
- **½ cup minced fresh parsley**
- **½ cup grated Parmesan cheese**

1. Cook tortellini according to package directions. Meanwhile, in a large saucepan, combine the bacon, cream, parsley and cheese; cook over medium heat until heated through.

2. Drain tortellini; toss with cream sauce. Serve immediately.

FREEZE IT

Barbecued Pork Sandwiches

These delicious sandwiches taste even better if the pork is prepared a day ahead so the flavors can blend. Growing up, we children welcomed Mother's pork sandwiches for any occasion, but especially for birthday celebrations.
—THELMA WAGGONER HOPKINSVILLE, KY

PREP: 20 MIN. • **COOK:** 4 HOURS
MAKES: 16 SERVINGS

- **1 boneless pork shoulder roast (4 to 5 pounds), cut into 1-inch cubes**
- **2 medium onions, coarsely chopped**
- **2 tablespoons chili powder**
- **½ teaspoon salt**
- **1½ cups water**
- **1 cup ketchup**
- **¼ cup white vinegar**
- **16 hamburger buns, split**

1. In a Dutch oven, combine the meat, onions, chili powder, salt if desired, water, ketchup and vinegar. Cover and simmer for 4 hours or until the meat is tender.

2. Skim off the excess fat. With a slotted spoon, remove meat, reserving cooking liquid. Shred the meat with two forks. Return to the cooking liquid and heat through. Serve on buns.

FREEZE OPTION *Cool pork mixture and freeze in freezer containers for up to 3 months. Thaw in the refrigerator; place in a saucepan and heat through. Serve on buns.*

Pork **shoulder** is a **flavorful** cut with plenty of **fatty marbling** throughout. Trim any excess fat before cooking. The meat needs a **long cook time** to become tender.

Chipotle Chili Dogs

START TO FINISH: 25 MIN.
MAKES: 6 SERVINGS

- **6 hot dogs**
- **½ pound ground beef**
- **¼ cup chopped onion**
- **1 garlic clove, minced**
- **1 can (8 ounces) tomato sauce**
- **2½ teaspoons minced chipotle peppers in adobo sauce**
- **¾ teaspoon chili powder**
- **¼ teaspoon salt**
- **⅛ teaspoon pepper**
- **6 hot dog buns, split**
- **3 tablespoons sour cream**
- **3 tablespoons salsa**
- **¾ cup shredded cheddar cheese**
- **2 green onions, chopped**

1. Cook hot dogs according to package directions. Meanwhile, in a large skillet, cook the beef, onion and garlic over medium heat until meat is no longer pink; drain.

2. Stir in the tomato sauce, chipotle peppers, chili powder, salt and pepper. Bring to a boil. Reduce heat; simmer, uncovered, for 4-5 minutes or until flavors are blended.

3. Place hot dogs in buns. Spoon chili over hot dogs. In a small bowl, combine sour cream and salsa; spoon over tops. Sprinkle with cheese and green onions.

"I created these dogs for the 125th anniversary of a small town in southern Minnesota. They have a medium spice level, and people of all ages love them."
—BARB TEMPLIN NORWOOD, MN

CHIPOLTE CHILI DOGS

LEMONY TORTELLINI BACON SALAD

Lemony Tortellini Bacon Salad

Summer meals shouldn't be complicated. We love this simple and tasty salad on warm nights. Add a glass of iced tea or lemonade and dinner couldn't be easier.
—SAMANTHA VICARS KENOSHA, WI

START TO FINISH: 20 MIN.
MAKES: 4 SERVINGS

- **2 cups frozen cheese tortellini (about 8 ounces)**
- **4 cups fresh broccoli florets**
- **¾ cup mayonnaise**
- **1 tablespoon balsamic vinegar**
- **2 teaspoons lemon juice**
- **¾ teaspoon dried oregano**
- **¼ teaspoon salt**
- **1 package (5 ounces) spring mix salad greens**
- **4 bacon strips, cooked and crumbled**

1. In a large saucepan, cook tortellini according to package directions, adding broccoli during the last 5 minutes of cooking. Meanwhile, in a small bowl, mix mayonnaise, vinegar, lemon juice, oregano and salt.
2. Drain tortellini and broccoli; gently rinse with cold water. Transfer to a large bowl. Add dressing; toss to coat. Serve over salad greens; sprinkle with bacon.

Save time, money and mess by purchasing **bacon** on sale and **freezing the cooked strips** in single layers separated by **waxed paper**. Reheat the needed quantity in the **microwave**.

Ham and Penne Milano

I came up with this recipe one night when I had to stretch leftover ham to feed my family of five. I added pasta and simply built the recipe as I went along. My family loves it!
—KATHLEEN MANCUSO NISKAYUNA, NY

START TO FINISH: 30 MIN.
MAKES: 8 SERVINGS

- **1 package (16 ounces) penne pasta**
- **2⅔ cups frozen broccoli florets**
- **2 garlic cloves, minced**
- **2 tablespoons butter**
- **3 tablespoons all-purpose flour**
- **1 can (14½ ounces) reduced-sodium chicken broth**
- **¼ cup 2% milk**
- **1½ pounds boneless fully cooked ham, julienned**
- **1 jar (7½ ounces) roasted sweet red peppers, drained and julienned**
- **⅔ cup grated Parmesan cheese**
- **½ cup chopped walnuts**
- **1 teaspoon pepper**

1. In a Dutch oven, cook pasta according to package directions, adding the broccoli during the last 5 minutes of cooking.
2. Meanwhile, in a large skillet, saute garlic in butter for 1 minute. Stir in flour until blended; gradually add chicken broth and milk. Bring to a boil; cook and stir for 1-2 minutes or until thickened. Stir in the ham, red peppers, cheese, walnuts and pepper.
3. Drain pasta and broccoli. Add ham mixture; toss to coat.

HAM AND PENNE MILANO

SAUSAGE BREAKFAST BURRITOS

Sausage Breakfast Burritos

Here's a fun way to serve scrambled eggs that will keep you going well into the day. The zippy flavor is sure to wake up everyone's taste buds.

—**BRENDA SPANN** GRANGER, IN

START TO FINISH: 20 MIN.
MAKES: 8 SERVINGS

- **1 pound bulk pork sausage**
- **1 small onion, chopped**
- **½ green pepper, chopped**
- **1 can (4 ounces) mushroom stems and pieces, drained**
- **1 tablespoon butter**
- **6 eggs, beaten**
- **8 flour tortillas (8 inches), warmed**
- **1 cup (4 ounces) shredded cheddar cheese**
- **Salsa, optional**

1. In a large skillet, brown sausage. Drain, reserving 2 tablespoons drippings. Saute the onion, green pepper and mushrooms in drippings until tender.
2. In another skillet, melt butter over medium-high heat. Add eggs; cook and stir until set.
3. Divide sausage mixture among tortillas; top with eggs and cheese. Fold bottom of tortilla over filling and roll up. Serve with salsa if desired.

Ham with Mixed Fruit

Apple pie filling and fruit cocktail create a sweet and chunky sauce that nicely complements ham steaks. I make this often for birthdays, and it's delicious.

—**RAYMOND HOLTMANN** GERMANTOWN, IL

START TO FINISH: 15 MIN.
MAKES: 8 SERVINGS

- **2 pounds fully cooked bone-in ham steak, cut into serving-size portions**
- **1 tablespoon canola oil**
- **1 can (21 ounces) apple pie filling**
- **1 can (15¼ ounces) fruit cocktail, drained**
- **¼ cup packed brown sugar**
- **¼ cup butter, melted**

1. In a large skillet, brown the ham steaks in oil.
2. Meanwhile, in a large microwave-safe bowl, combine the pie filling, fruit cocktail, brown sugar and butter. Cook until heated through, stirring twice. Serve with ham.

Ham 'n' Hominy Salad

I love collecting recipes, and this is one I found several years ago. It's one of my favorite salads.

—**ANITA FREED** KALAMAZOO, MI

START TO FINISH: 20 MIN.
MAKES: 4 SERVINGS

- **1 medium onion, chopped**
- **1 tablespoon butter**
- **1 tablespoon all-purpose flour**
- **½ cup water**
- **¼ cup cider vinegar**
- **¼ cup sugar**
- **¼ teaspoon salt**
- **⅛ teaspoon pepper**
- **1 can (15½ ounces) hominy, rinsed and drained**
- **1 cup cubed fully cooked ham**
- **½ cup chopped celery**
- **½ cup chopped green pepper**

1. In a large skillet, saute onion in butter until tender. Stir in flour until blended. Combine water, vinegar and sugar; whisk into the onion mixture. Bring to a boil; cook and stir for 2 minutes or until thickened.
2. Remove from heat; add remaining ingredients. Serve warm or cold.

Taco Pork Chops

You'll love these zesty pork chops. A short ingredient list makes them perfect for a weeknight. These tender, saucy chops are just right for the kids.

—**FAY BASWELL** LODI, CA

START TO FINISH: 20 MIN.
MAKES: 4 SERVINGS

- **4 boneless pork loin chops (6 ounces each)**
- **1 tablespoon canola oil**
- **1 can (8 ounces) tomato sauce**
- **1 cup water, divided**
- **1 medium onion, chopped**
- **1 envelope taco seasoning**
- **2 tablespoons all-purpose flour**

1. In a large skillet over medium heat, cook pork chops in oil for 2-3 minutes on each side or until lightly browned.
2. In a small bowl, combine the tomato sauce, 3⁄4 cup water, onion and taco seasoning. Pour over pork and bring to a boil. Reduce heat; cover and simmer for 4-5 minutes or until a thermometer reads 160°. Let meat stand 5 minutes before serving.
3. Remove pork to a serving plate and keep warm. Combine flour and remaining water until smooth. Stir into skillet. Bring to a boil; cook and stir for 2 minutes or until sauce is thickened. Serve with pork chops.

"I developed this delightful dish by tweaking my veal scallopine recipe. Thinly sliced pork is an economical success!"
—**MARY COKENOUR** MONTICELLO, UT

BALSAMIC PORK SCALLOPINE

Balsamic Pork Scallopine

PREP: 25 MIN. • **COOK:** 30 MIN.
MAKES: 12 SERVINGS

- **3 pounds pork sirloin cutlets**
- **1½ cups all-purpose flour**
- **½ cup olive oil**
- **2 tablespoons butter**
- **1 medium onion, chopped**
- **½ cup chopped roasted sweet red peppers**
- **6 garlic cloves, minced**
- **1 can (14½ ounces) reduced-sodium chicken broth**
- **½ cup minced fresh basil or 2 tablespoons dried basil**
- **½ cup balsamic vinegar**
- **½ teaspoon pepper**

NOODLES

- **1 package (16 ounces) egg noodles**
- **½ cup half-and-half cream**
- **¼ cup grated Romano cheese**
- **¼ cup butter, cubed**
- **½ teaspoon pepper**
- **¼ teaspoon garlic powder**

1. Dredge pork cutlets in flour. Heat oil and butter in a large skillet over medium-high heat; add pork and brown in batches. Set aside.
2. Add onion and red peppers to the pan; saute until onion is tender. Add garlic; cook 1 minute longer. Add the broth, basil, vinegar and pepper. Return pork to the pan, layering if necessary.
3. Cover and cook over low heat for 15-20 minutes or until meat is tender.
4. Meanwhile, in a Dutch oven, cook noodles according to package directions. Drain; stir in the cream, cheese, butter, pepper and garlic powder. Serve with pork.

Chili Sausage Supper

Here's a nice simple dinner, sized right for two, that's a snap to prepare. It's good cold-weather comfort food.

—**PHILLIS MOORE** EXCELSIOR SPRINGS, MO

PREP: 15 MIN. • **COOK:** 30 MIN.
MAKES: 2 SERVINGS

- **½ pound bulk pork sausage**
- **⅓ cup finely chopped onion**
- **⅓ cup chopped green pepper**
- **2 cups uncooked egg noodles**
- **1 cup canned diced tomatoes**
- **¾ cup water**
- **1½ teaspoons sugar**
- **½ teaspoon chili powder**
- **¼ teaspoon salt, optional**
- **½ cup sour cream**

1. In a large skillet, cook the sausage, onion and green pepper over medium heat until meat is no longer pink; drain. Stir in the noodles, tomatoes, water, sugar, chili powder and salt if desired. Bring to a boil. Reduce heat; cover and simmer for 30 minutes or until noodles are tender.

2. Gradually stir ½ cup hot sausage mixture into sour cream; return all to the pan, stirring constantly. Cook until heated through.

If you'd like to use a whole 14½-ounce **can of tomatoes** instead of splitting it up, just **double the recipe**. Use a whole **onion** or **green pepper** if desired.

Pork Chops with Apple Rings

With a delicious apple and dried fruit topping, these tender chops are special enough to serve to company, yet simple enough to fix anytime. The best part is that the apples don't have to be peeled: Just core and slice, and you're ready to go.

—**KATHLEEN HARRIS** GALESBURG, IL

START TO FINISH: 30 MIN.
MAKES: 6 SERVINGS

- **6 pork chops (½ inch thick)**
- **½ teaspoon celery salt**
- **½ teaspoon rubbed sage**
- **½ teaspoon salt**
- **¼ teaspoon pepper**
- **2 tablespoons butter**
- **2 medium unpeeled Golden Delicious apples, cored and cut into ½-inch rings**
- **¼ cup diced dried apricots**
- **2 tablespoons golden raisins**
- **2 tablespoons brown sugar**

1. Sprinkle pork chops with celery salt, sage, salt and pepper. In a large skillet, brown chops in butter on one side; turn. Top with apple rings. Sprinkle with apricots, raisins and brown sugar.

2. Cover chops and cook over low heat for 18-22 minutes or until meat juices run clear.

BAYOU SAUSAGE STEW

FREEZE IT

Bayou Sausage Stew

My husband and I worked on this recipe together. We make a big pot and freeze it to enjoy all winter long. We sometimes stir in sauteed shrimp for a delicious addition to this stew.

—**LISA NELSON** BLUFFTON, SC

PREP: 20 MIN. • **COOK:** 20 MIN.
MAKES: 9 SERVINGS

- **1 pound smoked sausage, halved lengthwise and cut into ¼-inch slices**
- **2 large onions, chopped**
- **1 large green pepper, chopped**
- **8 green onions, sliced**
- **1 cup minced fresh parsley**
- **¼ cup olive oil**
- **6 garlic cloves, minced**
- **1 cup white wine**
- **1 can (28 ounces) diced tomatoes, undrained**
- **1 package (16 ounces) frozen sliced okra**
- **1 can (8 ounces) tomato sauce**
- **2 tablespoons soy sauce**
- **1 tablespoon Louisiana-style hot sauce**
- **Hot cooked rice**

1. In a Dutch oven, saute the first five ingredients in oil until the vegetables are tender. Add garlic; cook 1 minute longer. Add wine, stirring to loosen browned bits from pan.

2. Stir in the tomatoes, okra, tomato sauce, soy sauce and hot sauce; bring to a boil. Reduce heat; simmer, uncovered, for 4-5 minutes or until okra is tender. Serve with rice.

FREEZE OPTION *Freeze cooled stew in freezer containers. To use, partially thaw in refrigerator overnight. Microwave, covered, on high in a microwave-safe dish until heated through, gently stirring and adding a little broth or water if necessary. Serve with rice.*

Pepperoni 'n' Tomato Pasta

PREP: 25 MIN. • **COOK:** 20 MIN.
MAKES: 8 SERVINGS

- **1 medium onion, chopped**
- **1 large green pepper, chopped**
- **1 cup sliced fresh mushrooms**
- **1 tablespoon olive oil**
- **2 cans (15 ounces each) tomato sauce**
- **2 cans (14½ ounces each) stewed tomatoes, chopped**
- **2 bay leaves**
- **1 tablespoon sugar**
- **½ teaspoon dried basil**
- **½ teaspoon dried oregano**
- **½ teaspoon fennel seed, crushed**
- **½ teaspoon crushed red pepper flakes**
- **¼ teaspoon pepper**
- **1 package (8 ounces) sliced pepperoni, quartered**
- **4 cups uncooked ziti or bow tie pasta**
- **½ cup grated Parmesan cheese**
- **1½ cups (6 ounces) shredded part-skim mozzarella cheese**

1. In a large saucepan, saute the onion, green pepper and mushrooms in oil until tender.
2. Stir in the tomato sauce, tomatoes, bay leaves, sugar and seasonings. Bring to a boil. Stir in pepperoni. Reduce heat; simmer, uncovered, for 15 minutes.
3. Meanwhile, cook pasta according to package directions. Drain and place in a large serving bowl. Discard bay leaves from sauce; stir in Parmesan cheese. Pour over pasta; toss to coat. Sprinkle with mozzarella cheese.

SWEET POTATO AND HAM HASH

Sweet Potato and Ham Hash

Tender sweet potatoes match up with ham, eggs and zippy seasonings for an impressive breakfast. Or serve it with salad and have an easy breakfast-for-dinner meal.
—**JUDY ARMSTRONG** PRAIRIEVILLE, LA

PREP: 20 MIN. • **COOK:** 20 MIN.
MAKES: 4 SERVINGS

- **2 cups cubed peeled sweet potatoes**
- **2 tablespoons butter**
- **1 tablespoon olive oil**
- **1 medium onion, chopped**
- **1 small sweet red pepper, chopped**
- **3 green onions, chopped**
- **1 red chili pepper, seeded and finely chopped**
- **3 garlic cloves, minced**
- **2 cups cubed fully cooked ham**
- **½ teaspoon pepper**
- **¼ teaspoon salt**
- **4 eggs**
- **¼ cup shredded white cheddar cheese**

1. In a large skillet, saute sweet potatoes in butter and oil until crisp-tender. Add the onion, red pepper, green onions and chili pepper. Saute 4-5 minutes longer or until tender. Add garlic; cook 1 minute longer. Stir in ham, pepper and salt.
2. With the back of a spoon, make four wells in the potato mixture; add an egg to each well. Sprinkle with cheese. Cover and cook for 4-5 minutes or until egg whites are completely set.

NOTE *Wear disposable gloves when cutting hot peppers; the oils can burn skin. Avoid touching your face.*

For a **variation**, add a dash of **cinnamon** to the **sweet potatoes** and use a pound of chopped **andouille** instead of the ham. Or prepare the **hash** with cubed skin-on **red potatoes** and **corned beef**.

PEPPERONI 'N' TOMATO PASTA

Cider-Glazed Pork Chops with Carrots

Treat the family to a new pork chop dinner that will please them so much, they'll think you took culinary classes. They'll never guess this simple main dish cost about $2 a serving!

—TASTE OF HOME TEST KITCHEN

PREP: 20 MIN. • **COOK:** 15 MIN.
MAKES: 4 SERVINGS

- **4 bone-in pork loin chops (7 ounces each)**
- **4 teaspoons olive oil, divided**
- **¾ cup apple cider or juice**
- **2 tablespoons brown sugar**
- **2 tablespoons cider vinegar**
- **2 tablespoons soy sauce**
- **3 garlic cloves, minced**
- **2 teaspoons prepared mustard**
- **½ teaspoon ground ginger**
- **8 small carrots, halved lengthwise**
- **½ teaspoon salt**
- **¼ teaspoon pepper**

1. In a large skillet, brown pork chops in 3 teaspoons oil on both sides.
2. In a small bowl, combine the cider, brown sugar, vinegar, soy sauce, garlic, mustard and ginger; pour over chops. Bring to a boil. Reduce heat; cover and simmer for 15-20 minutes or until chops are tender.
3. Meanwhile, place carrots in a greased 15-in. x 10-in. x 1-in. baking pan. Drizzle with remaining oil. Sprinkle with salt and pepper; toss to coat.
4. Bake, uncovered, at 425° for 15-20 minutes or until tender, turning once. Serve with pork chops.

Pork Chops with Creamy Mustard Noodles

A fast, creamy skillet sauce dresses up everyday pork chops and noodles. Chicken also works well with the zesty mix of mustards in this recipe.

—MARGARET BRACHER ROBERTSDALE, AL

START TO FINISH: 30 MIN.
MAKES: 4 SERVINGS

- **6 cups uncooked egg noodles**
- **½ teaspoon salt**
- **½ teaspoon pepper**
- **¼ teaspoon garlic powder**
- **¼ teaspoon dried thyme**
- **¼ teaspoon dried oregano**
- **4 boneless pork loin chops (6 ounces each)**
- **1 tablespoon olive oil**
- **1 can (10½ ounces) condensed beef broth, undiluted**
- **½ cup water**
- **⅔ cup whipped cream cheese**
- **2 tablespoons butter**
- **1 tablespoon spicy brown mustard**
- **1 tablespoon yellow mustard**
- **Minced fresh parsley**

1. Cook egg noodles according to package directions.
2. Meanwhile, combine the salt, pepper, garlic powder, thyme and oregano; sprinkle over pork chops. In a large skillet, brown chops in oil. Add broth and water. Bring to a boil. Reduce heat; cover and simmer for 8-10 minutes or until pork chops are tender, turning once. Remove chops and keep warm.
3. Stir the cream cheese, butter and mustards into the skillet. Cook and stir over medium heat until thickened. Drain noodles; add to skillet and toss to coat. Serve with pork chops. Garnish with parsley.

PORK CHOPS WITH CREAMY MUSTARD NOODLES

RAVIOLI WITH SAUSAGE & TOMATO CREAM SAUCE

Ravioli with Sausage & Tomato Cream Sauce

It tastes like you spent all day preparing this pasta, but it's ready in just 30 minutes! Family members request my ravioli often.

—**CHERYL WEGENER** FESTUS, MO

START TO FINISH: 25 MIN.
MAKES: 4 SERVINGS

- **1 package (9 ounces) refrigerated cheese ravioli**
- **¾ pound bulk Italian sausage**
- **1 jar (24 ounces) tomato basil pasta sauce**
- **½ cup heavy whipping cream**
- **2 bacon strips, cooked and crumbled**
- **2 tablespoons grated Parmesan cheese**
- **Minced fresh parsley**

1. Cook ravioli according to package directions. Meanwhile, cook sausage in a large skillet over medium heat until no longer pink; drain. Stir in the pasta sauce, cream and bacon. Bring to a boil. Reduce heat; simmer, uncovered, for 2 minutes or until slightly thickened.

2. Drain ravioli; stir into sauce. Top with Parmesan cheese and parsley.

Greek Pork Pockets

These are so easy to make for a quick lunch. And my kids prefer them to peanut butter and jelly any day!

—**DIANE HIXON** NICEVILLE, FL

START TO FINISH: 20 MIN.
MAKES: 4 SERVINGS

- **⅓ cup creamy Caesar salad dressing**
- **1 pound pork tenderloin, sliced**
- **1 teaspoon canola oil**
- **4 pita pocket halves**
- **½ cup chopped cucumber**
- **4 slices red onion, separated into rings**
- **¼ cup cucumber ranch salad dressing**

1. Place Caesar dressing in a small bowl; add pork and toss to coat. In a large nonstick skillet, heat oil over medium-high heat. Add pork; cook and stir 7-8 minutes or until meat is no longer pink.

2. Fill pitas with pork, cucumber and onion; drizzle with salad dressing.

Colorful Kielbasa

This stick-to-your-ribs dish is sure to satisfy the heartiest appetite. You can take it from stovetop to table in about 45 minutes, and most of the cooking is hands-free.

—**SCHELBY THOMPSON** CAMDEN, WY

PREP: 15 MIN. • **COOK:** 35 MIN.
MAKES: 4-6 SERVINGS

- **1 can (10¾ ounces) condensed cream of celery soup, undiluted**
- **1½ cups water**
- **1 tablespoon butter**
- **1 pound smoked kielbasa, cut into ½-inch pieces**
- **¾ cup uncooked long grain rice**
- **1 package (10 ounces) frozen peas**
- **1 jar (4½ ounces) sliced mushrooms, drained**
- **1 cup (4 ounces) shredded cheddar cheese**

1. In a large skillet, combine soup, water and butter; bring to a boil. Add kielbasa and rice. Reduce heat; simmer, covered, 18 minutes or until rice is almost tender.

2. Stir in peas and mushrooms. Cover and cook for 15 minutes or until rice is tender and peas are heated through. Sprinkle with cheese; cover and let stand until melted.

Check whether your **grocery store** offers its own **grated Parmesan** in the deli or **cheese** section. Often, you can get a **higher-quality** product for **less money** than the commercial brands.

"I'm always looking for quick and easy recipes that are impressive enough to serve company. These pork chops smothered in bacon and Swiss cheese certainly fit the bill." —KEITH MILLER FORT GRATIOT, MI

BACON-SWISS PORK CHOPS

EAT SMART

Bacon-Swiss Pork Chops

START TO FINISH: 25 MIN.
MAKES: 4 SERVINGS

- **2 bacon strips, chopped**
- **1 medium onion, chopped**
- **4 boneless pork loin chops (4 ounces each)**
- **½ teaspoon garlic powder**
- **¼ teaspoon salt**
- **2 slices reduced-fat Swiss cheese, halved**

1. In a nonstick skillet coated with cooking spray, cook bacon and onion over medium heat until bacon is crisp, stirring occasionally. Remove with a slotted spoon; drain on paper towels. Discard drippings.
2. Sprinkle pork chops with garlic powder and salt. Add pork chops to same pan; cook over medium heat 3-5 minutes on each side or until a thermometer reads 160°.
3. Top the pork chops with bacon mixture and cheese. Cook, covered, on low heat for 1-2 minutes or until cheese is melted.

PER SERVING *218 cal., 10 g fat (4 g sat. fat), 64 mg chol., 268 mg sodium, 4 g carb., 1 g fiber, 27 g pro.* ***Diabetic Exchanges:*** *4 lean meat, ½ fat.*

For a **sweet and spicy** variation, brush the **pork chops** with **barbecue sauce**, then top with the **bacon** mixture and **pepper jack** cheese instead of Swiss.

ASIAN PORK LINGUINE

EAT SMART

Asian Pork Linguine

Peanut butter, ginger and honey make an easy, authentic-tasting sauce for noodles. If I have fresh ginger on hand, I grate ¼ teaspoon to use in place of the ground ginger.
—LISA VARNER EL PASO, TX

START TO FINISH: 30 MIN.
MAKES: 5 SERVINGS

- **6 ounces uncooked linguine**
- **2 teaspoons cornstarch**
- **½ cup water**
- **¼ cup reduced-fat creamy peanut butter**
- **2 tablespoons reduced-sodium soy sauce**
- **1 tablespoon honey**
- **½ teaspoon garlic powder**
- **⅛ teaspoon ground ginger**
- **1 pound boneless pork loin chops, cubed**
- **3 teaspoons sesame oil, divided**
- **2 medium carrots, sliced**
- **1 medium onion, halved and sliced**

1. Cook linguine according to package directions. For sauce, in a small bowl, combine cornstarch and water until smooth. Whisk in the peanut butter, soy sauce, honey, garlic powder and ginger until blended; set aside.
2. In a large nonstick skillet or wok coated with cooking spray, stir-fry pork in 2 teaspoons oil until no longer pink. Remove and keep warm. Stir-fry carrots and onion in remaining oil until crisp-tender. Stir the sauce and add to the pan. Bring to a boil; cook and stir for 2 minutes or until thickened.
3. Return pork to the pan. Drain linguine; add to the pan and stir to coat.

PER SERVING *376 cal., 13 g fat (3 g sat. fat), 44 mg chol., 358 mg sodium, 39 g carb., 3 g fiber, 27 g pro.* ***Diabetic Exchanges:*** *3 lean meat, 2½ starch, 2 fat.*

Fish & Seafood

154

151

152

This chapter is brimming with **fresh dinner ideas**. Cook up some sweet, **buttery scallops**, heart-healthy **salmon**, **family-pleasing battered fish** fillets and more. Sample some of these ethnic and regional specialties. Healthy, **delicious** entrees abound!

Chilled Salmon with Cucumber-Dill Sauce

A friend from Boston shared this traditional New England dish. It's a refreshing hot-weather meal and a nice change of pace from heavy cookout food.
—SHERI SIDWELL ALTON, IL

PREP: 20 MIN. • **COOK:** 10 MIN. + CHILLING
MAKES: 4 SERVINGS

- **1½ cups water**
- **1 cup white wine or chicken broth**
- **4 green onions, sliced**
- **10 whole peppercorns**
- **4 salmon fillets (5 ounces each)**

DILL SAUCE

- **½ cup reduced-fat sour cream**
- **¼ cup chopped peeled cucumber**
- **4½ teaspoons snipped fresh dill or 1½ teaspoons dill weed**
- **2 teaspoons prepared horseradish**
- **1½ teaspoons lemon juice**
- **⅛ teaspoon salt**
- **⅛ teaspoon pepper**

1. In a large skillet, combine the water, wine, onions and peppercorns. Bring to a boil. Reduce heat; carefully add salmon. Cover and cook for 5-7 minutes or until fish flakes easily with a fork.

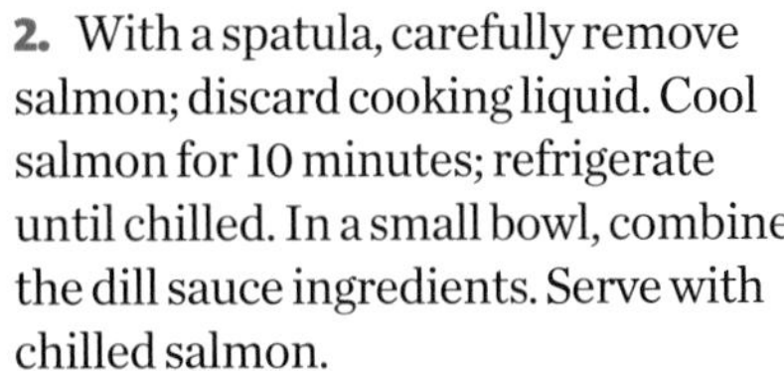

2. With a spatula, carefully remove salmon; discard cooking liquid. Cool salmon for 10 minutes; refrigerate until chilled. In a small bowl, combine the dill sauce ingredients. Serve with chilled salmon.

CHILLED SALMON WITH CUCUMBER-DILL SAUCE

EAT SMART

Tilapia with Strawberry-Thyme Sauce

Here's a delicious way to welcome spring. I like to serve the tilapia with polenta and a blend of leeks and green onions that I've roasted in the oven with a little olive oil, salt and pepper. And definitely add a bit of bacon or blue cheese: It lends a hint of saltiness to contrast with the sweet and tangy sauce.
—STEPHEN EXEL DES MOINES, IA

START TO FINISH: 30 MIN.
MAKES: 4 SERVINGS

- **1 cup quartered fresh strawberries**
- **½ cup white wine**
- **⅓ cup sugar**
- **¼ cup lemon juice**
- **1 fresh thyme sprig**
- **½ teaspoon sea salt, divided**
- **1 tablespoon all-purpose flour**
- **¼ teaspoon pepper**
- **4 tilapia fillets (4 ounces each)**
- **1 tablespoon olive oil**
- **Crumbled blue cheese or cooked bacon, optional**

1. In a small saucepan, combine the strawberries, wine, sugar, lemon juice, thyme sprig and 1/4 teaspoon salt. Bring to a boil. Reduce heat; simmer, uncovered, for 15-20 minutes or until slightly thickened. Discard thyme sprig.

2. Combine the flour, pepper and remaining salt; sprinkle over tilapia. In a large skillet, cook fillets in oil over medium-high heat for 3-4 minutes on each side or until fish flakes easily with a fork. Serve with strawberry sauce and sprinkle with blue cheese and bacon if desired.

PER SERVING *221 cal., 5 g fat (1 g sat. fat), 55 mg chol., 337 mg sodium, 23 g carb., 1 g fiber, 22 g pro.* ***Diabetic Exchanges:*** *3 lean meat, 1½ starch, ½ fat.*

Fettuccine with Bacon-Clam Sauce

Clams, garlic, smoky bacon and grated Parmesan cheese flavor this hearty pasta dish. It's been a favorite for years. Add a side salad and garlic breadsticks for a fabulous dinner.

—**DARLENE HICKS** ARCATA, CA

START TO FINISH: 25 MIN.
MAKES: 2 SERVINGS

- **4 ounces uncooked fettuccine**
- **1 can (6½ ounces) chopped clams**
- **1 tablespoon butter**
- **1 garlic clove, minced**
- **1 tablespoon minced fresh parsley**
- **½ teaspoon dried oregano**
- **¼ teaspoon pepper**
- **½ cup heavy whipping cream**
- **¼ cup grated Parmesan cheese**
- **2 bacon strips, cooked and crumbled**

1. Cook fettuccine according to package directions. Meanwhile, drain clams, reserving 1/4 cup juice. In a large saucepan, combine the butter, garlic, parsley, oregano, pepper, clams and reserved juice. Bring to a boil. Reduce heat; simmer, uncovered, for 5 minutes.

2. Stir in the cream and Parmesan cheese; cook 2-3 minutes longer or until heated through. Add bacon. Drain fettuccine; stir into sauce.

TERIYAKI MAHI MAHI

Sweet and Sour Shrimp in a Hurry

Quick, easy and convenient, this family-friendly recipe is proof you can whip up a delicious dinner in minutes.

—**TASTE OF HOME TEST KITCHEN**

START TO FINISH: 20 MIN.
MAKES: 4 SERVINGS

- **1 small onion, cut into thin wedges**
- **⅔ cup sweet-and-sour sauce, divided**
- **1 package (14 ounces) frozen sugar snap peas**
- **1 pound peeled and deveined cooked medium shrimp**
- **1 can (8¾ ounces) whole baby corn, drained**
- **4 teaspoons reduced-sodium soy sauce**
- **Hot cooked rice**

1. In a large nonstick skillet, cook onion in 2 tablespoons sweet-and-sour sauce over medium heat for 3 minutes. Stir in the peas; cook and stir for 3-5 minutes or until crisp-tender.

2. Add the shrimp, corn, soy sauce and remaining sweet-and-sour sauce; heat through. Serve with rice.

EAT SMART

Teriyaki Mahi Mahi

This recipe is good with rice, vegetables or salad, and it works well with cod or halibut fillets, too. Blot the fish thoroughly with paper towels before cooking to allow a nice brown crust to form.

—**MICHELLE IBARRIENTOS** TORRANCE, CA

START TO FINISH: 20 MIN.
MAKES: 4 SERVINGS

- **4 mahi mahi fillets (6 ounces each)**
- **¼ teaspoon garlic powder**
- **¼ teaspoon pepper**
- **1 tablespoon canola oil**
- **1 teaspoon minced fresh gingerroot**
- **¼ cup reduced-sodium teriyaki sauce**

1. Sprinkle mahi mahi with garlic powder and pepper. In a large skillet, cook mahi mahi in oil over medium-high heat for 4-5 minutes on each side or until fish flakes easily with a fork. Remove and keep warm.

2. In the same skillet, saute ginger for 30 seconds. Stir in teriyaki sauce; heat through. Serve over mahi mahi.

PER SERVING *192 cal., 5 g fat (1 g sat. fat), 124 mg chol., 470 mg sodium, 3 g carb., trace fiber, 33 g pro.* ***Diabetic Exchanges:*** *5 lean meat, 1/2 fat.*

"I created this salad to satisfy our family's love of shrimp. It has lots of contrasting textures, including taco-seasoned shrimp, crispy tortilla strips, cheese and hearty black beans."
—**ELLEN MORRELL** HAZLETON, PA

Shrimp Taco Salad

START TO FINISH: 30 MIN.
MAKES: 8 SERVINGS

- **1 pound uncooked large shrimp, peeled and deveined**
- **1 envelope taco seasoning, divided**
- **½ cup plus 3 tablespoons olive oil, divided**
- **1 small onion, finely chopped**
- **3 tablespoons cider vinegar**
- **2 tablespoons diced green or sweet red pepper**
- **6 garlic cloves, minced**
- **½ teaspoon ground coriander**
- **¼ teaspoon sugar**
- **3 corn tortillas (6 inches), cut into ¼-inch strips**
- **1 can (15 ounces) black beans, rinsed and drained**
- **1 package (8 ounces) ready-to-serve salad greens**
- **1 medium tomato, chopped**
- **2 cups (8 ounces) finely shredded Colby-Monterey Jack cheese**

1. Place shrimp in a large bowl; sprinkle with half of the taco seasoning. Set aside. In a small bowl, whisk 1/2 cup oil, onion, vinegar, green pepper, garlic, coriander and sugar; set aside.
2. In a large skillet, heat remaining oil over medium-high heat. Add tortilla chips; stir-fry until golden. Drain on paper towels. Sprinkle with remaining taco seasoning. In same skillet, cook and stir shrimp 8-10 minutes or until shrimp turn pink.
3. In a large bowl, combine the beans, salad greens, tomato, shrimp and tortilla strips. Just before serving, whisk dressing and pour over salad; sprinkle with cheese and toss to coat.

Caesar Shrimp and Pasta

Here's a five-ingredient entree that's ready in a dash. Creamy Caesar salad dressing coats pasta, shrimp and broccoli for a flavorful meal.
—**JO ANN BOYER** BLOOMINGDALE, OH

START TO FINISH: 20 MIN.
MAKES: 4 SERVINGS

- **3 cups uncooked bow tie pasta**
- **3 cups fresh broccoli florets**
- **1 pound peeled and deveined cooked medium shrimp**
- **2 tablespoons plus ½ cup reduced-fat creamy Caesar salad dressing, divided**
- **⅓ cup grated Parmesan cheese**

1. In a large saucepan, cook pasta according to package directions, adding the broccoli during the last 4 minutes of cooking.
2. Meanwhile, in a large skillet, cook shrimp in 2 tablespoons dressing over medium heat for 3-4 minutes or until heated through.
3. Drain pasta mixture; transfer to a large bowl. Add the shrimp, cheese and remaining dressing; toss to coat. Serve immediately.

Angel Hair Tuna

I got this easy dinner idea from a dear friend, and it quickly became a standby in our house. Just toss together a green salad and toast some garlic bread to make it complete.
—**COLLETTE BURCH** EDINBURG, TX

START TO FINISH: 20 MIN.
MAKES: 4 SERVINGS

- **2 packages (5.1 ounces each) angel hair pasta with Parmesan cheese dinner mix**
- **1 can (12 ounces) tuna, drained and flaked**
- **½ teaspoon Italian seasoning**
- **¾ cup crushed butter-flavored crackers (about 15)**
- **¼ cup butter, melted**

1. Prepare pasta dinner mixes according to package directions. Stir in the tuna and Italian seasoning. Transfer to a large serving bowl; cover and let stand for 5 minutes to thicken.
2. Toss cracker crumbs and butter; sprinkle over the top. Serve immediately.
EDITOR'S NOTE *This recipe was tested with Pasta Roni.*

CAESAR SHRIMP AND PASTA

TUNA STEAK SALAD

Tuna Steak Salad

START TO FINISH: 30 MIN.
MAKES: 4 SERVINGS

- **3 tablespoons plus ½ cup olive oil, divided**
- **3 tablespoons chopped shallots, divided**
- **½ teaspoon salt, divided**
- **¼ teaspoon pepper, divided**
- **1 pound tuna steaks (1 inch thick)**
- **¼ cup cider vinegar**
- **1 tablespoon Dijon mustard**
- **1½ teaspoons sugar**
- **1 package (5 ounces) spring mix salad greens**
- **1 cup cut fresh thin asparagus (1-inch pieces)**
- **1 cup grape tomatoes, halved**
- **2 tablespoons minced chives**

1. In a large resealable plastic bag, combine 3 tablespoons of olive oil, 1 tablespoon shallots, 1/4 teaspoon salt and 1/8 teaspoon pepper. Add tuna steaks. Seal and turn to coat; marinate 10 minutes.

2. Meanwhile, for dressing, combine the vinegar, mustard, sugar, and the remaining shallots, salt and pepper in a small bowl; slowly whisk in the remaining oil. Set aside.

3. Drain and discard marinade. In a large nonstick skillet, cook tuna over medium heat for 3-5 minutes on each side for medium-rare or until slightly pink in the center.

4. On salad plates, arrange the greens, asparagus and tomatoes. Cut tuna into bite-size pieces; add to salads. Drizzle salads with dressing. Sprinkle with chives.

For a **sweeter** dressing, substitute **rice vinegar** for the cider vinegar. Sprinkle salads with **sesame seeds** or **cashews** if desired.

SOUTHERN SHRIMP & GRITS

Southern Shrimp & Grits

Here's an old Southern stick-to-your-ribs dinner combining fresh shrimp, a medley of peppers, onion and creamy cheese grits. Use crab instead of or in addition to shrimp if you like. This meal is wonderful with corn bread and sliced tomatoes.
—**MELISSA HASS** GILBERT, SC

START TO FINISH: 30 MIN.
MAKES: 4 SERVINGS

- **2½ cups chicken broth**
- **1 cup quick-cooking grits**
- **1 medium onion, sliced**
- **1 package (14 ounces) frozen pepper strips, thawed**
- **4 teaspoons olive oil**
- **¾ pound uncooked large shrimp, peeled and deveined**
- **¼ cup minced fresh parsley**
- **1 teaspoon lemon juice**
- **1 cup (4 ounces) shredded sharp cheddar cheese**
- **½ cup sour cream**

1. In a large saucepan, bring the broth to a boil. Slowly stir in grits. Reduce heat; cook and stir for 5-7 minutes or until thickened.

2. Meanwhile, in a large skillet, saute onion and pepper strips in oil until crisp-tender. Add the shrimp, parsley and lemon juice; saute 3-4 minutes longer or until shrimp turn pink.

3. Stir cheese and sour cream into grits; serve with shrimp mixture.

CURRY SCALLOPS AND RICE

Curry Scallops and Rice

Buttery scallops, colorful peppers and a fast rice mix tinged with curry...what's not to love abou this stress-free main dish?
—TASTE OF HOME TEST KITCHEN

START TO FINISH: 30 MIN.
MAKES: 4 SERVINGS

- **1 package (6¼ ounces) curry rice pilaf mix**
- **¼ cup butter, divided**
- **1½ pounds sea scallops**
- **1 package (14 ounces) frozen pepper strips, thawed and chopped**
- **¼ cup minced fresh parsley**
- **¼ teaspoon salt**

1. Prepare pilaf mix according to package directions, using 1 tablespoon butter.
2. Meanwhile, in a large skillet, saute scallops in remaining butter until firm and opaque. Remove and keep warm.
3. In the same skillet, saute peppers until tender. Stir in the scallops, rice, parsley and salt.

Velvet Shrimp

Here's an easy, delicious way to get a meal on the table in a hurry. The clients of my cooking business request this dish time and again.
—VONDA NIXON ANCHORAGE, AK

PREP: 15 MIN. • **COOK:** 25 MIN.
MAKES: 6 SERVINGS

- **1 package (16 ounces) linguine**
- **½ cup thinly sliced green onions**
- **1 garlic clove, minced**
- **3 tablespoons butter**
- **4 teaspoons seafood seasoning**
- **1 pound uncooked medium shrimp, peeled and deveined**
- **1½ cups heavy whipping cream**
- **1 cup (4 ounces) shredded Muenster cheese**

1. Cook linguine according to package directions.
2. Meanwhile, in a large skillet over medium-low heat, cook onions and garlic in butter for 1 minute. Stir in seafood seasoning; cook 1 minute longer. Add shrimp; cook for 3-4 minutes or until shrimp turn pink. Remove and keep warm.
3. Add cream to the pan, stirring to loosen any browned bits. Bring to a boil. Reduce heat; simmer, uncovered, for 5 minutes or until cream is reduced to about 1¼ cups.
4. Stir in cheese just until melted. Return shrimp to the pan and heat through. Drain linguine; top with shrimp mixture.

EAT SMART

Salmon Salad Pitas

I know these pitas are good because my husband and sons don't even mind having them the next day as leftovers.
—**CHERYL BAINBRIDGE** BLOOMINGTON, IN

PREP: 25 MIN. + CHILLING
MAKES: 4 SERVINGS

- **1 salmon fillet (1 pound)**
- **¼ cup chopped celery**
- **¼ cup chopped seeded peeled cucumber**
- **¼ cup reduced-fat sour cream**
- **¼ cup fat-free mayonnaise**
- **1 tablespoon minced chives**
- **1 tablespoon minced fresh dill**
- **1 teaspoon Italian seasoning**
- **¼ teaspoon salt**
- **⅛ teaspoon white pepper**
- **4 romaine leaves**
- **4 whole wheat pita pocket halves**

1. Place 2 in. of water in a large skillet; bring to a boil. Reduce heat; carefully add salmon. Poach, uncovered, for 6-12 minutes or until fish is firm and flakes easily with a fork. Remove salmon with a slotted spatula. Cool.

2. In a large bowl, combine the celery, cucumber, sour cream, mayonnaise and seasonings. Flake the salmon; stir into salad mixture. Cover and refrigerate for at least 1 hour. Serve in lettuce-lined pita breads.

PER SERVING *331 cal., 15 g fat (4 g sat. fat), 74 mg chol., 522 mg sodium, 22 g carb., 3 g fiber, 27 g pro.* ***Diabetic Exchanges:*** *3 lean meat, 1½ starch, 1 fat.*

GARDEN TUNA MACARONI SALAD

Garden Tuna Macaroni Salad

The first time I served this fresh and crunchy salad at a barbecue, I received many wonderful compliments. Someone even suggested that I open a restaurant!
—**SCARLETT HILTON** SABINA, OH

START TO FINISH: 30 MIN.
MAKES: 4 SERVINGS

- **2 cups uncooked elbow macaroni**
- **1 can (6 ounces) light water-packed tuna, drained and flaked**
- **⅔ cup chopped sweet yellow pepper**
- **⅔ cup chopped celery**
- **½ cup shredded carrot**
- **¼ cup diced radishes**
- **2 green onions, chopped**
- **2 tablespoons minced fresh parsley**
- **¾ cup Miracle Whip**
- **½ cup ranch salad dressing**
- **¼ cup grated Parmesan cheese**
- **1 teaspoon coarsely ground pepper**

1. Cook macaroni according to package directions. Meanwhile, in a large bowl, combine the tuna, vegetables and parsley. Drain macaroni and rinse in cold water; add to tuna mixture.

2. In a small bowl, combine the Miracle Whip, ranch dressing, cheese and pepper. Pour over salad and toss to coat. Chill until serving.

If you're concerned about mercury, look for **skipjack tuna**. It's a species of small light tuna, and **smaller fish** contain less mercury than very large ones.

SHRIMP AND SCALLOP COUSCOUS

EAT SMART

Stuffed-Olive Cod

Take advantage of the olive bar in your supermarket and put a new twist on cod. This simple high-protein, low-fat entree is a weeknight lifesaver.

—**TRIA OLSEN** QUEEN CREEK, AZ

START TO FINISH: 25 MIN.
MAKES: 4 SERVINGS

- **4 cod fillets (6 ounces each)**
- **1 teaspoon dried oregano**
- **¼ teaspoon salt**
- **1 medium lemon, thinly sliced**
- **1 shallot, thinly sliced**
- **⅓ cup garlic-stuffed olives, halved**
- **2 tablespoons water**
- **2 tablespoons olive juice**

1. Place fillets in a large nonstick skillet coated with cooking spray. Sprinkle with oregano and salt; top with lemon and shallot.

2. Scatter olives around fish; add water and olive juice. Bring to a boil. Reduce heat to low; gently cook, covered, 8-10 minutes or until fish just begins to flake easily with a fork.

PER SERVING *163 cal., 3 g fat (trace sat. fat), 65 mg chol., 598 mg sodium, 4 g carb., trace fiber, 27 g pro.* ***Diabetic Exchange:*** *4 lean meat.*

EAT SMART

Shrimp and Scallop Couscous

This quick and satisfying skillet dish is a favorite of mine with its sensational blend of flavors. Great for using up those abundant summer veggies.

—**MARVIN MEUSER JR.** PRINCETON, IN

START TO FINISH: 30 MIN.
MAKES: 4 SERVINGS

- **2 medium zucchini, julienned**
- **1 medium green pepper, julienned**
- **2 tablespoons olive oil**
- **3 plum tomatoes, chopped**
- **4 green onions, chopped**
- **1 tablespoon minced fresh basil or 1 teaspoon dried basil**
- **3 teaspoons chili powder**
- **1 garlic clove, minced**
- **½ teaspoon dried oregano**
- **½ pound uncooked medium shrimp, peeled and deveined**
- **½ pound bay scallops**
- **¼ teaspoon salt**
- **⅛ teaspoon pepper**
- **Hot cooked couscous or rice**
- **Thinly sliced fresh basil leaves, optional**

1. In a large skillet, saute zucchini and green pepper in oil until tender. Add the tomatoes, onions, basil, chili powder, garlic and oregano. Bring to a boil. Reduce heat; simmer, uncovered, for 5 minutes.

2. Stir in the shrimp, scallops, salt and pepper. Return to a boil. Reduce heat; simmer, uncovered, for 5 minutes or until shrimp turn pink and scallops are opaque. Serve with couscous. Garnish with sliced basil if desired.

PER SERVING *201 cal., 9 g fat (1 g sat. fat), 88 mg chol., 342 mg sodium, 11 g carb., 3 g fiber, 21 g pro.* ***Diabetic Exchanges:*** *3 lean meat, 1½ fat, 1 vegetable.*

Because **scallops** are filter-feeders that live on plankton, farmed scallops **don't require feeding**. Their low environmental impact makes them a **green choice** that will **probably grow** in popularity.

STUFFED-OLIVE COD

Shrimp Burritos

These gooey, creamy and rich burritos are packed full of shrimp and cheese. Kids will dive right in!

—TASTE OF HOME TEST KITCHEN

START TO FINISH: 20 MIN.
MAKES: 4 SERVINGS

- **1 can (10¾ ounces) condensed cream of celery soup, undiluted**
- **3 ounces cream cheese, softened**
- **¼ cup milk**
- **¼ teaspoon paprika**
- **¼ teaspoon pepper**
- **⅛ teaspoon seafood seasoning**
- **1 pound cooked medium shrimp, peeled and deveined**
- **4 flour tortillas (10 inches), warmed**
- **½ cup shredded cheddar-Monterey Jack cheese**
- **1 cup torn romaine**

1. In a large skillet, combine the first six ingredients. Cook and stir over medium heat until cream cheese is melted. Stir in the shrimp and heat through.

2. Spoon 2/3 cup filling off center on each tortilla. Sprinkle each with 2 tablespoons cheese. Fold sides and ends over filling and roll up. Serve with lettuce.

SHRIMP BURRITOS

Lemon-Batter Fish

Here is a delicious classic. You'll love what the light and crispy batter does for your fresh catch.

—JACKIE HANNAHS BRETHREN, MI

START TO FINISH: 25 MIN.
MAKES: 5 SERVINGS

- **1½ cups all-purpose flour, divided**
- **1 teaspoon baking powder**
- **¾ teaspoon salt**
- **½ teaspoon sugar**
- **1 egg, beaten**
- **⅔ cup water**
- **⅔ cup lemon juice, divided**
- **2 pounds perch or walleye fillets, cut into serving-size pieces**
- **Oil for frying**
- **Lemon wedges, optional**

1. In a shallow bowl, combine 1 cup flour, baking powder, salt and sugar; set aside. Combine the egg, water and 1/3 cup lemon juice; stir into dry ingredients until smooth.

2. In separate shallow bowls, place remaining lemon juice and remaining flour. Dip fillets in lemon juice, then flour, and then coat with the batter.

3. In a large skillet over medium-high heat, heat 1 in. of oil. Fry fish, a few fillets at a time, for 2-3 minutes on each side or until golden brown and fish flakes easily with a fork. Drain on paper towels. Garnish with lemon wedges if desired.

EASY CRAB CAKES

EAT SMART

Easy Crab Cakes

Canned crabmeat makes these delicate patties simple enough for busy weeknight dinners. For something different, try forming the crab mixture into four thick patties instead of eight cakes.

—**CHARLENE SPELOCK** APOLLO, PA

START TO FINISH: 25 MIN.
MAKES: 4 SERVINGS

- **1 cup seasoned bread crumbs, divided**
- **2 green onions, finely chopped**
- **¼ cup finely chopped sweet red pepper**
- **1 egg, beaten**
- **¼ cup reduced-fat mayonnaise**
- **1 tablespoon lemon juice**
- **½ teaspoon garlic powder**
- **⅛ teaspoon cayenne pepper**
- **2 cans (6 ounces each) crabmeat, drained, flaked and cartilage removed**
- **1 tablespoon butter**

1. In a large bowl, combine ⅓ cup bread crumbs, green onions, red pepper, egg, mayonnaise, lemon juice, garlic powder and cayenne pepper; fold in crab.

2. Place remaining bread crumbs in a shallow bowl. Divide mixture into eight portions; shape into 2-in. balls. Gently coat in bread crumbs and shape into a ½-in.-thick patty.

3. In a large nonstick skillet, heat butter over medium-high heat. Add crab cakes; cook 3-4 minutes on each side or until golden brown.

PER SERVING *239 cal., 11 g fat (3 g sat. fat), 141 mg chol., 657 mg sodium, 13 g carb., 1 g fiber, 21 g pro.* ***Diabetic Exchanges:*** *3 lean meat, 2 fat, 1 starch.*

Serve **crab cakes** with lemon wedges, **cocktail sauce**, tartar sauce, or a homemade sauce of **mayo**, pickle juice and hot sauce.

POLISH CASSEROLE, PAGE 203

“When I first made this dish, my 2-year-old liked it so much that he wanted it for every meal! You can use most any pasta that will hold the sauce.”

—**CRYSTAL JO BRUNS** ILIFF, CO
about her recipe, Polish Casserole, on page 203

Oven Entrees

Beef & Ground Beef

Nothing says home cooking like the **oven-fresh aroma** of **tender pot roast** with all the trimmings, a **homemade meat loaf** or **golden-brown potpie**. Turn to this chapter for **homey chill-chasing recipes** that are guaranteed to satisfy!

Beef Tips & Caramelized Onion Casserole

Beef sweetened with rich caramelized onions makes this a recipe you'll want to cook again and again. It's great with mashed potatoes.

—**LINDA STEMEN** MONROEVILLE, IN

PREP: 40 MIN. • **BAKE:** 1½ HOURS
MAKES: 8 SERVINGS

- **4 pounds beef sirloin tip roast, cut into 1-inch cubes**
- **½ teaspoon salt**
- **½ teaspoon pepper**
- **2 tablespoons olive oil**
- **4 large sweet onions, halved and thinly sliced**
- **3 tablespoons butter**
- **4 garlic cloves, minced**
- **⅔ cup all-purpose flour**
- **2 cans (10½ ounces each) condensed beef consomme, undiluted**
- **1 can (14½ ounces) reduced-sodium beef broth**
- **2 tablespoons Worcestershire sauce**
- **2 bay leaves**
- **½ cup heavy whipping cream**
- **8 slices French bread (½ inch thick), toasted**
- **1 cup (4 ounces) shredded part-skim mozzarella cheese**

1. Sprinkle beef with salt and pepper. In a large skillet, brown meat in oil in batches; drain. Transfer to a greased 13x9-in. baking dish.
2. In the same skillet, cook onions in butter over medium-low heat for 25-30 minutes or until golden brown, stirring occasionally. Add garlic; cook 1 minute longer.
3. Preheat oven to 325°. Stir flour into onion mixture until blended; gradually add consomme and broth. Stir in Worcestershire sauce and bay leaves. Bring to a boil; cook and stir for 1 minute or until thickened. Pour over the beef.
4. Cover and bake 1 hour. Carefully stir in cream; discard bay leaves. Bake, uncovered, 25-35 minutes or until meat is tender. Place toast over beef mixture; sprinkle with cheese. Bake 5 minutes or until cheese is melted.

Meat Loaf Stew

Cooking hearty vegetables alongside makes this meat loaf an easy meal in one. I've made the recipe many times since I received it from a friend years ago.

—**MARIAN TOBIN** UNDERHILL, VT

PREP: 35 MIN. • **BAKE:** 1½ HOURS
MAKES: 6 SERVINGS

- **6 medium potatoes, peeled**
- **6 medium onions, peeled**
- **6 medium carrots, halved lengthwise**
- **½ cup milk**
- **1 egg, beaten**
- **½ cup dry bread crumbs**
- **1 tablespoon chopped onion**
- **½ teaspoon salt**
- **½ teaspoon pepper**
- **1½ pounds lean ground beef (90% lean)**
- **1 can (10¾ ounces) condensed tomato soup, undiluted**
- **1⅓ cups water**
- **1 tablespoon brown sugar**
- **½ teaspoon ground mustard**

1. Place potatoes, whole onions and carrots in a Dutch oven. Cover with water. Bring to a boil; boil for 15 minutes.
2. Meanwhile, in a large bowl, combine milk, egg, bread crumbs, chopped onion, salt and pepper. Crumble beef over mixture and mix well. Shape into a loaf in a large roasting pan. Drain vegetables; arrange around loaf. Combine the soup, water, brown sugar and mustard; pour over meat loaf and vegetables.
3. Cover and bake at 350° for 1½ hours or until a thermometer reads 160° and vegetables are tender.

To ensure a **tender meat loaf**, mix all ingredients well before adding the ground meat. Then **lightly mix** just until combined.

FREEZE IT

Flank Steak Santa Fe

This recipe is a favorite for special family dinners. It's a fresh and zesty blend of Southwest flavors.

—**TANYA JOHNSON** SAN DIEGO, CA

PREP: 20 MIN. • **BAKE:** 1½ HOURS
MAKES: 6-8 SERVINGS

- **¾ pound bulk spicy pork sausage or uncooked chorizo**
- **2 eggs, lightly beaten**
- **1½ cups unseasoned croutons**
- **⅓ cup sliced green onions**
- **⅓ cup minced fresh parsley**
- **1 beef flank steak (1½ to 2 pounds)**
- **3 tablespoons canola oil**
- **1 jar (16 ounces) picante sauce or salsa verde**
- **Additional picante sauce or salsa verde, optional**

1. Crumble sausage into a large skillet; cook for 6-8 minutes over medium heat until fully cooked. Drain. Cool sausage to room temperature; stir in the eggs, croutons, onions and parsley.
2. Cut steak horizontally from a long side to within ½ in. of opposite side. Open steak so it lies flat; cover with plastic wrap. Flatten to ½-in. thickness. Spread with sausage mixture. Roll up jelly-roll style, starting with long side; tie with string.
3. In a large skillet, brown steak in oil. Place in a greased 13-in. x 9-in. baking dish. Spread picante sauce over steak.
4. Cover and bake at 350° for 1½ to 1¾ hours or until meat is tender. Garnish with additional picante sauce if desired.

FREEZE OPTION *Cool flank steak and sauce. Freeze in a resealable plastic freezer bag. To use, partially thaw in refrigerator overnight. Place in a baking dish with sauce. Cover and reheat in a preheated 350° oven until a thermometer inserted in the beef reads 165°. Serve as directed.*

Reuben Casserole

Here's a great dish to serve on St. Patrick's Day. It features corned beef, sauerkraut and all of the other ingredients that make Reuben sandwiches popular. It disappears quickly when I take it potlucks.

—**MARGERY BRYAN** MOSES LAKE, WA

PREP: 10 MIN. • **BAKE:** 25 MIN.
MAKES: 4 SERVINGS

- **1 can (14 ounces) sauerkraut, rinsed and well drained**
- **1¼ cups chopped cooked corned beef**
- **1 cup (8 ounces) sour cream**
- **1 small onion, chopped**
- **1 garlic clove, minced**
- **1 cup (4 ounces) shredded Swiss cheese**
- **2 slices rye bread, cubed**
- **2 tablespoons butter, melted**

1. In a large bowl, combine the sauerkraut, corned beef, sour cream, onion and garlic.
2. Transfer to a greased 11-in. x 7-in. baking dish. Sprinkle with cheese and bread; drizzle with butter. Bake, uncovered, at 350° for 25-30 minutes or until heated through.

Blue Cheese-Crusted Sirloin Steaks

START TO FINISH: 30 MIN.
MAKES: 4 SERVINGS

- **2 tablespoons butter, divided**
- **1 medium onion, chopped**
- **1 beef top sirloin steak (1 inch thick and 1½ pounds)**
- **¾ teaspoon salt**
- **½ teaspoon pepper**
- **⅓ cup crumbled blue cheese**
- **2 tablespoons soft bread crumbs**

1. In a large ovenproof skillet, heat 1 tablespoon butter over medium heat. Add onion; cook and stir until tender. Transfer to a small bowl.
2. Cut steak into four equal portions; season with salt and pepper.In the same skillet, heat remaining butter over medium heat. Brown steaks, about 5 minutes on each side. Meanwhile, add blue cheese and bread crumbs to onion; mix well. Spread over steaks.
3. Broil steaks 4-6 in. from the heat for 3-5 minutes or until steaks reach desired doneness (for medium-rare, a thermometer should read 145°; medium, 160°; well-done, 170°).

FLANK STEAK SANTA FE

BLUE CHEESE-CRUSTED SIRLOIN STEAKS

Sirloin with Bearnaise Sauce

A classic bearnaise sauce is typically made with clarified butter, but using regular cold butter works great for me. I've been cooking my whole life, and when I want an extra-special meal, I serve this beef.

—WILLA GOVORO NEVADA, MO

PREP: 20 MIN.
BAKE: 2½ HOURS + STANDING
MAKES: 12 SERVINGS

- **½ teaspoon garlic salt**
- **½ teaspoon pepper**
- **1 beef sirloin tip roast (5 to 6 pounds)**

BEARNAISE SAUCE

- **¼ cup white wine vinegar**
- **½ cup chopped green onions**
- **1 tablespoon minced fresh tarragon or 1 teaspoon dried tarragon**
- **¼ teaspoon pepper**
- **4 egg yolks**
- **1 tablespoon cold water**
- **¼ teaspoon salt**
- **⅛ teaspoon cayenne pepper**
- **¾ cup cold butter**
- **1 tablespoon minced fresh parsley**

1. Combine garlic salt and pepper; sprinkle over roast. Place on a rack in a shallow roasting pan. Bake, uncovered, at 325° for 2½ to 3 hours or until meat reaches desired doneness (for medium-rare, a thermometer should read 145°; medium, 160°; well-done, 170°). Let stand for 10-15 minutes before slicing.

2. Meanwhile, in a saucepan, combine the vinegar, green onions, tarragon and pepper; bring to a boil. Strain, reserving liquid; discard green onions and tarragon.

3. In top of a double boiler or a metal bowl over simmering water, whisk egg yolks, water and vinegar mixture until blended; cook until mixture is just thick enough to coat a metal spoon and temperature reaches 160°, whisking constantly.

4. Whisk in butter, 1 tablespoon at a time, until melted. Whisk in parsley. Keep warm. Cut roast into thin slices; serve with sauce.

SIRLOIN WITH BEARNAISE SAUCE

Beef 'n' Cheese French Bread

This open-faced sandwich is sure to be a hit with kids of all ages. My family loves eating supper when I make this entree. And I love that it's so easy!

—BECKY STUBBS LARNED, KS

START TO FINISH: 30 MIN.
MAKES: 8 SERVINGS

- **1 pound ground beef**
- **½ cup chopped onion**
- **1 cup salsa**
- **1 medium green pepper, chopped**
- **2 cans (2¼ ounces each) sliced ripe olives, drained**
- **1 teaspoon salt**
- **1 teaspoon chili powder**
- **1 teaspoon minced garlic**
- **½ teaspoon ground cumin**
- **1 loaf (1 pound) unsliced French bread**
- **2 cups (8 ounces) shredded sharp cheddar cheese**

1. In a large skillet, cook beef and onion over medium heat until meat is no longer pink; drain. Stir in the salsa, green pepper, olives, salt, chili powder, garlic and cumin. Remove from the heat.

2. Cut bread in half lengthwise; place on a baking sheet. Spread meat mixture over cut sides; sprinkle with cheese. Bake at 450° for 10-15 minutes or until cheese is melted.

FREEZE IT

Gyro Meat Loaf with Tzatziki Sauce

PREP: 20 MIN. • **BAKE:** 55 MIN. + STANDING
MAKES: 8 SERVINGS

- **1 package (10 ounces) frozen chopped spinach, thawed and squeezed dry**
- **1 cup dry bread crumbs**
- **1 small onion, finely chopped**
- **2 eggs, lightly beaten**
- **¼ cup grated Romano cheese**
- **2 teaspoons dried oregano**
- **1½ teaspoons garlic powder**
- **½ teaspoon salt**
- **2 pounds ground beef or ground lamb**
- **1 cup refrigerated tzatziki sauce**

1. Preheat oven to 350°. In a large bowl, combine the first eight ingredients. Crumble beef over mixture and mix well. Shape into a loaf and place in a greased 11-in. x 7-in. baking dish.

2. Bake, uncovered, for 55-60 minutes or until no pink remains and a thermometer reads 160°. Let stand 15 minutes before slicing. Serve with tzatziki sauce.

FREEZE OPTION *Securely wrap and freeze cooled meat loaf in plastic wrap and foil. To use, partially thaw in refrigerator overnight. Unwrap meat loaf; reheat on a greased shallow baking pan in a preheated 350° oven until heated through and a thermometer inserted in center reads 165°.*

"I love this spin on a classic meat loaf because I can sneak spinach in on my meat-and-potatoes family. I also get to make a whole other meal the next night with the leftovers–gyros. Serve the meat loaf with Greek-style potatoes or a Greek salad."
—**MANDY RIVERS** LEXINGTON, SC

GYRO MEAT LOAF WITH TZATZIKI SAUCE

EAT SMART

Bacon-Cheddar Meat Loaves

It's easy to get your family eating healthier with these fun little meat loaves. No one will guess they're light—they're topped with bacon and melted cheese!
—**TONYA VOWELS** VINE GROVE, KY

PREP: 20 MIN. • **BAKE:** 40 MIN.
MAKES: 4 SERVINGS

- **4 egg whites**
- **½ cup crushed reduced-fat butter-flavored crackers (about 12 crackers)**
- **⅓ cup plus 8 teaspoons shredded reduced-fat cheddar cheese, divided**
- **¼ cup chopped onion**
- **½ teaspoon salt**
- **¼ teaspoon pepper**
- **1 pound lean ground beef (90% lean)**
- **2 turkey bacon strips, cut in half**

1. In a large bowl, combine the egg whites, crackers, 1/3 cup cheese, onion, salt and pepper. Crumble beef over mixture and mix well. Shape into four small loaves; place in an ungreased 11-in. x 7-in. baking dish. Top each with a half-strip of bacon.

2. Bake at 350° for 35-40 minutes or until no pink remains and a thermometer reads 160°. Sprinkle meat loaves with remaining cheese; bake 2-3 minutes longer or until cheese is melted.

PER SERVING *296 cal., 15 g fat (6 g sat. fat), 86 mg chol., 672 mg sodium, 9 g carb., trace fiber, 30 g pro.* ***Diabetic Exchanges:*** *4 lean meat, 1/2 starch, 1/2 fat.*

FREEZE IT

Italian Spiral Meat Loaf

Take a classic comfort food to delicious new heights with this impressive recipe. Sausage, pizza sauce and mozzarella give meat loaf an Italian accent.

—**MEGAN KRUMM** SCHERERVILLE, IN

PREP: 40 MIN. • **BAKE:** 1¼ HOURS
MAKES: 12 SERVINGS

- **2 eggs, lightly beaten**
- **1 cup pizza sauce, divided**
- **1 cup seasoned bread crumbs**
- **1 medium onion, chopped**
- **1 medium green pepper, chopped**
- **1 teaspoon dried oregano**
- **1 garlic clove, minced**
- **½ teaspoon salt**
- **¼ teaspoon pepper**
- **2 pounds lean ground beef (90% lean)**
- **1 pound bulk Italian sausage**
- **½ pound sliced deli ham**
- **2 cups (8 ounces) shredded part-skim mozzarella cheese, divided**
- **1 jar (6 ounces) sliced mushrooms, drained**

1. Preheat oven to 375°. In a large bowl, combine the eggs, ¾ cup pizza sauce, bread crumbs, onion, green pepper, oregano, garlic, salt and pepper. Crumble beef and sausage over mixture and mix well.

2. On a piece of parchment paper, pat beef mixture into a 12-in. x 10-in. rectangle. Layer the ham, 1½ cups cheese and mushrooms over beef mixture to within 1 in. of edges. Roll up jelly-roll style, starting with a short side and peeling parchment paper away as you roll. Seal seam and ends. Place seam side down in a greased 13x9-in. baking dish; brush with remaining pizza sauce.

3. Bake, uncovered, 1 hour. Sprinkle with remaining cheese. Bake 15-20 minutes or until no pink remains and a thermometer reads 160°. Using two large spatulas, carefully transfer meat loaf to a serving platter.

FREEZE OPTION *Securely wrap and freeze cooled meat loaf in plastic wrap and foil. To use, partially thaw in refrigerator overnight. Unwrap meat loaf; reheat on a greased shallow baking pan in a preheated 350° oven until heated through and a thermometer inserted in center reads 165°.*

You can **customize** the meat loaf recipe by substituting **basil** for half of the oregano, using **turkey Italian sausage** instead of pork, or **pepperoni** instead of ham.

Caraway Beef Roast

It seems there aren't many beef roasts that are both extra-special and extra-easy. This one is, though. I like to make it for Sunday dinner.

—**BEVERLY SWANSON** RED OAK, IA

PREP: 20 MIN. • **BAKE:** 3 HOURS
MAKES: 12 SERVINGS

- **1 boneless beef rump roast or chuck roast (3 pounds)**
- **3 tablespoons canola oil**
- **1 cup hot water**
- **1½ teaspoons beef bouillon granules**
- **¼ cup ketchup**
- **1 tablespoon dried minced onion**
- **1 tablespoon Worcestershire sauce**
- **2 teaspoons caraway seeds**
- **1 teaspoon salt**
- **½ teaspoon pepper**
- **2 bay leaves**
- **2 tablespoons all-purpose flour**
- **¼ cup cold water**
- **Cooked potatoes and carrots, optional**

1. In an ovenproof Dutch oven over medium heat, brown roast in oil on all sides; drain.

2. In a small bowl, combine the hot water and bouillon; add the ketchup, onion, Worcestershire sauce, caraway, salt and pepper. Pour over roast. Add bay leaves.

3. Cover and bake at 325° for 3 hours or until tender. Remove roast to a serving platter; keep warm.

4. In a small bowl, combine flour and cold water until smooth. Stir into pan juices; bring to a boil. Cook and stir for 1-2 minutes or until thickened, adding water to thin if necessary. Discard bay leaves. Serve with cooked potatoes and carrots if desired.

PERSONAL POT ROASTS

Personal Pot Roasts

Do you want a pot roast with big old-fashioned flavor, that doesn't serve eight? Then try this one that I enjoy making for my husband, Art, and myself.

—**MARIAN PLATT** SEQUIM, WA

PREP: 10 MIN. • **BAKE:** 2 HOURS
MAKES: 2 SERVINGS

- **2 beef shanks (about 1½ pounds)**
- **3 tablespoons all-purpose flour, divided**
- **1½ cups cold water, divided**
- **½ cup beef broth**
- **1 tablespoon onion soup mix**
- **1 garlic clove, minced**
- **1 teaspoon Worcestershire sauce**
- **¼ teaspoon dried thyme**
- **1 large potato, peeled and cut into eighths**
- **2 medium carrots, cut into 2-inch pieces**
- **6 pearl onions**
- **Salt and pepper to taste**

1. Sprinkle meat with 1 tablespoon flour; place in a shallow 2-qt. baking dish. Mix 1 cup water, broth, soup mix, garlic, Worcestershire sauce and thyme; pour over meat. Cover and bake at 325° for 1½ hours.

2. Turn meat; add the potato, carrots and onions. Cover; return to oven for 30-45 minutes or until meat and vegetables are tender. Remove meat and vegetables and keep warm.

3. To prepare gravy, skim fat from pan juices. Measure 1 cup of the juices and place in a small saucepan. Combine remaining flour and cold water; stir into juices. Bring to a boil; cook and stir for 2 minutes or until thickened. Season with salt and pepper. Serve with meat and vegetables.

"My kids love meatballs with rigatoni or spaghetti. The baked cheese sauce in this recipe just takes it over the top."
—JENNIFER ROSS CLINTON, OH

MEATBALL RIGATONI ALFREDO

Meatball Rigatoni Alfredo

PREP: 1¼ HOURS • **BAKE:** 20 MIN.
MAKES: 6 SERVINGS

- **1 egg, lightly beaten**
- **¾ cup seasoned bread crumbs**
- **⅓ cup water**
- **¼ cup grated Parmesan cheese**
- **4½ teaspoons each minced fresh thyme, oregano and basil or 1½ teaspoons each dried thyme, oregano and basil**
- **1½ teaspoons pepper**
- **½ teaspoon salt**
- **1½ pounds ground beef**
- **1 tablespoon canola oil**
- **1 small onion, chopped**
- **3 garlic cloves, minced**
- **⅓ cup dry red wine or beef broth**
- **1 can (28 ounces) crushed tomatoes**
- **1 tablespoon minced fresh parsley**
- **12 ounces uncooked rigatoni or large tube pasta**

ALFREDO TOPPING

- **¼ cup butter, cubed**
- **2 tablespoons all-purpose flour**
- **2 cups half-and-half cream**
- **1 cup grated Parmesan cheese, divided**
- **1 teaspoon minced fresh thyme or ¼ teaspoon dried thyme**
- **1 teaspoon minced fresh oregano or ¼ teaspoon dried oregano**

1. In a large bowl, combine the egg, bread crumbs, water, cheese and seasonings. Crumble beef over mixture and mix well. Shape into 1½-in. balls. In a Dutch oven, brown meatballs in oil in batches; remove and keep warm.
2. Drain, reserving 1 tablespoon drippings. In the drippings, saute onion until tender. Add garlic; cook 1 minute longer. Add wine; cook and stir for 3 minutes.
3. Return meatballs to the pan; stir in tomatoes and parsley. Bring to a boil. Reduce heat; cover and simmer for 25-30 minutes or until meat is no longer pink.
4. Cook rigatoni according to package directions. Meanwhile, in a small saucepan, melt butter. Stir in flour until smooth; gradually add cream. Bring to a boil; cook and stir for 1-2 minutes or until thickened. Remove sauce from the heat. Stir in ¾ cup Parmesan cheese.
5. Drain rigatoni. Add meatballs and sauce; stir to coat. Transfer to a greased 13-in. x 9-in. baking dish.
6. Top with the sauce; sprinkle with thyme, oregano and remaining Parmesan cheese. Bake casserole, uncovered, at 400° for 20-25 minutes or until bubbly.

Black Bean Tamale Pie

Corn bread mix makes this tamale pie a snap to whip up. For a change of pace, try topping it with lettuce, guacamole or extra salsa. My husband really likes this recipe, so I make it often.
—**LAURA MORRIS** ST. JOSEPH, MO

PREP: 20 MIN. • **BAKE:** 20 MIN.
MAKES: 6-8 SERVINGS

- **½ pound ground beef**
- **½ cup chopped onion**
- **½ cup chopped green pepper**
- **1 can (15 ounces) black beans, rinsed and drained**
- **1 cup salsa**
- **1 package (8½ ounces) corn bread/muffin mix**
- **¼ cup milk**
- **1 egg**
- **2 cups (8 ounces) shredded cheddar cheese, divided**
- **Sour cream and sliced ripe olives, optional**

1. In a large skillet, cook the beef, onion and green pepper over medium heat until meat is no longer pink; drain. Stir in beans and salsa; set aside.
2. In a large bowl, combine the muffin mix, milk, egg and 1 cup cheese. Pour into a greased 9-in. pie plate. Bake at 375° for 5-6 minutes.
3. Spoon beef mixture over crust, leaving a ½-in. edge. Bake for 15-18 minutes or until crust is golden brown. Sprinkle with remaining cheese. Bake 1-2 minutes longer or until cheese is melted. Serve with sour cream and olives if desired.

BLACK BEAN TAMALE PIE

GRANDMA'S POTPIE

Grandma's Potpie

My husband and father-in-law are both picky eaters, but they always enjoy this savory beef potpie with a flaky golden crust. The recipe came from my husband's grandmother.

—**ANNETTE WHEATLEY** SYRACUSE, NY

PREP: 30 MIN. • **BAKE:** 45 MIN.
MAKES: 6 SERVINGS

- **1½ pounds ground beef**
- **1 teaspoon onion powder**
- **Salt to taste**
- **1 cup diced peeled potatoes**
- **1 cup frozen mixed vegetables, thawed**
- **¼ cup butter, cubed**
- **¼ cup all-purpose flour**
- **1 can (14½ ounces) beef broth**

CRUST

- **2 cups all-purpose flour**
- **1 tablespoon baking powder**
- **1 teaspoon salt**
- **¼ cup shortening**
- **¾ cup milk**
- **1 tablespoon butter, melted**

1. In a large skillet, cook beef over medium heat until no longer pink; drain. Stir in onion powder and salt. Transfer to a greased 9-in.-square baking dish. Top with potatoes and mixed vegetables.

2. Meanwhile, in a small saucepan, melt the butter. Stir in flour until smooth; gradually add broth. Bring to a boil. Cook and stir for 2 minutes or until thickened. Pour over vegetables.

3. For crust, in a small bowl, combine the flour, baking powder and salt in a bowl. Cut in shortening until mixture resembles coarse crumbs. Stir in milk until a soft dough forms.

4. On a floured surface, roll dough into a 9-in. square. Place over filling; flute edges and cut slits in top. Brush with melted butter. Bake at 350° for 45 minutes or until golden brown.

Chuck Roast with Homemade Noodles

The whole family loves my mom's tender beef and hearty noodles. Simmered in beef broth, the noodles taste wonderfully old-fashioned. Mom has to make a huge batch since even the grandchildren gobble them up.

—**GLORIA GRANT** STERLING, IL

PREP: 30 MIN. • **BAKE:** 2½ HOURS
MAKES: 8 SERVINGS

- **1 boneless beef chuck roast (3 to 4 pounds)**
- **½ cup chopped onion**
- **2 tablespoons canola oil**
- **3 cups water, divided**
- **1 cup all-purpose flour**
- **½ teaspoon salt**
- **1 egg**
- **2 tablespoons milk**
- **1 can (14 ounces) beef broth**
- **Pepper to taste**

1. In a Dutch oven, brown roast and onion in oil. Add 1 cup of water. Cover and bake at 325° for 2½ to 3 hours or until the meat is tender.

2. Meanwhile, for noodles, combine flour and salt in a bowl; make a well in the center. Beat egg and milk; pour into well. Stir to form a stiff dough. Turn onto a well-floured surface; roll into a 15-in. x 12-in. rectangle. Cut into ⅛-in. strips. Cover and refrigerate until ready to cook.

3. Remove roast and keep warm; add broth and remaining water to pan. Bring to a boil; add noodles. Cook for 8-10 minutes or until tender. Drain; season with pepper. Serve noodles with the roast.

EDITOR'S NOTE *Uncooked noodles may be stored in the refrigerator for 2-3 days or frozen for up to 1 month.*

Round Steak with Potatoes

Have a delicious steak and potatoes dinner tonight! Baking the round steak for an extended amount of time guarantees tender results.

—TARYN KUEBELBECK PLYMOUTH, MN

PREP: 20 MIN. • **BAKE:** 2½ HOURS
MAKES: 6 SERVINGS

- **2 pounds beef top round steak**
- **1 teaspoon salt**
- **½ teaspoon pepper**
- **2 tablespoons canola oil**
- **1 can (10¾ ounces) condensed golden mushroom soup, undiluted**
- **1¼ cups water**
- **1 cup chopped celery**
- **1 cup chopped sweet red pepper**
- **½ cup chopped onion**
- **¼ teaspoon dried thyme**
- **12 small red potatoes**

1. Cut steak into six pieces; sprinkle with salt and pepper. In an ovenproof Dutch oven, brown meat in oil on both sides. Stir in the soup, water, celery, red pepper, onion and thyme. Cover and bake at 350° for 1 hour.

2. Add potatoes; cover and bake 1½ hours longer or until steak and vegetables are tender.

Round steak is cut from the rear leg, a well-exercised muscle. This **affordable cut** benefits from **long, slow cooking** in liquid to make it **tender**.

ROUND STEAK WITH POTATOES

Steak Potpie

On cool nights, nothing hits the spot like a steaming homemade potpie—especially one you can get on the table so quickly. The pinwheel crust on top has become my signature.

—KRISTIN SHAW CASTLETON, NY

PREP: 25 MIN. • **BAKE:** 20 MIN.
MAKES: 6 SERVINGS

- **2 tablespoons butter**
- **1¼ pounds beef top sirloin steak, cut into ½-inch cubes**
- **¼ teaspoon pepper**
- **1 package (16 ounces) frozen vegetables for stew**
- **2 tablespoons water**
- **½ teaspoon dried thyme**
- **1 jar (12 ounces) mushroom or beef gravy**
- **1 tube (8 ounces) refrigerated crescent rolls**

1. Preheat oven to 375°. In a 10-in. ovenproof skillet, heat butter over medium-high heat. Brown beef in batches; remove from pan. Sprinkle with pepper; keep warm.

2. In same skillet, combine vegetables, water and thyme; stir in gravy. Bring to a boil. Reduce heat; simmer, uncovered, until vegetables are thawed. Stir in beef; remove from heat.

3. Unroll crescent dough and separate into eight triangles. Starting from the wide end of each triangle, roll up a third of the length and place over beef mixture with pointed ends toward the center.

4. Bake, uncovered, 16-18 minutes or until golden brown.

STEAK POTPIE

Meatball Pizza

I always keep meatballs and pizza crusts in the freezer to make this pizza at the spur of the moment. Add a tossed salad and you have a delicious dinner.

—MARY HUMENIUK-SMITH PERRY HALL, MD

START TO FINISH: 25 MIN.
MAKES: 6-8 SLICES

- **1 prebaked 12-inch pizza crust**
- **1 can (8 ounces) pizza sauce**
- **1 teaspoon garlic powder**
- **1 teaspoon Italian seasoning**
- **¼ cup grated Parmesan cheese**
- **1 small onion, halved and sliced**
- **12 frozen fully cooked homestyle meatballs (½ ounce each), thawed and halved**
- **1 cup (4 ounces) shredded part-skim mozzarella cheese**
- **1 cup (4 ounces) shredded cheddar cheese**

1. Place the crust on an ungreased 12-in. pizza pan. Spread with pizza sauce; top with garlic powder, Italian seasoning, Parmesan cheese and onion. Arrange the meatball halves over top; sprinkle with cheeses.

2. Bake at 350° for 12-17 minutes or until heated through and cheese is melted.

For a **fun pizza variation,** skip the onion and spread a little leftover cooked **spaghetti** over the sauce.

Taco Lasagna

If you like foods with Southwestern flair, this recipe just might become a new favorite. I never have leftovers when I take it to potlucks.

—**TERRI KEENAN** TUSCALOOSA, AL

PREP: 20 MIN. • **BAKE:** 25 MIN.
MAKES: 9 SERVINGS

- **1 pound ground beef**
- **½ cup chopped green pepper**
- **½ cup chopped onion**
- **⅔ cup water**
- **1 envelope taco seasoning**
- **1 can (15 ounces) black beans, rinsed and drained**
- **1 can (14½ ounces) Mexican diced tomatoes, undrained**
- **6 flour tortillas (8 inches)**
- **1 can (16 ounces) refried beans**
- **3 cups (12 ounces) shredded Mexican cheese blend**

1. In a large skillet, cook the beef, green pepper and onion over medium heat until meat is no longer pink; drain. Add water and taco seasoning; bring to a boil. Reduce heat; simmer, uncovered, for 2 minutes. Stir in black beans and tomatoes. Simmer, uncovered, for 10 minutes.

2. Place two tortillas in a greased 13-in. x 9-in. baking dish. Spread with half of the refried beans and beef mixture; sprinkle with 1 cup cheese. Repeat layers. Top with remaining tortillas and cheese.

3. Cover and bake at 350° for 25-30 minutes or until heated through and cheese is melted.

BISCUIT BOWL CHILI

Biscuit Bowl Chili

Kids love to help make these biscuit bowls almost as much as they love eating them. For a different meal another time, bake the yummy little cups as directed and stuff them with taco fixings or sloppy joe filling.

—**CASSY RAY** PARKERSBURG, WV

PREP: 20 MIN. • **COOK:** 30 MIN.
MAKES: 8 SERVINGS

- **1 tube (16.3 ounces) large refrigerated flaky biscuits**
- **2 teaspoons cornmeal**
- **1 pound lean ground beef (90% lean)**
- **½ cup chopped onion**
- **1 can (16 ounces) kidney beans, rinsed and drained**
- **1 can (11½ ounces) V8 juice**
- **1 cup ketchup**
- **2 teaspoons chili powder**
- **½ teaspoon salt**
- **¼ to ½ teaspoon cayenne pepper**
- **¼ teaspoon crushed red pepper flakes**
- **¼ teaspoon pepper**
- **½ cup shredded cheddar cheese**

1. Preheat oven to 350°. Place two muffin tins upside down; spray bottoms and sides of eight alternating muffin cups. On a work surface, roll or press biscuits into 4-in. circles. Sprinkle both sides with cornmeal, pressing lightly to adhere. Place biscuits over greased muffin cups, shaping biscuits around cups.

2. Bake 11-13 minutes or until lightly browned. Carefully remove biscuit bowls from pans; cool on a wire rack.

3. Meanwhile, in a large skillet, cook beef and onion over medium heat 6-8 minutes or until beef is no longer pink; drain. Stir in beans, V8 juice, ketchup and seasonings. Bring to a boil. Reduce heat; simmer, covered, 10 minutes. Serve in biscuit bowls; top with cheese.

EAT SMART

Feta Stuffed Peppers

PREP: 35 MIN. • **BAKE:** 30 MIN.
MAKES: 3 SERVINGS

- **3 large green peppers**
- **½ pound lean ground beef (90% lean)**
- **1 small onion, chopped**
- **1 can (14½ ounces) diced tomatoes, undrained**
- **2 cups chopped fresh spinach**
- **¾ cup uncooked whole wheat orzo pasta**
- **2 tablespoons minced fresh oregano or 2 teaspoons dried oregano**
- **¼ teaspoon salt**
- **¼ teaspoon pepper**
- **6 tablespoons crumbled feta cheese**

1. Cut peppers in half lengthwise and remove seeds. In a Dutch oven, cook peppers in boiling water for 3-5 minutes. Drain and rinse in cold water; invert onto paper towels.
2. In a large skillet, cook beef and onion over medium heat until meat is no longer pink. Stir in the tomatoes, spinach, orzo, oregano, salt and pepper. Bring to a boil. Reduce heat; cover and simmer for 5-7 minutes or until orzo is tender.
3. Spoon into peppers. Place in an 11-in. x 7-in. baking dish coated with cooking spray. Cover and bake at 350° for 30-35 minutes or until peppers are tender.
4. Sprinkle with cheese; bake 5 minutes longer or until cheese is softened.

PER SERVING *369 cal., 10 g fat (4 g sat. fat), 55 mg chol., 567 mg sodium, 46 g carb., 13 g fiber, 26 g pro.* ***Diabetic Exchanges:*** *3 starch, 2 lean meat, ½ fat.*

"One of my favorite meals when I was younger was a recipe my mother made called Quick Chili Rice Casserole. I put a Greek spin on it and stuffed it in a pepper . It works great paired with a garden salad and fresh bread."
—**SACHA MORGAN** WOODSTOCK, GA

FETA STUFFED PEPPERS

Ultimate Pastrami Sandwiches

This peerless pastrami sandwich was adapted from a menu favorite at Primanti Bros. Restaurant in Pittsburgh. The marketing office graciously shared the basic ingredients—grilled cold cuts, cheese, fried potatoes and tomatoes—all stacked between slices of chewy Italian bread. From there, we created the spot-on copy, including our version of the secret coleslaw topping.
—TASTE OF HOME TEST KITCHEN

PREP: 25 MIN. + STANDING • **BAKE:** 5 MIN.
MAKES: 4 SERVINGS

- **½ cup sugar, divided**
- **½ cup cider vinegar, divided**
- **4 cups shredded cabbage**
- **3½ cups frozen waffle-cut fries**
- **¼ teaspoon salt**
- **¼ teaspoon celery seed**
- **¼ teaspoon pepper**
- **1 pound sliced deli pastrami**
- **4 slices provolone cheese**
- **8 slices Italian bread (¾ inch thick), toasted**
- **2 medium tomatoes, thinly sliced**

1. In a large bowl, combine ¼ cup of the sugar and vinegar; add cabbage and toss to coat. Cover and let stand for 30 minutes. Meanwhile, bake fries according to package directions.
2. Drain cabbage. In a small bowl, combine the salt, celery seed, pepper and remaining sugar and vinegar; pour over cabbage and toss to coat.
3. On an ungreased baking sheet, divide pastrami into four stacks; top each with cheese. Bake at 450° for 2-3 minutes or until cheese is melted. Place pastrami on four toast slices. Layer with fries, coleslaw, tomato slices and remaining toast. Serve sandwiches immediately.

ULTIMATE PASTRAMI SANDWICHES

We love these versatile meatballs over noodles with creamy Swedish-style gravy. But they're also great additions to soups, stews and spaghetti sauce.
—**STACY THOMAS** ANCHORAGE, AK

FREEZE IT

Flavorful Swedish Meatballs

PREP: 20 MIN. • **BAKE:** 20 MIN.
MAKES: 2 BATCHES (6 SERVINGS EACH)

- **2 eggs, lightly beaten**
- **¼ cup ketchup**
- **¾ cup dry bread crumbs**
- **2 tablespoons dried parsley flakes**
- **2 tablespoons Worcestershire sauce**
- **1 teaspoon onion powder**
- **1 teaspoon garlic powder**
- **1 teaspoon pepper**
- **½ teaspoon salt**
- **½ teaspoon chili powder**
- **2 pounds ground beef**
- **1 pound ground pork**

ADDITIONAL INGREDIENTS (FOR EACH BATCH)

- **1 envelope brown gravy mix**
- **½ cup sour cream**
- **Dash each nutmeg and pepper**
- **Hot cooked noodles**

1. In a large bowl, combine the first 10 ingredients. Crumble meat over mixture and mix well. Shape into 1-in. balls (about 6 dozen).
2. Place on greased racks in shallow baking pans. Bake at 400° for 20 minutes or until a thermometer reads 160°.
3. In a large skillet, prepare gravy mix according to package directions. Add half of the meatballs; cover and cook for 10 minutes or until heated through. Remove from the heat; stir in the sour cream, nutmeg and pepper. Serve with noodles.
FREEZE OPTION *Cool half of the meatballs; place in a freezer container. Freeze for up to 3 months. Thaw completely in refrigerator. Proceed as directed, increasing cooking time as needed to thoroughly heat meatballs.*

Sweet Potato Shepherd's Pie

When I was a child, shepherd's pie was one of my favorites. I made our family recipe healthier with sweet potato instead of white, and changed the veggies and spices to better complement the fluffy sweet potato topping.
—**TANYA MARCKETTI** GOLDEN, CO

PREP: 25 MIN. • **BAKE:** 25 MIN.
MAKES: 2 SERVINGS

- **1 large sweet potato**
- **½ pound lean ground beef (90% lean)**
- **¼ cup chopped onion**
- **1 can (8¾ ounces) whole kernel corn, drained**
- **½ cup tomato sauce**
- **Dash each ground cinnamon, allspice and nutmeg**
- **1 tablespoon butter**
- **1 tablespoon 2% milk**
- **⅛ teaspoon salt**
- **⅛ teaspoon pepper**

1. Scrub and pierce sweet potato; place on a microwave-safe plate. Microwave, uncovered, on high for 10-12 minutes or until tender, turning once.
2. Meanwhile, in a large skillet, cook beef and onion until meat is no longer pink; drain. Add the corn, tomato sauce and spices. Place in a 1-qt. baking dish coated with cooking spray; set aside.
3. When cool enough to handle, cut potato in half; scoop out the pulp and place in a small bowl. Mash with butter, milk, salt and pepper. Spread evenly over meat mixture.
4. Bake, uncovered, at 350° for 25-30 minutes or until heated through.
NOTE *This recipe was tested in a 1,100-watt microwave.*

SWEET POTATO SHEPHERD'S PIE

APPLE MEAT LOAF

Apple Meat Loaf

I put a little twist on the wonderful meat loaf my mom made when I was a kid. Apple gives it a bit of a sweet flavor and helps keep it moist.

—**DEBORAH WILLIAMS** PEORIA, AZ

PREP: 15 MIN. • **BAKE:** 40 MIN.
MAKES: 3 SERVINGS

- **1 small onion, finely chopped**
- **2 teaspoons butter**
- **¾ cup shredded peeled apple**
- **½ cup soft bread crumbs**
- **1 egg, beaten**
- **4 teaspoons ketchup**
- **1 teaspoon Dijon mustard**
- **½ teaspoon salt**
- **¼ teaspoon pepper**
- **Dash ground allspice**
- **¾ pound lean ground beef (90% lean)**

1. In a small skillet, saute onion in butter until tender. In a large bowl, combine the apple, bread crumbs, egg, ketchup, mustard, salt, pepper and allspice. Stir in onion. Crumble beef over mixture and mix well. Shape into a 6-in. x 5-in. loaf.

2. Place in an 8-in.-square baking dish coated with cooking spray. Bake, uncovered, at 350° for 40-45 minutes or until no pink remains and a thermometer reads 160°.

Perfect Pot Roast

I serve this flavorful fork-tender beef with its rich gravy at least once a month. Although I wouldn't say meats are my specialty, everyone who tries my pot roast asks for seconds.

—**MELODY SROUFE** WICHITA, KS

PREP: 20 MIN. • **BAKE:** 2½ HOURS
MAKES: 8-10 SERVINGS

- **1 teaspoon seasoned salt**
- **½ teaspoon onion powder**
- **¼ teaspoon pepper**
- **⅛ teaspoon garlic powder**
- **1 beef chuck pot roast (3 to 4 pounds)**
- **1 tablespoon olive oil**
- **¾ cup water**
- **1 large onion, chopped**
- **¼ cup chopped green pepper**
- **2 garlic cloves, minced**
- **2 bay leaves**
- **2 teaspoons dried parsley flakes**
- **¼ teaspoon dried thyme**
- **All-purpose flour**

1. Combine first four ingredients; rub onto roast. In a skillet, brown roast in oil. Place in a roasting pan. Add water, onion, green pepper, garlic and seasonings. Cover and bake at 325° for 2½ to 3 hours or until roast is tender.

2. Remove and keep warm. Discard bay leaf. Skim fat from pan juices. Measure juices and transfer to a saucepan.

3. For each cup of juices, combine 1 tablespoon flour with 2 tablespoons water; mix well. Stir flour mixture into pan. Bring to a boil; cook and stir for 2 minutes or until thickened. Serve gravy with roast.

CLASSIC BEEF WELLINGTONS

Classic Beef Wellingtons

Perfect for any holiday dinner, this impressive entree is also incredibly easy. I love that it bakes hands-free while I do the last-minute dinner preparations.

—**KERRY DINGWALL** PONTE VEDRA, FL

PREP: 20 MIN. + CHILLING • **BAKE:** 25 MIN.
MAKES: 4 SERVINGS

- **4 beef tenderloin steaks (6 ounces each)**
- **¾ teaspoon salt, divided**
- **½ teaspoon pepper, divided**
- **2 tablespoons olive oil, divided**
- **1¾ cups sliced fresh mushrooms**
- **1 medium onion, chopped**
- **1 package (17.3 ounces) frozen puff pastry, thawed**
- **1 egg, lightly beaten**

1. Sprinkle steaks with 1/2 teaspoon salt and 1/4 teaspoon pepper. In a large skillet, brown steaks in 1 tablespoon oil for 2-3 minutes on each side. Remove from skillet and refrigerate until chilled.

2. In the same skillet, saute mushrooms and onion in remaining oil until tender. Stir in remaining salt and pepper; cool to room temperature.

3. Preheat oven to 425°. On a lightly floured surface, roll each puff pastry sheet into a 14-in. x 9½-in. rectangle. Cut into two 7-in. squares (use scraps to make decorative cutouts if desired). Place a steak in the center of each square; top with mushroom mixture. Lightly brush pastry edges with water. Bring opposite corners of pastry over steak; pinch seams to seal tightly.

4. Place in a greased 15-in. x 10-in. x 1-in. baking pan. Cut four small slits in top of pastry. Arrange cutouts over top if desired. Brush with egg.

5. Bake 25-30 minutes or until pastry is golden brown and meat reaches desired doneness (for medium-rare, a thermometer should read 145°; medium, 160°; well-done, 170°).

EAT SMART

Berry Nice Brisket

Cranberry juice and cranberry sauce make this brisket tender and tasty. It's wonderful for a holiday buffet.

—**CAROL HUNIHAN** ALAMOSA, CO

PREP: 15 MIN.
BAKE: 3 HOURS + STANDING
MAKES: 10-12 SERVINGS

- **¼ cup all-purpose flour**
- **1 can (14½ ounces) beef broth**
- **1 can (14 ounces) whole-berry cranberry sauce**
- **1 cup cranberry juice**
- **3 garlic cloves, minced**
- **1 tablespoon minced fresh rosemary or 1 teaspoon dried rosemary, crushed**
- **1 large onion, thinly sliced**
- **1 fresh beef brisket (3 to 4 pounds)**
- **½ teaspoon salt**
- **¼ teaspoon pepper**

1. In a large bowl, combine flour and broth until smooth. Stir in the cranberry sauce, cranberry juice, garlic and rosemary. Pour into a large roasting pan. Top with onion slices.

2. Season the brisket with salt and pepper. Place fat side up in the pan. Cover and bake at 350° for 3 to 3½ hours or until meat is tender, basting occasionally.

3. Remove brisket to a serving platter and let stand for 15 minutes. Thinly slice meat across the grain; serve with onion and pan juices.

NOTE *This is a fresh beef brisket, not corned beef.*

PER SERVING *219 cal., 5 g fat (2 g sat. fat), 48 mg chol., 298 mg sodium, 18 g carb., 1 g fiber, 24 g pro.* ***Diabetic Exchanges:*** *3 lean meat, 1 starch.*

BERRY NICE BRISKET

Poultry

Discover **classic casseroles**, good-for-you baked **chicken dishes**, and **dinnertime dazzlers** like **roasted turkey** breast and an easy Chicken Cordon Bleu that's oven-ready in just 20 minutes. These recipes prove you don't have to compromise **good taste** for **ease of preparation**.

EAT SMART FREEZE IT

Savory Turkey Potpies

This is the ultimate in comfort food on a cold, rainy day. You can use chicken in place of turkey. I like to serve the potpies with a fresh green salad or cranberry sauce on the side.

—JUDY WILSON SUN CITY WEST, AZ

PREP: 25 MIN. • **BAKE:** 20 MIN.
MAKES: 8 SERVINGS

- **1 small onion, chopped**
- **¼ cup all-purpose flour**
- **3 cups chicken stock**
- **3 cups cubed cooked turkey breast**
- **1 package (16 ounces) frozen peas and carrots**
- **2 medium red potatoes, cooked and cubed**
- **3 tablespoons minced fresh parsley**
- **1 tablespoon minced fresh thyme**
- **¼ teaspoon pepper**
- **1 sheet refrigerated pie pastry**
- **Additional fresh parsley or thyme leaves, optional**
- **1 egg**
- **1 teaspoon water**
- **½ teaspoon kosher salt**

1. In a Dutch oven coated with cooking spray, saute onion until tender. In a small bowl, whisk flour and stock until smooth; gradually stir into Dutch oven. Bring to a boil; cook and stir 2 minutes or until thickened. Remove from heat. Add turkey, peas and carrots, potatoes, parsley, thyme and pepper; stir gently.

2. Preheat oven to 425°. Divide turkey mixture among eight 10-oz. ramekins. On a lightly floured surface, unroll pastry. Cut out eight 3-in. circles. Gently press parsley into pastries if desired. Place over turkey mixture. Beat egg and water; brush over tops. Sprinkle with salt.

3. Place ramekins on a baking sheet. Bake 20-25 minutes or until crusts are golden brown.

FREEZE OPTION *Securely wrap and freeze baked and cooled potpies in plastic wrap and foil. To use, partially thaw in refrigerator overnight. Remove from refrigerator 30 minutes before baking. Preheat oven to 425°. Unwrap potpies; bake in oven until heated through and a thermometer inserted in center reads 165°. Cover top with foil to prevent overbrowning if necessary.*

PER SERVING *279 cal., 9 g fat (3 g sat. fat), 77 mg chol., 495 mg sodium, 28 g carb., 3 g fiber, 22 g pro.* ***Diabetic Exchanges:*** *2 starch, 2 lean meat, ½ fat.*

Chicken Alfredo Stromboli

I combined my favorite fettuccine Alfredo recipe with the flavors of chicken Alfredo pizza to come up with this satisfying open-faced sandwich.

—TRACY HAVEN HENRYVILLE, IN

START TO FINISH: 25 MIN.
MAKES: 2 SERVINGS

- **1 mini French bread baguette (5 ounces), halved lengthwise**
- **6 ounces boneless skinless chicken breast, cubed**
- **1 teaspoon olive oil**
- **4 teaspoons butter, softened, divided**
- **⅓ cup canned mushroom stems and pieces, drained**
- **¼ teaspoon salt**
- **¼ teaspoon garlic powder**
- **¼ teaspoon pepper**
- **¼ cup sour cream**
- **¼ cup grated Parmesan cheese**
- **½ cup shredded part-skim mozzarella cheese**

1. Place bread, cut side up, on an ungreased baking sheet. Broil 4-6 in. from the heat for 2-3 minutes or until lightly toasted; set aside.

2. In a small skillet, saute chicken in oil and 1 teaspoon butter until no longer pink. Add the mushrooms, salt, garlic powder and pepper; heat through.

3. In a small bowl, combine the sour cream, Parmesan cheese and remaining butter; spread over bread halves. Top with chicken mixture and sprinkle with mozzarella cheese. Broil for 1-2 minutes or until cheese is melted.

CHICKEN ALFREDO STROMBOLI

Baked Chicken and Acorn Squash

With its colorful acorn squash and sweet peaches, this eye-pleasing main dish is ideal for fall. The fragrance of rosemary-seasoned chicken baking is heavenly, and my family says it's every bit as delicious as it smells.

—**CONNIE SVOBODA** ELKO, MN

PREP: 20 MIN. • **BAKE:** 1 HOUR
MAKES: 4 SERVINGS

- **2 small acorn squash (1¼ pounds each)**
- **2 to 4 garlic cloves, minced**
- **2 tablespoons canola oil, divided**
- **4 bone-in chicken thighs (about 1½ pounds)**
- **4 chicken drumsticks**
- **¼ cup packed brown sugar**
- **1 tablespoon minced fresh rosemary or 1 teaspoon dried rosemary, crushed**
- **1 teaspoon salt**
- **1 can (15¼ ounces) sliced peaches, undrained**

1. Cut squash in half lengthwise; discard seeds. Cut each half widthwise into ½-in. slices; discard ends. Place slices in an ungreased 13-in. x 9-in. baking dish. Sprinkle with garlic and drizzle with 1 tablespoon oil.

2. In a large skillet, brown chicken in remaining oil. Arrange chicken over squash. Combine the brown sugar, rosemary and salt; sprinkle over chicken. Bake, uncovered, at 350° for 45 minutes, basting occasionally with pan juices.

3. Pour peaches over the chicken and squash. Bake, uncovered, 15 minutes longer or until a thermometer inserted in chicken reads 180°.

BAKED CHICKEN AND ACORN SQUASH

Easy Chicken Cordon Bleu

PREP: 20 MIN. • **BAKE:** 30 MIN.
MAKES: 8 SERVINGS

- **8 boneless skinless chicken breast halves (4 ounces each)**
- **¼ teaspoon salt**
- **⅛ teaspoon pepper**
- **3 tablespoons butter**
- **1 package (17.3 ounces) frozen puff pastry, thawed**
- **8 slices Swiss cheese**
- **8 slices fully cooked ham**
- **1 egg**
- **1 tablespoon water**

1. Sprinkle chicken with salt and pepper. In a large skillet, brown chicken in butter for 1-2 minutes on each side. Remove to paper towels to drain.

2. On a lightly floured surface, roll each pastry sheet into a 12-in. square. Cut into four 6-in. squares. Place a chicken breast in the center of each square; top with cheese and ham.

3. Whisk egg and water; lightly brush over pastry edges. Bring two sides of pastry over chicken, overlapping one over the other; press seams to seal. Pinch together ends and fold under.

4. Transfer to a greased 15-in. x 10-in. x 1-in. baking pan; brush tops of bundles with egg mixture. Bake at 400° for 30-35 minutes or until a thermometer reads 165°.

In **traditional** Chicken Cordon Bleu, the chicken is **cut into a pocket** and then **stuffed** with ham and Swiss, **breaded** and **fried**. The layered and baked version is much simpler.

"I make my easy version of Chicken Cordon Bleu by wrapping the chicken, ham and Swiss in puff pastry and then baking it. What a yummy finish, and it's less messy than breading and browning the chicken on the stovetop."
—**SHARON LAABS** HARTFORD, WI

EASY CHICKEN CORDON BLEU

"Our family of five enjoys trying different ethnic cuisines. This Italian specialty has a little Mexican zip. Be careful not to overcook the manicotti. If the filled shells happen to break, just place them in the pan break-side down."
—**KEELY JANKUNAS** CORVALLIS, MT

Mexican Chicken Manicotti

PREP: 25 MIN. • **BAKE:** 40 MIN.
MAKES: 7 SERVINGS

- **1 package (8 ounces) manicotti shells**
- **2 cups cubed cooked chicken**
- **2 cups (8 ounces) shredded Monterey Jack cheese, divided**
- **1½ cups (6 ounces) shredded cheddar cheese**
- **1 cup (8 ounces) sour cream**
- **1 small onion, diced, divided**
- **1 can (4 ounces) chopped green chilies, divided**
- **1 can (10¾ ounces) condensed cream of chicken soup, undiluted**
- **1 cup salsa**
- **⅔ cup milk**

1. Cook manicotti according to package directions. Meanwhile, in a large bowl, combine chicken, 1½ cups Monterey Jack cheese, cheddar cheese, sour cream, half of the onion and 6 tablespoons chilies.
2. In another bowl, combine the soup, salsa, milk and remaining onion and chilies. Spread ½ cup in a greased 13-in. x 9-in. baking dish.
3. Drain manicotti and rinse in cold water; stuff each with about ¼ cupful of chicken mixture. Arrange over sauce in baking dish. Pour remaining sauce over shells.
4. Cover casserole and bake at 350° for 30 minutes. Uncover; sprinkle with remaining Monterey Jack cheese. Bake 10 minutes longer or until cheese is melted.

Chicken Burgers with Sesame Slaw

This chicken burger gets an Asian flavor twist from ginger, garlic and sesame. It's topped off with a fabulous coleslaw. If you like, serve the coleslaw as a side with grilled chicken breasts, fish fillets or chops.
—**DEBORAH BIGGS** OMAHA, NE

START TO FINISH: 25 MIN.
MAKES: 2 SERVINGS

- **½ pound ground chicken**
- **1 teaspoon minced fresh gingerroot**
- **¾ teaspoon minced garlic**
- **½ teaspoon kosher salt**
- **1¼ cups coleslaw mix**
- **2 tablespoons thinly sliced green onion**
- **2 tablespoons Asian toasted sesame salad dressing**
- **1 tablespoon mayonnaise**
- **1¼ teaspoons black sesame seeds or sesame seeds**
- **2 sesame seed hamburger buns, split**

1. Crumble chicken into a small bowl. Sprinkle with ginger, garlic and salt; mix well. Shape into two patties.
2. Broil 4-6 in. from the heat for 4-6 minutes on each side or until a thermometer reads 165° and juices run clear. In a large bowl, combine the coleslaw mix, onion, salad dressing, mayonnaise and sesame seeds. Serve burgers on buns with coleslaw.

CHICKEN BURGERS WITH SESAME SLAW

Stacked Enchilada

Here's my easy stacked version of a classic Tex-Mex dish. Loaded with chicken, black beans and green pepper, this tortilla pie is both delicious and simple to prepare.
—**REBECCA PEPSIN** LONGMONT, CO

PREP: 20 MIN. • **BAKE:** 20 MIN.
MAKES: 4 SERVINGS

- **⅔ cup chopped green pepper**
- **2 teaspoons canola oil**
- **1 garlic clove, minced**
- **1 cup shredded cooked chicken**
- **1 cup canned black beans, rinsed and drained**
- **⅓ cup thinly sliced green onions**
- **½ cup enchilada sauce**
- **½ cup picante sauce**
- **4 corn tortillas (6 inches)**
- **1 cup shredded cheddar cheese**
- **Sour cream and shredded lettuce, optional**

1. In a large skillet, saute pepper in oil for 3 minutes. Add garlic and cook 2 minutes longer or until pepper is crisp-tender. Stir in the chicken, beans and onions; heat through. Transfer to a bowl and keep warm.
2. In the same skillet, combine enchilada and picante sauces. Coat both sides of one tortilla with sauce mixture; place in a greased 9-in. pie plate. Top with a third of the chicken mixture and 1/4 cup cheese. Repeat layers twice. Top with remaining tortilla, sauce and cheese.
3. Cover and bake at 350° for 18-22 minutes or until heated through. Remove to a serving plate and cut into wedges. Serve with sour cream and lettuce if desired.

EAT SMART

Chicken 'n' Summer Squash Packets

These fun meal-in-one packets are an ideal way to use up your garden bounty. Tender chicken and seasoned veggies are tucked inside each foil pack.
—**SHARON SALVADOR** LAKEPORT, CA

PREP: 20 MIN. • **BAKE:** 25 MIN.
MAKES: 4 SERVINGS

- **4 boneless skinless chicken breast halves (4 ounces each)**
- **¼ teaspoon salt, divided**
- **¼ teaspoon pepper, divided**
- **1 medium onion, sliced**
- **2 tablespoons Dijon mustard**
- **1 small zucchini, sliced**
- **1 small yellow summer squash, sliced**
- **2 cups sliced fresh mushrooms**
- **¾ teaspoon dried basil**
- **⅛ teaspoon garlic powder**
- **⅛ teaspoon paprika**
- **1 tablespoon butter**
- **1 tablespoon grated Parmesan cheese**

1. Flatten chicken to 1/4-in. thickness; sprinkle with 1/8 teaspoon each salt and pepper. Cut eight 15-in. x 12-in. rectangles of heavy-duty foil; place one rectangle on top of another to make four. Divide onion slices among the four rectangles; top with chicken, mustard, zucchini, yellow squash and mushrooms.
2. Combine the basil, garlic powder, paprika and remaining salt and pepper; sprinkle over vegetables. Dot with butter. Fold foil around vegetable mixture and seal tightly. Place packets on a baking sheet.
3. Bake at 425° for 25-30 minutes or until a thermometer reads 165°. Open foil carefully to allow steam to escape. Sprinkle with Parmesan cheese.
PER SERVING *206 cal., 7 g fat (3 g sat. fat), 71 mg chol., 449 mg sodium, 10 g carb., 3 g fiber, 27 g pro.* ***Diabetic Exchanges:*** *3 lean meat, 2 vegetable, 1 fat.*

BRUSCHETTA CHICKEN

EAT SMART

Bruschetta Chicken

We enjoy serving this tasty chicken to company as well as family. It's a flavorful way to use up summer tomatoes and basil.

—CAROLIN CATTOI-DEMKIW
LETHBRIDGE, AB

PREP: 10 MIN. • **BAKE:** 30 MIN.
MAKES: 4 SERVINGS

- **½ cup all-purpose flour**
- **½ cup egg substitute**
- **4 boneless skinless chicken breast halves (4 ounces each)**
- **¼ cup grated Parmesan cheese**
- **¼ cup dry bread crumbs**
- **1 tablespoon butter, melted**
- **2 large tomatoes, seeded and chopped**
- **3 tablespoons minced fresh basil**
- **1 tablespoon olive oil**
- **2 garlic cloves, minced**
- **½ teaspoon salt**
- **¼ teaspoon pepper**

1. Preheat oven to 375°. Place flour and egg substitute in separate shallow bowls. Dip chicken in flour, then in egg substitute; place in a greased 13-in. x 9-in. baking dish. In a small bowl, mix cheese, bread crumbs and butter; sprinkle over chicken.

2. Loosely cover baking dish with foil. Bake 20 minutes. Uncover; bake 5-10 minutes longer or until a thermometer reads 165°.

3. Meanwhile, in a small bowl, toss tomatoes with the remaining ingredients. Spoon over chicken; bake 3-5 minutes or until tomato mixture is heated through.

If you prefer, **use 2 eggs** instead of the egg substitute. Each serving will have **20 additional calories** and 105 more milligrams of **cholesterol**.

PER SERVING *316 cal., 11 g fat (4 g sat. fat), 75 mg chol., 563 mg sodium, 22 g carb., 2 g fiber, 31 g pro.* ***Diabetic Exchanges:*** *3 lean meat, 1½ fat, 1 starch, 1 vegetable.*

Honey Mustard Chicken

Try different styles of mustard, such as dijon, sweet hot mustard or even Chinese — each will give your dish a different taste sensation. For spicier chicken, you can substitute cayenne pepper for some or all of the chili powder.

—RICHARD GALLOP PUEBLO, CO

PREP: 15 MIN. • **BAKE:** 45 MIN.
MAKES: 6 SERVINGS

- **½ cup honey**
- **¼ cup prepared mustard**
- **1 envelope ranch salad dressing mix**
- **1 tablespoon dried parsley flakes**
- **1½ teaspoons Italian seasoning**
- **½ teaspoon dried basil**
- **½ teaspoon chili powder**
- **¼ teaspoon garlic powder**
- **¼ teaspoon pepper**
- **6 chicken drumsticks**
- **6 bone-in chicken thighs**

1. For sauce, in a small bowl, combine the first nine ingredients. Set aside ½ cup for serving. Place chicken in a greased 15-in. x 10-in. x 1-in. baking pan; drizzle with remaining sauce.

2. Bake, uncovered, at 350° for 45-50 minutes or until a thermometer reads 180°, basting occasionally with pan juices. Warm reserved sauce; serve with chicken.

HONEY MUSTARD CHICKEN

EAT SMART FREEZE IT

Chicken Florentine Meatballs

PREP: 40 MIN. • **COOK:** 20 MIN.
MAKES: 6 SERVINGS

- **2 eggs, lightly beaten**
- **1 package (10 ounces) frozen chopped spinach, thawed and squeezed dry**
- **½ cup dry bread crumbs**
- **¼ cup grated Parmesan cheese**
- **1 tablespoon dried minced onion**
- **1 garlic clove, minced**
- **¼ teaspoon salt**
- **⅛ teaspoon pepper**
- **1 pound ground chicken**
- **1 medium spaghetti squash**

SAUCE

- **½ pound sliced fresh mushrooms**
- **2 teaspoons olive oil**
- **1 can (14½ ounces) diced tomatoes, undrained**
- **1 can (8 ounces) tomato sauce**
- **2 tablespoons minced fresh parsley**
- **1 garlic clove, minced**
- **1 teaspoon dried oregano**
- **1 teaspoon dried basil**

1. In a large bowl, combine the first eight ingredients. Crumble chicken over mixture and mix well. Shape into 1½-in. balls.

2. Place meatballs on a rack in a shallow baking pan. Bake, uncovered, at 400° for 20-25 minutes or until no longer pink. Meanwhile, cut squash in half lengthwise; discard seeds. Place squash cut side down on a microwave-safe plate. Microwave, uncovered, on high for 15-18 minutes or until tender.

3. For sauce, in a large nonstick skillet, saute mushrooms in oil until tender. Stir in the remaining ingredients. Bring to a boil. Reduce heat; simmer, uncovered, for 8-10 minutes or until slightly thickened. Add meatballs and heat through.

4. When squash is cool enough to handle, use a fork to separate strands. Serve with meatballs and sauce.

FREEZE OPTION *Place individual portions of cooled meatball mixture in freezer containers. To use, partially thaw in refrigerator overnight. Microwave, covered, on high in a microwave-safe dish until heated through, gently stirring and adding a little water if necessary.*

NOTE *This recipe was tested in a 1,100-watt microwave.*

PER SERVING *303 cal., 12 g fat (3 g sat. fat), 123 mg chol., 617 mg sodium, 31 g carb., 7 g fiber, 22 g pro.* ***Diabetic Exchanges:*** *3 lean meat, 2 starch, ½ fat.*

CHICKEN FLORENTINE MEATBALLS

"Served over squash with a chunky mushroom-tomato sauce, these tender meatballs are tops when it comes to great flavor."
—**DIANE NEMITZ** LUDINGTON, MI

Hot Chicken Salad

When I got married, I was happy to receive this simple yet delicious recipe from my mom. Her sister had given it to her.
—**MICHELLE WISE** SPRING MILLS, PA

PREP: 15 MIN. • **BAKE:** 30 MIN.
MAKES: 6 SERVINGS

- **2½ cups diced cooked chicken**
- **2 cups cooked rice**
- **1 cup diced celery**
- **1 cup sliced fresh mushrooms**
- **1 can (8 ounces) sliced water chestnuts, drained**
- **1 tablespoon finely chopped onion**
- **1 teaspoon lemon juice**
- **½ teaspoon dried rosemary, crushed**
- **¼ teaspoon pepper**
- **¾ cup mayonnaise**
- **1 can (10¾ ounces) condensed cream of chicken soup, undiluted**

TOPPING

- **3 tablespoons butter**
- **½ cup cornflake crumbs**
- **½ cup slivered almonds**

1. In a large bowl, combine the first nine ingredients. In a small bowl, combine the mayonnaise and soup. Pour over chicken mixture; stir gently to coat. Spoon into a greased 2-qt. baking dish.

2. In a small skillet, melt butter. Add cornflakes and almonds; cook and stir until lightly browned. Sprinkle over the top. Bake, uncovered, at 350° for 30-35 minutes or until casserole is heated through.

EAT SMART

Pizza Pasta

You can toss in red pepper flakes, olives, artichokes or any of your favorite pizza toppings. Kids love this casserole, and best of all, it only takes 10 minutes to prep for the oven.

—**KERRIE DEVAY** NEW ORLEANS, LA

PREP: 10 MIN. • **BAKE:** 65 MIN.
MAKES: 6 SERVINGS

- **4 cups uncooked multigrain bow tie pasta**
- **2 cans (14½ ounces each) fire-roasted diced tomatoes, undrained**
- **¾ cup water**
- **12 slices turkey pepperoni, quartered**
- **1 tablespoon prepared pesto**
- **¼ teaspoon pepper**
- **¾ cup shredded Italian cheese blend**

1. In a large bowl, combine the pasta, tomatoes, water, pepperoni, pesto and pepper. Transfer to an 11-in. x 7-in. x 2-in. baking dish coated with cooking spray.

2. Cover and bake at 350° for 45 minutes. Stir; cover and bake 15 minutes longer or until pasta is tender. Top with cheese. Bake, uncovered, for 4-6 minutes or until cheese is melted.

PER SERVING *318 cal., 7 g fat (2 g sat. fat), 15 mg chol., 584 mg sodium, 47 g carb., 5 g fiber, 16 g pro.* ***Diabetic Exchanges:*** *2½ starch, 1 medium-fat meat, 1 vegetable.*

Chicken with Country Gravy

My mother, grandson and I worked together to create our signature oven-fried chicken. We tweaked the ingredients and seasonings each time, until we made this cherished recipe.

—**LINDA FOREMAN** LOCUST GROVE, OK

PREP: 15 MIN. • **BAKE:** 50 MIN.
MAKES: 2 SERVINGS

- **2 tablespoons butter**
- **2 tablespoons canola oil**
- **¼ cup all-purpose flour**
- **¼ teaspoon paprika**
- **Dash each seasoned salt, garlic powder, salt and pepper**
- **2 chicken leg quarters**

GRAVY

- **1 tablespoon all-purpose flour**
- **⅔ cup milk**
- **¼ teaspoon salt**
- **¼ tablespoon pepper**

1. Place butter and oil in a large ovenproof skillet. Place in a 425° oven for 5 minutes. Meanwhile, in a shallow bowl, combine flour and seasonings; add chicken, one piece at a time, and turn to coat.

2. Carefully place chicken, skin side down, in hot skillet. Bake, uncovered, for 25-30 minutes on each side or until a thermometer reads 180°. Remove and keep warm.

3. Transfer 1 tablespoon of drippings from the skillet to a small saucepan; stir in flour until smooth. Gradually stir in the milk, salt and pepper. Bring to a boil; cook and stir for 2 minutes or until thickened. Serve with chicken.

Herbed Turkey Breast

Like most, I always serve turkey for our family's Thanksgiving meal. But instead of roasting a whole bird, I opt for a turkey breast since most of us prefer white meat. The herb butter basting sauce keeps it so moist, and it's easy to carve.

—RUBY WILLIAMS BOGALUSA, LA

PREP: 10 MIN.
BAKE: 1½ HOURS + STANDING
MAKES: 10-12 SERVINGS

- **½ cup butter, cubed**
- **¼ cup lemon juice**
- **2 tablespoons reduced-sodium soy sauce**
- **2 tablespoons finely chopped green onions**
- **1 tablespoon rubbed sage**
- **1 teaspoon dried thyme**
- **1 teaspoon dried marjoram**
- **¼ teaspoon pepper**
- **1 bone-in turkey breast (5½ to 6 pounds)**

1. In a small saucepan, combine the first eight ingredients; bring to a boil. Remove from the heat. Place turkey in a shallow roasting pan; drizzle with butter mixture.

2. Bake, uncovered, at 325° for 1½ to 2 hours or until a thermometer reads 170°, basting every 30 minutes. Let stand for 10 minutes before carving.

Chorizo-Stuffed Turkey Breast with Mexican Grits

This recipe features a wonderful combination of well-seasoned ingredients. Unique and impressive, it's just perfect for company.

—VERONICA GANTLEY NORFOLK, VA

PREP: 30 MIN.
BAKE: 1¼ HOURS + STANDING
MAKES: 6 SERVINGS

- **1 boneless skinless turkey breast half (2 pounds)**
- **½ pound uncooked chorizo, crumbled**
- **2 tablespoons olive oil**
- **1 teaspoon salt, divided**
- **1 teaspoon pepper, divided**
- **2 cups water**
- **1 cup milk**
- **1 cup quick-cooking grits**
- **1 can (4 ounces) chopped green chilies**
- **½ cup shredded Mexican cheese blend**
- **Minced fresh parsley, optional**

1. Cover turkey with plastic wrap; flatten to ½-in. thickness. Remove plastic. Spread chorizo over turkey to within 1 in. of edges. Roll up jelly-roll style, starting with a short side; tie with kitchen string.

2. Rub with oil. Sprinkle with ½ teaspoon salt and ½ teaspoon pepper. In a large ovenproof skillet, brown turkey on all sides. Bake at 350° for 1¼ to 1½ hours or until a thermometer reads 170°. Cover and let stand for 10 minutes before slicing.

3. In a large saucepan, bring the water, milk and remaining salt to a boil. Slowly stir in grits. Reduce heat; cook and stir for 5-7 minutes or until thickened. Stir in the chilies, cheese and remaining pepper. Serve grits with turkey. Sprinkle with parsley if desired.

CHORIZO-STUFFED TURKEY BREAST WITH MEXICAN GRITS

HONEY-GLAZED HENS WITH FRUIT STUFFING

Honey-Glazed Hens with Fruit Stuffing

PREP: 30 MIN. • **BAKE:** 1 HOUR + STANDING
MAKES: 4 SERVINGS

- **½ cup butter, cubed**
- **¼ cup chopped onion**
- **¼ cup chopped celery**
- **4 cups cubed day-old bread**
- **½ cup dried fruit bits**
- **½ cup water**
- **⅛ teaspoon ground allspice**

CORNISH HENS

- **4 Cornish game hens (20 to 24 ounces each)**
- **¼ teaspoon salt**
- **⅛ teaspoon pepper**
- **2 tablespoons butter, melted**
- **1 tablespoon honey**

1. In a large skillet over medium heat, melt butter. Add onion and celery; cook and stir until tender. Stir in the bread, fruit bits, water and allspice; cover and cook for 2-3 minutes or until heated through.

2. Loosely stuff hens with stuffing. Tuck wings under hens; tie drumsticks together. Sprinkle with salt and pepper. Place breast side up on a rack in a shallow roasting pan. Combine butter and honey; drizzle over hens.

3. Bake, uncovered, at 350° for 1 to 1½ hours or until a thermometer reads 180° for hens and 165° for stuffing, basting occasionally with pan drippings. Cover loosely with foil if hens brown too quickly. Cover and let stand for 10 minutes before serving.

EAT SMART

Sausage Penne Bake

No one will guess a dish this cheesy and satisfying could be healthy, but this one's chock-full of eggplant, whole wheat pasta, tomatoes and fabulous flavor.
—**BARBARA KEMPEN** CAMBRIDGE, MN

PREP: 35 MIN. • **BAKE:** 20 MIN.
MAKES: 8 SERVINGS

- **2 cups uncooked whole wheat penne pasta**
- **¾ pound Italian turkey sausage links, casings removed**
- **1 small eggplant, peeled and cut into ½-inch cubes**
- **1 medium onion, chopped**
- **½ cup dry red wine or chicken broth**
- **3 garlic cloves, minced**
- **1 can (28 ounces) crushed tomatoes**
- **2 cups (8 ounces) shredded part-skim mozzarella cheese, divided**
- **3 tablespoons chopped ripe olives**
- **2 teaspoons dried basil**
- **¼ teaspoon pepper**
- **½ cup grated Parmesan cheese**

1. Cook pasta according to package directions. Meanwhile, in a large skillet, cook the sausage, eggplant and onion over medium heat until meat is no longer pink; drain.

2. Add wine and garlic, stirring to loosen browned bits from pan. Stir in tomatoes. Bring to a boil. Reduce heat; simmer, uncovered, for 10 minutes or until slightly thickened. Drain pasta. Add the pasta, 1½ cups mozzarella cheese, olives, basil and pepper to skillet.

3. Transfer to a 3-qt. baking dish coated with cooking spray. Sprinkle with Parmesan cheese and remaining mozzarella cheese. Bake, uncovered, at 350° for 20-25 minutes or until heated through.

PER SERVING *325 cal., 11 g fat (5 g sat. fat), 46 mg chol., 623 mg sodium, 35 g carb., 7 g fiber, 23 g pro.* ***Diabetic Exchanges:*** *3 lean meat, 1½ starch, 1 vegetable, 1 fat.*

PINEAPPLE CHICKEN FOR A CROWD

Pineapple Chicken for a Crowd

I came up with this recipe years ago by combining a couple of our family's favorite dishes. Easy, economical and versatile, it's great for potlucks. I can make the sauce ahead and use all wings or leg quarters when they're on sale. This is a welcome entree at senior citizen fellowship dinners.

—**PHYLLIS MINTER** WAKEFIELD, KS

PREP: 30 MIN. • **BAKE:** 1 HOUR
MAKES: 12 SERVINGS

- **4 cups unsweetened pineapple juice**
- **2½ cups sugar**
- **2 cups white vinegar**
- **1½ cups water**
- **1 cup packed brown sugar**
- **⅔ cup cornstarch**
- **½ cup ketchup**
- **6 tablespoons reduced-sodium soy sauce**
- **2 teaspoon chicken bouillon granules**
- **¾ teaspoon ground ginger**
- **2 broiler/fryer chickens (3 to 3½ pounds each), cut up**
- **3 tablespoons canola oil**
- **1 can (8 ounces) pineapple chunks, drained**
- **1 medium green pepper, julienned**

1. Preheat oven to 350°. In a large saucepan, combine first 10 ingredients; stir until smooth. Bring to a boil; cook and stir 2 minutes or until thickened. Set aside. In a large skillet over medium-high heat, brown chicken in oil on all sides.

2. Place the chicken in two greased 13x9-in. baking dishes. Pour sauce over chicken. Bake, uncovered, 45 minutes. Add pineapple and green pepper; bake 15 minutes longer or until chicken juices run clear.

Serve the chicken with **hot cooked rice** for a classic accompaniment. If you like **pineapple**, substitute a larger can.

EAT SMART

Italian Mushroom Meat Loaf

Healthful oats and flaxseed amp up the nutrition in this tasty Italian meat loaf.

—**KYLIE WERNING** CANDLER, NC

PREP: 30 MIN. • **BAKE:** 1 HOUR
MAKES: 8 SERVINGS

- **1 egg, lightly beaten**
- **¼ pound fresh mushrooms, chopped**
- **½ cup old-fashioned oats**
- **½ cup chopped red onion**
- **¼ cup ground flaxseed**
- **½ teaspoon pepper**
- **1 package (19½ ounces) Italian turkey sausage links, casings removed, crumbled**
- **1 pound lean ground beef (90% lean)**
- **1 cup marinara or spaghetti sauce**

1. In a large bowl, combine the egg, mushrooms, oats, onion, flax and pepper. Crumble turkey and beef over mixture and mix well.

2. Shape into a 10-in. x 4-in. loaf. Place in a 13-in. x 9-in. baking dish coated with cooking spray. Bake, uncovered, at 350° for 50 minutes; drain. Top with marinara sauce. Bake 10-15 minutes longer or until no pink remains and a thermometer reads 165°.

PER SERVING *261 cal., 14 g fat (3 g sat. fat), 103 mg chol., 509 mg sodium, 10 g carb., 2 g fiber, 25 g pro.* ***Diabetic Exchanges:*** *3 lean meat, ½ starch.*

CHICKEN CLUB PIZZA

Chicken Club Pizza

Pizza topped with lettuce, tomatoes and cool ranch dressing? You're in for a treat! Fresh veggies give the cheesy crust a welcoming crunch.

—**DEBBIE REID** CLEARWATER, FL

START TO FINISH: 25 MIN.
MAKES: 8 SLICES

- **1 prebaked 12-inch pizza crust**
- **4 ounces cream cheese, softened**
- **1 shallot, minced**
- **2 cups shredded rotisserie chicken**
- **1½ cups (6 ounces) shredded Monterey Jack cheese**
- **1 cup (4 ounces) shredded sharp cheddar cheese**
- **8 slices ready-to-serve fully cooked bacon, cut into 1-inch pieces**
- **¼ cup sour cream**
- **3 tablespoons 2% milk**
- **2 teaspoons ranch salad dressing mix**
- **1 cup shredded lettuce**
- **1 plum tomato, seeded and chopped**

1. Place crust on an ungreased pizza pan. Combine cream cheese and shallot; spread over crust. Top with chicken, cheeses and bacon.

2. Bake at 425° for 12-15 minutes or until edges are lightly browned and cheese is melted.

3. Meanwhile, in a small bowl, combine the sour cream, milk and dressing mix. Sprinkle lettuce and tomato over pizza; drizzle with dressing.

GREEN BEAN CHICKEN CASSEROLE

FREEZE IT

Green Bean Chicken Casserole

My husband, who claims to be strictly a meat-and-potatoes man, asked for seconds the first time I threw together this comforting all-in-one meal. My daughter and several guests raved about it, too.

—**DELISSA MINGEE** WARR ACRES, OK

PREP: 15 MIN. • **BAKE:** 25 MIN.
MAKES: 2 CASSEROLES (4-6 SERVINGS EACH)

- **1 package (6 ounces) long grain and wild rice mix**
- **4 cups cubed cooked chicken**
- **1¾ cups frozen French-style green beans**
- **1 can (10¾ ounces) condensed cream of mushroom soup, undiluted**
- **1 can (10¾ ounces) condensed cream of broccoli soup, undiluted**
- **1 can (4 ounces) mushroom stems and pieces, drained**
- **⅔ cup chopped onion**
- **⅔ cup chopped green pepper**
- **1 envelope onion soup mix**
- **¾ cup shredded Colby cheese**

ADDITIONAL INGREDIENT (FOR EACH CASSEROLE)

- **⅔ cup French-fried onions**

1. Prepare wild rice according to package directions. Stir in the chicken, beans, soups, mushrooms, onion, green pepper and soup mix. Spoon into two greased 1½-qt. baking dishes. Sprinkle with cheese.

2. Cover and bake at 350° for 25-30 minutes or until heated through. Uncover and sprinkle with French-fried onions; bake 5 minutes longer or until onions are golden.

FREEZE OPTION *Cover and freeze one casserole for up to 3 months. Completely thaw in the refrigerator. Remove from the refrigerator 30 minutes before baking. Cover and bake at 350° for 60-65 minutes or until heated through. Uncover and sprinkle with French-fried onions; bake 5 minutes longer.*

EAT SMART

French Onion Turkey Shepherd's Pie

PREP: 40 MIN. • **BAKE:** 30 MIN.
MAKES: 4 SERVINGS

- **1 pound potatoes, peeled and cubed**
- **2 large onions, peeled, halved and thinly sliced**
- **½ teaspoon salt, divided**
- **1 tablespoon canola oil**
- **2¼ cups reduced-sodium beef broth, divided**
- **¼ teaspoon pepper**
- **1 pound extra-lean ground turkey**
- **2 tablespoons all-purpose flour**
- **2 tablespoons brandy or additional reduced-sodium beef broth**
- **1 tablespoon stone-ground mustard**
- **1 tablespoon Worcestershire sauce**
- **1 cup frozen peas**
- **⅓ cup shredded Gruyere or Swiss cheese**

1. Place potatoes in a large saucepan and cover with water. Bring to a boil. Reduce heat; cover and cook for 10-15 minutes or until tender.

2. Meanwhile, in a large skillet, saute onions and ¼ teaspoon salt in oil until softened. Reduce heat to medium-low; cook, stirring occasionally, for 30 minutes or until deep golden brown.

3. Drain potatoes. Mash with ¼ cup broth and pepper; set aside and keep warm.

4. In a nonstick skillet, cook turkey over medium heat until no longer pink; drain. Add the flour, brandy, mustard, Worcestershire sauce and remaining broth and salt. Cook and stir for 5-7 minutes or until thickened. Stir in peas and onion mixture.

5. Transfer to a 1½-qt. baking dish coated with cooking spray; spread with potato mixture. Bake, covered, at 375° for 20 minutes. Sprinkle with cheese. Bake, uncovered, 10-15 minutes longer or until golden brown.

PER SERVING *360 cal., 9 g fat (2 g sat. fat), 58 mg chol., 803 mg sodium, 32 g carb., 4 g fiber, 37 g pro.* ***Diabetic Exchanges:*** *4 lean meat, 1½ starch, 1 vegetable, 1 fat.*

FRENCH ONION TURKEY SHEPHERD'S PIE

Pork

Here is **the comfort food everyone craves**: fabulous **lasagna**, make-ahead **breakfast casserole**, creamy, **cheesy sausage pasta**, magnificent **glazed ham** and more. These easy, satisfying recipes are **so tempting**, you'll want to **try them all**!

PIZZA RING

Hearty Ham Loaf

This recipe comes from my father's side of the family. It brings back memories of my childhood days in Nebraska. It's a simple dish to make and good for many occasions. I hope you'll enjoy this old-fashioned meat loaf in your home as well, so it can create fond memories for you, too.

—COLLEEN DEMUTH LE MARS, IA

PREP: 15 MIN. • **BAKE:** 1¼ HOURS
MAKES: 10-12 SERVINGS

- **1 cup coarsely crushed saltines (about 25 crackers)**
- **1 cup 2% milk**
- **2 eggs, lightly beaten**
- **⅛ teaspoon pepper**
- **1½ pounds ground ham**
- **1 pound ground pork**

BASTING SAUCE

- **½ cup packed brown sugar**
- **1 teaspoon ground mustard**
- **2½ tablespoons vinegar**
- **¼ cup water**

1. In a large bowl, combine the crackers, milk, eggs and pepper. Crumble ham and pork over mixture and mix well. Press into a 9-in. x 5-in. loaf pan. Bake at 350° for 1¼ hours or until a thermometer reads 160°.

2. Meanwhile, combine the sauce ingredients in a small saucepan; bring to a boil. Boil for 2 minutes. Baste loaf occasionally after the first 20 minutes of baking.

Pizza Ring

Mom made a ring with chicken and broccoli one night. I said I'd rather have pizza. That's how this recipe was born!

—TRICIA RICHARDSON SPRINGDALE, AR

START TO FINISH: 30 MIN.
MAKES: 8 SERVINGS

- **1 pound bulk Italian sausage**
- **1 can (15 ounces) pizza sauce, divided**
- **1½ cups (6 ounces) shredded part-skim mozzarella cheese, divided**
- **4 ounces Canadian bacon, chopped**
- **2 tubes (8 ounces each) refrigerated crescent rolls**

1. Cook sausage in a large skillet over medium heat until no longer pink; drain. Stir in ½ cup pizza sauce, 1 cup cheese and Canadian bacon.

2. Unroll crescent dough and separate into triangles. On an ungreased 14-in. pizza pan, arrange triangles in a ring with points toward the outside and wide ends overlapping at the center, leaving a 4-in. opening. Press overlapping dough to seal.

3. Spoon filling onto wide end of triangles. Fold pointed end of triangles over filling, tucking the points under to form a ring (filling will be visible).

4. Bake at 375° for 12-15 minutes or until golden brown and heated through. Sprinkle with remaining cheese. Bake 5 minutes longer or until cheese is melted. Serve with remaining pizza sauce.

Experiment with the **crescent ring** to create your own flavors. For **chicken club**, try cubed cooked chicken, crispy **bacon**, shredded **Swiss** and your favorite **seasoned** mayonnaise.

Company Lasagna

I love having this in the fridge when guests come over. It's so easy, I can focus on socializing, not stress about dinner.
—**RENEE VAUGHAN** GALENA, OH

PREP: 40 MIN. + CHILLING
BAKE: 50 MIN. + STANDING
MAKES: 12 SERVINGS

- **1 pound bulk pork sausage**
- **2 cans (one 28 ounces, one 14½ ounces) stewed tomatoes, undrained**
- **1 can (6 ounces) tomato paste**
- **2 tablespoons dried oregano**
- **4 garlic cloves, minced**
- **¼ teaspoon salt**
- **¼ teaspoon pepper**
- **4 cups (16 ounces) shredded part-skim mozzarella cheese, divided**
- **3 cups (24 ounces) 2% cottage cheese**
- **1 cup grated Parmesan cheese**
- **2 eggs, lightly beaten**
- **3 tablespoons dried parsley flakes**
- **12 no-cook lasagna noodles**

1. In a Dutch oven, cook sausage over medium heat until no longer pink; drain. Stir in the tomatoes, tomato paste, oregano, garlic, salt and pepper. Bring to a boil. Reduce heat; simmer, uncovered, for 15-20 minutes or until thickened.
2. Meanwhile, in a large bowl, combine 2 cups mozzarella cheese, cottage cheese, Parmesan cheese, eggs and parsley.
3. Spread 1 cup meat mixture into a greased 13-in. x 9-in. baking dish. Layer with three noodles, 1¼ cups meat mixture and 1 cup cheese mixture. Repeat three times. Top with remaining mozzarella cheese. Cover lasagna and refrigerate for 8 hours or overnight.
4. Remove from the refrigerator 30 minutes before baking. Cover and bake at 350° for 30 minutes. Uncover and bake 20-25 minutes longer or until bubbly and cheese is melted. Let stand 10 minutes before cutting.

COMPANY LASAGNA

Easy Breakfast Strata

PREP: 20 MIN. + CHILLING • **BAKE:** 30 MIN.
MAKES: 12 SERVINGS

- **1 pound bulk pork sausage**
- **1 large green pepper, chopped**
- **1 medium onion, chopped**
- **1 loaf (1 pound) herb or cheese bakery bread, cubed**
- **1 cup (4 ounces) shredded cheddar cheese**
- **6 eggs**
- **2 cups 2% milk**
- **1 teaspoon ground mustard**

1. In a large skillet, cook the sausage, pepper and onion over medium heat until meat is no longer pink; drain.
2. Place bread in a greased 13-in. x 9-in. baking dish. Top with sausage mixture; sprinkle with cheese. In a large bowl, whisk the eggs, milk and mustard. Pour over the top. Cover and refrigerate overnight.
3. Remove casserole from the refrigerator 30 minutes before baking. Bake, uncovered, at 350° for 30-35 minutes or until a knife inserted in center comes out clean. Let stand 5 minutes before cutting.

EASY BREAKFAST STRATA

DEBRA'S CAVATINI

FREEZE IT

Debra's Cavatini

I love this recipe because it makes two hearty casseroles. I add a little something different every time I make it, such as extra garlic, to give it an added boost of Italian flavor.

—DEBRA BUTCHER DECATUR, IN

PREP: 45 MIN. • **BAKE:** 35 MIN.
MAKES: 2 CASSEROLES (6 SERVINGS EACH)

- **1 package (16 ounces) penne pasta**
- **1 pound ground beef**
- **1 pound bulk Italian pork sausage**
- **1¾ cups sliced fresh mushrooms**
- **1 medium onion, chopped**
- **1 medium green pepper, chopped**
- **2 cans (14½ ounces each) Italian diced tomatoes**
- **1 jar (23½ ounces) Italian sausage and garlic spaghetti sauce**
- **1 jar (16 ounces) chunky mild salsa**
- **1 package (8 ounces) sliced pepperoni, chopped**
- **1 cup (4 ounces) shredded Swiss cheese, divided**
- **4 cups (16 ounces) shredded part-skim mozzarella cheese, divided**
- **1½ cups shredded Parmesan cheese, divided**
- **1 jar (24 ounces) three-cheese spaghetti sauce**

1. Cook pasta according to the package directions. Meanwhile, in a Dutch oven, cook beef, sausage, mushrooms, onion and green pepper over medium heat until meat is no longer pink; drain.

2. Drain pasta; add to the meat mixture. Stir in the tomatoes, sausage and garlic spaghetti sauce, salsa and pepperoni.

3. Preheat oven to 350°. Divide half of pasta mixture between two greased 13-in. x 9-in. baking dishes. Sprinkle each with 1/4 cup Swiss, 1 cup cheese and 1/3 cup Parmesan. Spread 3/4 cup of three-cheese spaghetti sauce over each. Top with the remaining pasta mixture and three-cheese spaghetti sauce. Sprinkle with remaining cheeses.

4. Cover and bake 25 minutes. Uncover; bake 10 minutes or until cheese is melted.

FREEZE OPTION *Cover unbaked casserole and freeze for up to 3 months. To use, thaw in refrigerator overnight. Remove from refrigerator 30 minutes before baking. Preheat oven to 350°. Bake casserole, covered, 45 minutes. Uncover; bake 10 minutes or until cheese is melted.*

If you have a **half-pound** package of **mushrooms**–about double what's called for–feel free to **toss them all** into this **big** recipe.

Ham 'n' Cheese Egg Loaf

My family has enjoyed slices of this attractive brunch loaf for many years. Every crumb disappears fast whenever I serve it at gatherings.

—**CONNIE BAIR** EAST WENATCHEE, WA

PREP: 15 MIN. • **BAKE:** 55 MIN. + STANDING
MAKES: 6-8 SERVINGS

- **6 eggs**
- **¾ cup 2% milk**
- **1 teaspoon prepared mustard**
- **1½ cups all-purpose flour**
- **2½ teaspoons baking powder**
- **¼ teaspoon salt**
- **6 bacon strips, cooked and crumbled**
- **1 cup cubed fully cooked ham**
- **4 ounces cheddar cheese, cut into ½-inch cubes**
- **4 ounces Monterey Jack cheese, cut into ½-inch cubes**

1. In a large bowl, beat eggs until frothy, about 1 minute. Beat in milk and mustard. Combine the flour, baking powder and salt; add to egg mixture and beat until smooth. Stir in bacon, ham and cheeses. Transfer to a greased and floured 9-in. x 5-in. loaf pan.

2. Bake, uncovered, at 350° for 55-60 minutes or until a toothpick inserted near the center comes out clean. Let stand for 10-15 minutes before cutting. Run a knife around edge of pan to remove. Slice and serve warm.

THE BEST DERNED SOUTHWESTERN CASSEROLE

The Best Derned Southwestern Casserole

If you want to add a little spice to life—and to dinner—serve this hearty main dish. It's full of Tex-Mex goodness and is simply irresistible.

—**VALERIE IGAL** OAK HILL, VA

PREP: 35 MIN. • **BAKE:** 45 MIN. + STANDING
MAKES: 12 SERVINGS

- **1½ pounds uncooked chorizo or bulk spicy pork sausage**
- **1 small onion, chopped**
- **1 can (15 ounces) black beans, rinsed and drained**
- **1 can (15 ounces) tomato sauce**
- **1 can (11 ounces) Mexicorn, drained**
- **2 cans (4 ounces each) chopped green chilies**
- **1 cup salsa**
- **¼ cup minced fresh cilantro**
- **3 teaspoons each ground cumin, chili powder and paprika**
- **2 teaspoons garlic powder**
- **12 corn tortillas (6 inches)**
- **2 large tomatoes, sliced**
- **2 cups (8 ounces) shredded Monterey Jack or cheddar-Monterey Jack cheese**

1. Preheat oven to 375°. Crumble chorizo into a large skillet; add onion. Cook over medium heat until meat is fully cooked; drain. Add beans, tomato sauce, corn, chilies, salsa, cilantro and seasonings; heat through.

2. Place six tortillas in the bottom of a greased 13-in. x 9-in. baking dish. Layer with 3½ cups meat mixture, the tomatoes and 1 cup cheese. Top with remaining tortillas, meat mixture and cheese.

3. Cover and bake 40 minutes. Uncover; bake 5-10 minutes or until heated through. Let stand 10 minutes before cutting.

"A true comfort food that's impossible to resist, this main dish is hearty and saucy with flavors that blend so nicely together. Many shepherd's pie recipes call for beef, so this pork version is a tasty change of pace."

—**MICHELLE ROSS** STANWOOD, WA

Potato Pork Pie

PREP: 50 MIN. • **BAKE:** 35 MIN.
MAKES: 6 SERVINGS

- **2 pounds potatoes, peeled and cubed**
- **⅓ cup heavy whipping cream**
- **4 tablespoons butter, divided**
- **¾ teaspoon salt**
- **⅛ teaspoon pepper**
- **1 medium onion, chopped**
- **1 garlic clove, minced**
- **¼ cup all-purpose flour**
- **1 can (14½ ounces) beef broth**
- **1 tablespoon Dijon mustard**
- **1 teaspoon dried thyme**
- **3 tablespoons minced fresh parsley, divided**
- **2½ cups cubed cooked pork**

1. Place potatoes in a large saucepan and cover with water; bring to a boil. Cover and cook for 15-20 minutes or until tender. Drain well. Mash potatoes with cream, 2 tablespoons butter, salt and pepper. Spread 1½ cups of mashed potatoes into a greased shallow 1½-qt. baking dish.

2. In a large skillet, saute onion in remaining butter until tender. Add garlic; cook 1 minute longer. Stir in flour until blended. Gradually stir in broth, mustard, thyme and 2 tablespoons parsley. Bring to a boil; cook and stir for 2 minutes or until thickened. Stir in pork; heat through. Pour over the potato crust.

3. Pipe or spoon the remaining mashed potatoes over top of casserole. Bake, uncovered, at 375° for 35-40 minutes or until the potatoes are lightly browned. Sprinkle with remaining parsley.

Chops with Mushroom Gravy

After driving my family crazy trying new recipes, I always return to this classic standby. These pork chops come out great every time. We love the rich gravy over the chops and mashed potatoes.

—**LORAINE VAN BROECK** GENEVA, IL

PREP: 25 MIN. • **BAKE:** 50 MIN.
MAKES: 6-8 SERVINGS

- **½ cup all-purpose flour**
- **1 to 2 teaspoons paprika**
- **1½ teaspoons salt**
- **¼ teaspoon pepper**
- **6 to 8 boneless pork loin chops (1 inch thick)**
- **¼ cup butter**
- **1 medium onion, chopped**
- **½ cup chopped green pepper**
- **1 can (4 ounces) mushroom stems and pieces, drained**
- **2 cups milk**
- **2 tablespoons lemon juice**
- **Hot mashed potatoes**

1. In a large resealable plastic bag, combine the first four ingredients; set aside 3 tablespoons. Add pork chops to bag, one at a time, and toss to coat.

2. In a large skillet, brown chops in butter on both sides; transfer to a greased 13-in. x 9-in. baking dish. In the same pan, saute the onion, green pepper and mushrooms until tender. Stir in reserved flour mixture; gradually add milk until blended. Bring to a boil; cook and stir for 2 minutes or until thickened. Remove from the heat; stir in lemon juice. Pour over chops.

3. Cover and bake at 350° for 50-60 minutes or until the meat is. Serve with potatoes.

CHOPS WITH MUSHROOM GRAVY

FREEZE IT

Polish Casserole

When I first made this dish, my 2-year-old liked it so much that he wanted it for every meal! You can use most any pasta that will hold the sauce.

—**CRYSTAL JO BRUNS** ILIFF, CO

PREP: 25 MIN. • **BAKE:** 45 MIN.
MAKES: 2 CASSEROLES (6 SERVINGS EACH)

- **4 cups uncooked penne pasta**
- **1½ pounds smoked Polish sausage or kielbasa, cut into ½-inch slices**
- **2 cans (10¾ ounces each) condensed cream of mushroom soup, undiluted**
- **1 jar (16 ounces) sauerkraut, rinsed and well drained**
- **3 cups (12 ounces) shredded Swiss cheese, divided**
- **1⅓ cups 2% milk**
- **4 green onions, chopped**
- **2 tablespoons Dijon mustard**
- **4 garlic cloves, minced**

1. Cook pasta according to package directions; drain and transfer to a large bowl. Stir in the sausage, soup, sauerkraut, 2 cups cheese, milk, onions, mustard and garlic.
2. Spoon into two greased 8-in.-square baking dishes; sprinkle with remaining cheese. Bake, uncovered, at 350° for 45-50 minutes or until golden brown and bubbly.
FREEZE OPTION *Cover and freeze one casserole for up to 3 months. Thaw in the refrigerator overnight. Remove from the refrigerator 30 minutes before baking. Bake casserole, uncovered, at 350° for 50-55 minutes or until golden brown and bubbly.*

FREEZE IT

Jack Cheese Oven Omelet

Although it's easy, this omelet makes it look like you fussed. Sometimes I toss in mushrooms and cheddar cheese for a different flavor.

—**LAUREL ROBERTS** VANCOUVER, WA

PREP: 20 MIN. • **BAKE:** 35 MIN.
MAKES: 6 SERVINGS

- **8 bacon strips, diced**
- **4 green onions, sliced**
- **8 eggs**
- **1 cup 2% milk**
- **½ teaspoon seasoned salt**
- **2½ cups (10 ounces) shredded Monterey Jack cheese, divided**

1. In a large skillet, cook bacon until crisp. Drain, reserving 1 tablespoon drippings. Set bacon aside. Saute onion in the drippings until tender; set aside.
2. In a large bowl, beat eggs. Add the milk, seasoned salt, 2 cups cheese, bacon and sauteed onions. Transfer to a greased shallow 2-qt. baking dish.
3. Bake, uncovered, at 350° for 35-40 minutes or until set. Sprinkle with remaining cheese.
FREEZE OPTION *Freeze unbaked omelet until firm; cover with foil. To use, remove from freezer 30 minutes before baking (do not thaw). Preheat oven to 350°. Bake as directed, increasing time as necessary for a knife inserted near the center to come out clean. Sprinkle with 1/2 cup of shredded cheese.*

POLISH CASSEROLE

When I was expecting our daughter, I made and froze these tasty quiches as well as several other dishes. After her birth, it was nice to have dinner in the freezer when my husband and I were too tired to cook.
—**CHRISTENA PALMER** GREEN RIVER, WY

HAM 'N' CHEESE QUICHE

FREEZE IT

Ham 'n' Cheese Quiche

PREP: 20 MIN. • **BAKE:** 35 MIN.
MAKES: 2 QUICHES (6 SERVINGS EACH)

- **1 package (14.1 ounces) refrigerated pie pastry**
- **2 cups diced fully cooked ham**
- **2 cups (8 ounces) shredded sharp cheddar cheese**
- **2 teaspoons dried minced onion**
- **4 eggs**
- **2 cups half-and-half cream**
- **½ teaspoon salt**
- **¼ teaspoon pepper**

1. Preheat oven to 400°. Unroll pastry sheets into two 9-in. pie plates; flute edges. Line unpricked pastry shells with a double thickness of heavy-duty foil. Fill with pie weights, dried beans or uncooked rice.
2. Bake 10-12 minutes or until light golden brown. Remove foil and weights; bake 3-5 minutes longer or until bottom is golden brown. Cool on wire racks.
3. Divide ham, cheese and onion between shells. In a large bowl, whisk eggs, cream, salt and pepper until blended. Pour into shells. Cover edges loosely with foil.
4. Bake 35-40 minutes or until a knife inserted near the center comes out clean. Let stand for 5-10 minutes before cutting.

FREEZE OPTION *Cover and freeze unbaked quiche. To use, remove from freezer 30 minutes before baking (do not thaw). Preheat oven to 350°. Place quiche on a baking sheet; cover edge loosely with foil. Bake as directed, increasing time as necessary for a knife inserted near the center to come out clean.*

NOTE *Let pie weights cool before storing. Beans and rice may be reused for pie weights, but not for cooking.*

Pork Chops with Scalloped Potatoes

Mom always managed to put a delicious, hearty meal on the table for our family and the farmhands. This all-in-one main dish has a flavor that reminds me of home.

—**BERNICE MORRIS** MARSHFIELD, MO

PREP: 25 MIN. • **BAKE:** 1½ HOURS
MAKES: 6 SERVINGS

- **3 tablespoons butter**
- **3 tablespoons all-purpose flour**
- **1½ teaspoons salt**
- **¼ teaspoon pepper**
- **1 can (14½ ounces) chicken broth**
- **6 pork rib or loin chops (¾ inch thick)**
- **2 tablespoons canola oil**
- **Additional salt and pepper, optional**
- **6 cups thinly sliced peeled potatoes**
- **1 medium onion, sliced**
- **Paprika and minced fresh parsley, optional**

1. In a small saucepan, melt butter; stir in the flour, salt and pepper until smooth. Add broth. Bring to a boil; cook and stir for 1 minute or until thickened. Remove from the heat and set aside. In a large skillet, brown pork chops in oil; sprinkle with additional salt and pepper if desired.
2. In a greased 13-in. x 9-in. baking dish, layer potatoes and onion. Pour broth mixture over layers. Place pork chops on top.
3. Cover and bake at 350° for 1 hour; uncover and bake 30 minutes longer or until meat and potatoes are tender. If desired, sprinkle with paprika and parsley before serving.

To **thinly slice the potatoes** to a consistent thickness, use a mandolin or the **slicing blade** on your box grater.

PORK CHOPS WITH SCALLOPED POTATOES

HAM & ZUCCHINI ITALIANO

Ham & Zucchini Italiano

I strongly believe dinner should be three things: healthy, delicious and simple. With fresh zucchini, ham and marinara sauce baked with cheese, you can accomplish all three in the time it takes to describe this tasty dish.

—**MADISON MAYBERRY** AMES, IA

START TO FINISH: 30 MIN.
MAKES: 4 SERVINGS

- **3 medium zucchini, cut diagonally into ¼-inch slices**
- **1 tablespoon olive oil**
- **1 teaspoon dried basil**
- **½ teaspoon salt**
- **¼ teaspoon pepper**
- **½ pound smoked deli ham, cut into strips**
- **1 cup marinara or spaghetti sauce**
- **¾ cup shredded part-skim mozzarella cheese**

1. In a large skillet, saute zucchini in oil until crisp-tender. Sprinkle with basil, salt and pepper.
2. Place half of zucchini in a greased 8-in. baking dish. Layer with half of the ham, marinara sauce and cheese. Repeat layers.
3. Bake, uncovered, at 450° for 10-12 minutes or until heated through and cheese is melted. Serve with a slotted spoon.

Try **switching up** the casserole with yellow summer squash, **roasted red peppers**, capicola or other **Italian meats**, and **provolone**.

Pork Tenderloin with Roasted Potatoes

My mother found this delicious recipe many years ago, when I was a teenager. Now I make it for my husband, Bob, who adores it.

—**KIM WILSON** PLAINFIELD, IL

PREP: 15 MIN. + MARINATING
BAKE: 25 MIN. • **MAKES:** 2 SERVINGS

- **¼ cup olive oil**
- **2 garlic cloves, minced**
- **1½ teaspoons dried rosemary, crushed**
- **½ teaspoon salt**
- **¼ teaspoon pepper**
- **1 pork tenderloin (about ¾ pound)**
- **2 medium red potatoes, cut into chunks**

1. In a small bowl, mix oil, garlic, rosemary, salt and pepper. Place half of the marinade in each of two resealable plastic bags. Add pork to one bag and potatoes to the other bag. Seal bags and turn to coat; refrigerate 8 hours or overnight.
2. Preheat oven to 425°. Drain and discard marinades. Place meat and potatoes in a greased 2-qt. broiler-safe baking dish. Bake, uncovered, 20-25 minutes or until potatoes are almost tender. Broil 5 in. from heat for 4-5 minutes or until potatoes are tender and a thermometer inserted in pork reads 160°. Let stand 5 minutes before slicing.

PORK WITH BLUEBERRY HERB SAUCE

EAT SMART

Pork with Blueberry Herb Sauce

A delicious way to use up blueberries, this tangy, sweet-savory sauce would also be great over chicken. The blend of berries and balsamic is wonderful!
—**LIBBY WALP** CHICAGO, IL

PREP: 15 MIN. • **COOK:** 20 MIN.
MAKES: 4 SERVINGS

- **1 garlic clove, minced**
- **1 teaspoon pepper**
- **½ teaspoon salt**
- **⅛ teaspoon cayenne pepper**
- **4 boneless pork loin chops (6 ounces each)**
- **2 cups fresh blueberries**
- **¼ cup packed brown sugar**
- **2 tablespoons minced fresh parsley**
- **1 tablespoon balsamic vinegar**
- **2 teaspoons butter**
- **1 teaspoon minced fresh thyme or ¼ teaspoon dried thyme**
- **1 teaspoon fresh sage or ¼ teaspoon dried sage**

1. In a small bowl, combine the garlic, pepper, salt and cayenne; sprinkle over pork.

2. In a large ovenproof skillet coated with cooking spray, brown pork chops. Bake, uncovered at 350° for 10-15 minutes or until a thermometer reads 160°. Remove pork and keep warm.

3. Add remaining ingredients to the pan. Cook and stir over medium heat until thickened, about 8 minutes. Serve with pork.

PER SERVING *343 cal., 12 g fat (5 g sat. fat), 87 mg chol., 364 mg sodium, 25 g carb., 2 g fiber, 33 g pro.* ***Diabetic Exchanges:*** *5 lean meat, 1 starch, 1/2 fruit.*

Sausage Florentine Potpie

I created this tasty comfort food after someone requested chicken potpie, but all I had was sausage in the freezer.
—**KENDRA DOSS** COLORADO SPRINGS, CO

PREP: 30 MIN. • **BAKE:** 25 MIN. + STANDING
MAKES: 6 SERVINGS

- **1 pound bulk Italian sausage**
- **2½ cups sliced fresh mushrooms**
- **1 medium red onion, chopped**
- **3 garlic cloves, minced**
- **1 can (10¾ ounces) reduced-fat reduced-sodium condensed cream of mushroom soup, undiluted**
- **1 package (10 ounces) frozen chopped spinach, thawed and squeezed dry**
- **1 cup half-and-half cream**
- **1 cup shredded part-skim mozzarella cheese**
- **½ cup shredded Parmesan cheese**

TOPPING

- **5 sheets phyllo dough (14 inches x 9 inches)**
- **2 tablespoons butter, melted**
- **1 egg**
- **1 tablespoon water**

1. In a large skillet, cook the sausage, mushrooms, onion and garlic over medium heat until no longer pink; drain. Add the soup, spinach, cream and cheeses; cook and stir until cheese is melted.

2. Transfer to a greased 11-in. x 7-in. baking dish. Place a phyllo sheet over top; brush with some of the butter. Repeat with remaining phyllo dough and butter. Crimp edges of dough.

3. Whisk egg and water; brush over top. Bake, uncovered, at 350° for 25-30 minutes or until golden brown. Let the potpie stand for 10 minutes before serving.

MEATY RIGATONI BAKE

Meaty Rigatoni Bake

I created this super-easy Italian dish from ingredients that I had on hand. My husband and I are empty-nesters, so I'm always interested in recipes that make a small amount.

—**MARY GROSSMAN** CLOQUET, MN

PREP: 20 MIN. • **BAKE:** 25 MIN.
MAKES: 3 SERVINGS

- **1 cup uncooked rigatoni or large tube pasta**
- **½ pound bulk Italian sausage**
- **1½ cups spaghetti sauce**
- **1 can (4 ounces) mushroom stems and pieces, drained**
- **½ cup shredded Italian cheese blend**
- **8 slices pepperoni**

1. Cook pasta according to package directions. Meanwhile, crumble sausage into a large skillet. Cook over medium heat until no longer pink; drain. Stir in the spaghetti sauce and mushrooms. Drain pasta; add to sausage mixture.
2. Transfer to a 1-qt. baking dish coated with cooking spray. Top with cheese and pepperoni. Cover and bake at 350° for 25-30 minutes or until heated through.

Dogs in a Sweater

For a delightful twist on an old favorite, try these skewered hot dogs wrapped with breadstick dough and baked. They're fun to dip in ketchup, mustard or ranch dressing. Children will love these.

—**TASTE OF HOME TEST KITCHEN**

START TO FINISH: 30 MIN.
MAKES: 12 SERVINGS

- **1 tube (11 ounces) refrigerated breadsticks**
- **12 wooden pop sticks**
- **12 hot dogs**
- **Ketchup, mustard and/or ranch dressing**

1. Separate breadstick dough; roll each piece into a 15-in. rope. Insert a Popsicle stick into each hot dog lengthwise. Starting at one end, wrap dough in a spiral around hot dog; pinch ends to seal.
2. Place 1 in. apart on a baking sheet coated with cooking spray. Bake at 350° for 18-20 minutes. Serve with condiments of your choice.

Bacon & Tomato-Topped Meat Loaf

PREP: 30 MIN. • **BAKE:** 1 HOUR
MAKES: 6 SERVINGS

- **1 small onion, finely chopped**
- **1 celery rib, finely chopped**
- **1 small green pepper, finely chopped**
- **1 tablespoon canola oil**
- **1 garlic clove, minced**
- **1 egg, lightly beaten**
- **1 tablespoon prepared horseradish**
- **1 tablespoon dry red wine or beef broth**
- **1 teaspoon prepared mustard**
- **1 teaspoon Worcestershire sauce**
- **1 cup soft bread crumbs**
- **1 tablespoon all-purpose flour**
- **1 tablespoon brown sugar**
- **1 teaspoon salt**
- **1 teaspoon Cajun seasoning**
- **1 teaspoon pepper**
- **½ teaspoon chili powder**
- **1 pound lean ground beef (90% lean)**
- **½ pound bulk pork sausage**
- **½ pound bacon strips**

TOPPING

- **1 can (14½ ounces) diced tomatoes, drained**
- **1 can (8 ounces) tomato sauce**

1. In a large skillet, saute the onion, celery and green pepper in oil until tender. Add garlic; cook 1 minute longer. Transfer to a large bowl and cool slightly.
2. Add the egg, horseradish, wine, mustard, Worcestershire sauce, bread crumbs, flour, brown sugar and seasonings. Crumble beef and sausage over mixture and mix well. Pat into an ungreased 9-in. x 5-in. loaf pan. Place bacon strips over the meat loaf; tuck in ends.
3. Bake meat loaf, uncovered, at 350° for 55 minutes. Combine tomatoes and tomato sauce; spoon over loaf. Bake 5-10 minutes longer or until no pink remains and a thermometer reads 160°.

"I started with a meat loaf recipe I had that includes horseradish and added a few other complementary flavors. The results were a tender meat loaf with visible bits of veggies and plenty of savory flavor."
—**CHERYL MORING** NEW EDINBURG, AR

BACON & TOMATO-TOPPED MEAT LOAF

EAT SMART

Pork Tenderloin with Cranberry-Pear Chutney

Cranberries and pears go great with pork, and the brilliant color of the chutney just radiates festivity.

—AMANDA REED NASHVILLE, TN

PREP: 45 MIN. + MARINATING
BAKE: 25 MIN.
MAKES: 4 SERVINGS (1 CUP CHUTNEY)

- **3 green onions, chopped**
- **2 tablespoons lemon juice**
- **2 tablespoons olive oil**
- **1 tablespoon honey**
- **2 teaspoons grated lemon peel**
- **1 garlic clove, minced**
- **1 teaspoon salt**
- **1 teaspoon minced fresh sage or ¼ teaspoon dried sage leaves**
- **1 teaspoon minced fresh rosemary or ¼ teaspoon dried rosemary, crushed**
- **1 teaspoon pepper**
- **1 pork tenderloin (1 pound)**

CHUTNEY

- **1 cup fresh or frozen cranberries, thawed**
- **1 cup chopped peeled ripe pear**
- **½ cup sugar**
- **¼ cup water**
- **2 tablespoons minced fresh mint or 2 teaspoons dried mint**

1. In a large resealable plastic bag, combine the first 10 ingredients. Add the pork; seal bag and turn to coat. Refrigerate for at least 8 hours or overnight.

2. For chutney, in a small saucepan, combine all ingredients. Bring to a boil. Reduce heat; cover and simmer for 20 minutes. Uncover; simmer 20-25 minutes longer or until desired consistency, stirring occasionally. Cool to room temperature.

3. Meanwhile, drain and discard marinade. Place pork on a rack in a shallow roasting pan. Bake at 425° for 25-35 minutes or until a thermometer reads 160°. Let stand for 5 minutes before slicing. Serve with chutney.

PER SERVING *306 cal., 7 g fat (2 g sat. fat), 63 mg chol., 342 mg sodium, 38 g carb., 3 g fiber, 23 g pro.* ***Diabetic Exchanges:*** *3 lean meat, 1 starch, 1 fruit, 1/2 fat.*

PORK TENDERLOIN WITH CRANBERRY-PEAR CHUTNEY

Roast Pork and Potatoes

We used to raise hogs. I received this delicious home-style recipe from a fellow farmer who also served pork frequently.

—DENISE COLLINS CHILLICOTHE, OH

PREP: 20 MIN.
BAKE: 2½ HOURS + STANDING
MAKES: 8-10 SERVINGS

- **1 envelope onion soup mix**
- **2 garlic cloves, minced**
- **1 tablespoon dried rosemary, crushed**
- **½ teaspoon salt**
- **½ teaspoon pepper**
- **¼ teaspoon ground cloves**
- **3 cups water, divided**
- **1 bone-in pork loin roast (4 to 5 pounds)**
- **2 to 3 pounds small red potatoes, cut in half**
- **1½ cups sliced onions**

1. In a large bowl, combine the first six ingredients. Stir in 1/2 cup water; let stand for 3 minutes.

2. Place roast, fat side up, on a greased rack in a roasting pan. Pour remaining water into the pan. Combine potatoes and onions; spoon around the roast. Brush vegetables and roast with seasoning mixture.

3. Bake, uncovered, at 325° for 2½ to 3 hours or until a thermometer reads 160° and potatoes are tender. Baste and stir potatoes occasionally. Tent with foil if browning too fast.

4. Thicken the cooking juices for gravy if desired. Let the roast stand for 10 minutes before slicing.

Jeweled Buffet Ham

Cranberry sauce and mandarin oranges make a beautiful, aromatic glaze for baked ham. This recipe is a gururanteed crowd-pleaser!

—**AGNES WARD** STRATFORD, ON

PREP: 10 MIN. • **BAKE:** 2½ HOURS
MAKES: 15 SERVINGS

- **1 bone-in fully cooked spiral-sliced ham (7 pounds)**
- **1 can (14 ounces) whole-berry cranberry sauce**
- **1 can (11 ounces) mandarin oranges, drained**
- **1 can (8 ounces) jellied cranberry sauce**
- **½ cup orange juice**
- **½ teaspoon garlic powder**
- **⅛ teaspoon hot pepper sauce**

1. Place ham on a rack in a shallow roasting pan. Bake, uncovered, at 325° for 2 hours.
2. In a large saucepan, combine the remaining ingredients. Cook and stir over medium heat until heated through. Brush ham with some of the glaze; bake 30-60 minutes longer or until a thermometer reads 140°, brushing occasionally with the remaining glaze.

PARSNIP & HAM AU GRATIN

Parsnip & Ham au Gratin

Parsnips, thyme and a hint of roasted garlic give this entree a harvest-time feel. The crunchy bread crumb topping makes it special.

—**TASTE OF HOME TEST KITCHEN**

PREP: 20 MIN. • **BAKE:** 1 HOUR
MAKES: 6 SERVINGS

- **1 pound medium parsnips, peeled and sliced**
- **1 pound Yukon Gold potatoes, peeled and sliced**
- **2 cups cubed fully cooked ham**
- **1 can (10¾ ounces) condensed cream of mushroom with roasted garlic soup, undiluted**
- **⅔ cup 2% milk**
- **½ cup grated Parmesan cheese, divided**
- **½ teaspoon dried thyme**
- **¼ teaspoon pepper**
- **¼ cup dry bread crumbs**
- **2 tablespoons butter, melted**

1. Arrange the parsnips, potatoes and ham in a greased 13-in. x 9-in. baking dish. Combine the soup, milk, 1/4 cup cheese, thyme and pepper; pour over parsnip mixture.
2. In a small bowl, combine the bread crumbs, butter and remaining cheese. Sprinkle over top.
3. Cover and bake at 375° for 40 minutes. Uncover; bake 20-25 minutes longer or until potatoes are tender.

Fish & Seafood

215

220

225

It's easy to **give dinner an upgrade** with the delectable **seafood** dishes that follow. From a **fresh-tasting** tuna melt that's **packed with veggies** to a **buttery** crab casserole that's the **ultimate in indulgence**, you're sure to discover **delicious** new recipes your family will cherish.

Salmon Broccoli Bake

A good friend gave me this convenient recipe that uses canned salmon, leftover wild rice and frozen broccoli. I often serve the casserole with a wilted spinach salad.
—**BRIGITTE SCHALLER** FLEMINGTON, MO

PREP: 15 MIN. • **BAKE:** 35 MIN.
MAKES: 4 SERVINGS

- **1 cup chopped onion**
- **1 tablespoon butter**
- **1½ cups cooked wild rice**
- **1 can (7½ ounces) salmon, drained, bones and skin removed**
- **1 egg, beaten**
- **½ cup mayonnaise**
- **½ cup grated Parmesan cheese**
- **3 cups frozen chopped broccoli, thawed and drained**
- **1½ cups (6 ounces) shredded cheddar cheese, divided**

1. In a large skillet, saute onion in butter until tender. Remove from the heat; stir in rice and salmon. Combine egg and mayonnaise; stir into the salmon mixture.
2. Spoon half into a greased 2-qt. baking dish; top with half of the Parmesan cheese and broccoli. Sprinkle with 1 cup cheddar cheese. Top with remaining salmon mixture, Parmesan cheese and broccoli.
3. Bake the casserole, uncovered, at 350° for 30 minutes. Sprinkle with remaining cheddar cheese and bake 5 minutes longer or until the cheese is melted.

Canned salmon is a convenient way to include **more fish in your diet**. If you don't mind the **fine pin bones**, leave them in to boost the dish's **calcium content**. Discard the vertebrae.

VEGGIE-TUNA NOODLE CASSEROLE

Veggie-Tuna Noodle Casserole

Add zucchini, fresh tomatoes and basil to create a healthier version of tuna noodle casserole. It's a flavorful way to use what's in the garden.
—**HEIDI FARNWORTH** RIVERTON, UT

PREP: 30 MIN. • **BAKE:** 35 MIN.
MAKES: 6 SERVINGS

- **3 cups uncooked egg noodles**
- **2 medium zucchini, cut into ¼-inch slices**
- **2 teaspoons olive oil, divided**
- **1 celery rib, chopped**
- **1 garlic clove, minced**
- **2 cans (5 ounces each) tuna, drained and flaked**
- **½ cup reduced-fat sour cream**
- **½ cup reduced-fat mayonnaise**
- **4 green onions, thinly sliced**
- **2 teaspoons Dijon mustard**
- **½ teaspoon dried thyme**
- **¼ teaspoon salt**
- **¼ teaspoon pepper**
- **1 cup (4 ounces) shredded Monterey Jack cheese**
- **1 medium tomato, chopped**
- **2 tablespoons minced fresh basil**

1. Cook noodles according to package directions. Meanwhile, in a large skillet, saute zucchini in 1 teaspoon oil until crisp-tender; remove from skillet and set aside.
2. In the same pan, saute celery in remaining oil until crisp-tender. Add garlic; cook 1 minute longer.
3. Drain noodles; place in a large bowl. Stir in the tuna, sour cream, mayonnaise, green onions, mustard, thyme, salt, pepper and celery mixture.
4. Spoon half of the noodle mixture into a greased 11-in. x 7-in. baking dish; top with half of the zucchini. Repeat the layers.
5. Cover the casserole and bake at 375° for 30 minutes. Uncover; sprinkle with cheese. Bake 5-10 minutes longer or until cheese is melted. Combine tomato and basil; sprinkle over the top.

"This is an amazing dish. It's easy, yet so elegant. The veggies steam the fish from below, and covering the fillets with a crunchy topping keeps them moist."
—**KELLY REMINGTON** ARCATA, CA

CRUSTED RED SNAPPER

EAT SMART

Crusted Red Snapper

PREP: 25 MIN. • **BAKE:** 20 MIN.
MAKES: 6 SERVINGS

- **2 medium tomatoes, chopped**
- **1 each medium green, sweet yellow and red peppers, chopped**
- **1 cup chopped leeks (white portion only)**
- **½ cup chopped celery leaves**
- **2 garlic cloves, minced**
- **6 red snapper fillets (4 ounces each)**

TOPPING

- **½ cup panko (Japanese) bread crumbs**
- **½ cup coarsely crushed baked Parmesan and Tuscan herb potato chips**
- **¼ cup grated Parmesan cheese**
- **½ teaspoon salt**
- **½ teaspoon paprika**
- **¼ teaspoon cayenne pepper**
- **¼ teaspoon pepper**
- **2 tablespoons butter, melted**

1. In a 15-in. x 10-in. x 1-in. baking pan coated with cooking spray, combine the tomatoes, peppers, leeks, celery leaves and garlic; arrange fillets over vegetable mixture.

2. In a small bowl, combine the bread crumbs, chips, cheese, salt, paprika, cayenne and pepper; stir in butter. Sprinkle over fillets. Bake, uncovered, at 425° for 18-22 minutes or until fish flakes easily with a fork.

PER SERVING *237 cal., 7 g fat (3 g sat. fat), 53 mg chol., 396 mg sodium, 16 g carb., 3 g fiber, 26 g pro.* ***Diabetic Exchanges:*** *3 lean meat, 1 vegetable, 1 fat, ½ starch.*

Red snapper has experienced overfishing in the south Atlantic, but fish from **the Gulf** or **Hawaii** is still a good choice, as is **yellowtail** snapper.

Bacon & Tomato-Topped Haddock

Bacon presents a compelling argument for anyone who doesn't like fish. And for those who do, it just got even better.
—**SHERRI MELOTIK** OAK CREEK, WI

PREP: 25 MIN. • **COOK:** 10 MIN.
MAKES: 5 SERVINGS

- **6 bacon strips, chopped**
- **1 medium onion, thinly sliced**
- **1 garlic clove, minced**
- **1 cup panko (Japanese) bread crumbs**
- **2 plum tomatoes, chopped**
- **¼ cup minced fresh parsley**
- **2 tablespoons olive oil**
- **1 tablespoon butter, melted**
- **5 haddock fillets (6 ounces each)**
- **2 tablespoons lemon juice**
- **¼ teaspoon salt**

1. In a large skillet, cook bacon over medium heat until partially cooked but not crisp. Add onion and garlic; cook until golden brown, stirring mixture occasionally.

2. Remove from the heat; stir in bread crumbs, tomatoes and parsley. Set aside. Preheat oven to 400°. Spread the oil and butter in an ungreased 15in. x 10-in. x 1-in. baking pan. Place fillets in pan. Drizzle with lemon juice and sprinkle with salt. Top with bread crumb mixture.

3. Bake, uncovered, 10-15 minutes or until fish flakes easily with a fork.

BACON & TOMATO-TOPPED HADDOCK

FISH TACOS WITH AVOCADO SAUCE

Fish Tacos with Avocado Sauce

PREP: 30 MIN. + MARINATING
BROIL: 10 MIN. • **MAKES:** 4 SERVINGS

- **¼ cup lemon juice**
- **1 tablespoon olive oil**
- **3 garlic cloves, minced**
- **1 pound halibut or tilapia fillets**

SAUCE

- **2 medium ripe avocados, divided**
- **¼ cup fat-free sour cream**
- **¼ cup reduced-fat mayonnaise**
- **1 tablespoon lime juice**
- **1 garlic clove, minced**
- **1 teaspoon dill weed**
- **¼ teaspoon ground cumin**
- **¼ teaspoon dried oregano**
- **¼ teaspoon dried parsley flakes**
- **Dash cayenne pepper**

SALSA

- **1 medium tomato, seeded and chopped**
- **1 small red onion, chopped**
- **4½ teaspoons chopped seeded jalapeno pepper**
- **1 tablespoon minced fresh cilantro**
- **1½ teaspoons lime juice**
- **1 garlic clove, minced**
- **⅛ teaspoon salt**

TACOS

- **8 flour tortillas (6 inches)**
- **2 cups shredded cabbage**

1. In a large resealable plastic bag, combine the lemon juice, oil and garlic. Add the halibut; seal bag and turn to coat. Refrigerate for 30 minutes.

2. For sauce and salsa, peel and cube avocados. In a small bowl, mash 1/4 cup avocado. Stir in the remaining sauce ingredients. Place remaining avocados in a small bowl; stir in the remaining salsa ingredients. Refrigerate sauce and salsa until serving.

3. Drain fish and discard marinade. Broil halibut 4-6 in. from the heat for 8-10 minutes or until fish flakes easily with a fork. Place fish on the center of each tortilla. Top each with 1/4 cup cabbage, about 1 tablespoon sauce and 1/4 cup salsa.

NOTE *Wear disposable gloves when cutting hot peppers; the oils can burn skin. Avoid touching your face.*

EAT SMART

Baked Walleye

We live close to Lake Erie, which is nicknamed the Walleye Capital of the World. I came up with this recipe as a way to serve the succulent fish.
—**JOYCE SZYMANSKI** MONROE, MI

PREP: 15 MIN. • **BAKE:** 30 MIN.
MAKES: 4 SERVINGS

- **¾ cup chopped onion**
- **¾ cup chopped green pepper**
- **¾ cup chopped celery**
- **1 tablespoon dried parsley flakes**
- **½ teaspoon garlic powder**
- **½ teaspoon pepper**
- **½ teaspoon seasoned salt**
- **1 cup reduced-sodium V8 juice**
- **1 pound walleye fillets**

1. In a small saucepan, bring the first eight ingredients to a boil. Reduce heat; simmer, uncovered, until vegetables are crisp-tender, stirring occasionally.

2. Place fish in a greased 13-in. x 9-in. baking pan. Pour vegetable mixture over th e top. Cover and bake at 350° for 30 minutes or until fish flakes easily with a fork.

PER SERVING *137 cal., 1 g fat (0 sat. fat), 82 mg chol., 314 mg sodium, 9 g carb., 0 fiber, 22 g pro.* ***Diabetic Exchanges:*** *3 lean meat, 1½ vegetable.*

SMOKED SALMON AND EGG WRAPS

Smoked Salmon and Egg Wraps

These hearty breakfast roll-ups are great when you're serving a crowd. Everyone enjoys the smoked salmon flavor, which is accented by a hint of dill in the eggs.
—**MARY LOU WAYMAN** SALT LAKE CITY, UT

START TO FINISH: 25 MIN.
MAKES: 10 SERVINGS

- **12 eggs**
- **¼ cup snipped fresh dill or 4 teaspoons dill weed**
- **2 tablespoons 2% milk**
- **½ teaspoon seasoned salt**
- **10 flour tortillas (8 inches)**
- **1 package (4 ounces) smoked salmon or lox**
- **½ cup finely chopped red onion**
- **6 ounces Havarti cheese, thinly sliced**

1. In a large bowl, whisk the eggs, dill, milk and seasoned salt. Coat a large nonstick skillet with cooking spray and place over medium heat. Add egg mixture. Cook and stir over medium heat until eggs are completely set.

2. Spoon a scant ⅓ cup egg mixture down the center of each tortilla. Top with salmon, onion and cheese. Fold opposite sides of tortilla over filling (sides will not meet in center). Roll up tortilla, beginning at one of the open ends. Place the wraps, seam side down, in a 15-in. x 10-in. x 1-in. baking pan coated with cooking spray.

3. Cover and bake at 350° for 10 minutes or until cheese is melted.

Fresh 'n' Fruity Salmon Salad

Celebrate spring with a light and nutritious salad perfect for a lady's lunch. If you like, customize the salad with a berry-flavored goat cheese.

—**SHELISA TERRY** HENDERSON, NV

START TO FINISH: 20 MIN.
MAKES: 2 SERVINGS

- **2 salmon fillets (6 ounces each)**
- **2 tablespoons reduced-fat raspberry vinaigrette**
- **3 cups fresh baby spinach**
- **¾ cup sliced fresh strawberries**
- **2 slices red onion, separated into rings**
- **2 tablespoons crumbled goat cheese**
- **2 tablespoons chopped pecans, toasted**
- **Additional reduced-fat raspberry vinaigrette**

1. Place salmon on a broiler pan coated with cooking spray; drizzle with vinaigrette. Broil 3-4 in. from the heat for 10-15 minutes or until fish flakes easily with a fork.

2. Divide spinach between two serving plates. Top with strawberries, onion, cheese and pecans. Flake the salmon; sprinkle over salads. Drizzle with additional vinaigrette.

Cajun Pecan Catfish

This is one of our favorite recipes. It's quick, easy and delicious. Just serve with a side salad and biscuits, with mixed fruit for dessert.

—**JAN WILKINS** BLYTHEVILLE, AR

START TO FINISH: 25 MIN.
MAKES: 4 SERVINGS

- **2 tablespoons olive oil**
- **2 teaspoons lemon juice**
- **1 teaspoon Cajun seasoning**
- **½ teaspoon dried thyme**
- **⅓ cup finely chopped pecans**
- **2 tablespoons grated Parmesan cheese**
- **1 tablespoon dry bread crumbs**
- **1 tablespoon dried parsley flakes**
- **4 catfish fillets (6 ounces each)**

1. In a small bowl, combine the oil, lemon juice, Cajun seasoning and thyme. In another bowl, combine the pecans, cheese, bread crumbs, parsley and 1 tablespoon of the oil mixture.

2. Place catfish on a greased 15-in. x 10-in. x 1-in. baking pan. Brush with remaining oil mixture. Spread pecan mixture over fillets. Bake at 425° for 10-15 minutes or until fish flakes easily with a fork.

Pecans have a **higher fat content** than other nuts, so be careful that they don't go rancid. They'll **stay fresh** for twice as long **in the freezer** as they would at room temperature.

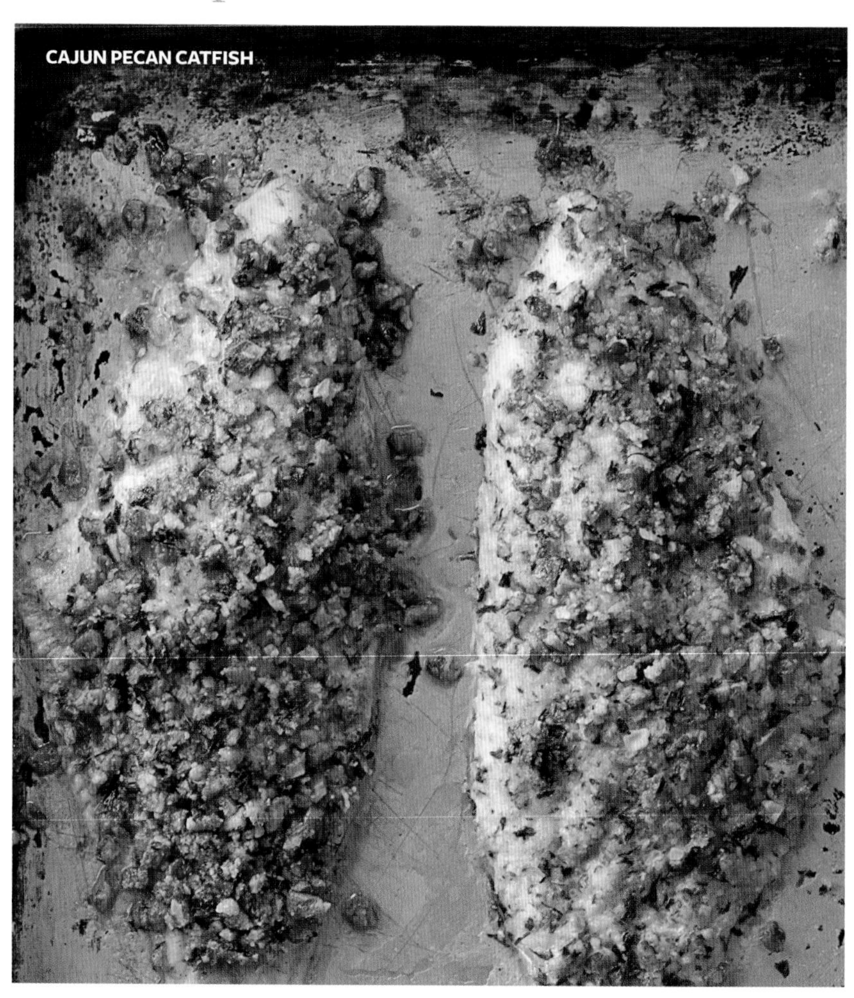

CAJUN PECAN CATFISH

SALMON WITH TOMATO-DILL SAUCE

Salmon with Tomato-Dill Sauce

Dinner doesn't get much easier than with this lovely main course. The creamy and fresh-tasting sauce complements the salmon nicely.

—JANET RYAN THORNTON, CO

PREP: 10 MIN. • **BAKE:** 25 MIN.
MAKES: 2 SERVINGS

- **2 salmon fillets (6 ounces each)**
- **⅓ cup mayonnaise**
- **1½ teaspoons milk**
- **½ teaspoon lemon-pepper seasoning**
- **¼ teaspoon dill weed**
- **1 plum tomato, diced**

1. Place the salmon in a small greased baking dish. Bake, uncovered, at 350° for 20-25 minutes or until fish flakes easily with a fork.
2. Combine the mayonnaise, milk, lemon-pepper and dill; stir in tomato. Spoon over salmon. Bake 5 minutes longer or until heated through.

French Riviera Trout

I love the versatility of this easy dish. If you don't care for trout, use salmon fillets or chicken breasts. Instead of green beans and tomatoes, toss in some broccoli florets and chopped eggplant. Have fun with it.

—ELIZABETH YARNELL DENVER, CO

PREP: 35 MIN. • **BAKE:** 25 MIN.
MAKES: 2 SERVINGS

- **4 small red potatoes, cut into 1-inch pieces**
- **1 cup cut fresh green beans (2-inch pieces)**
- **8 to 10 frozen pearl onions**
- **½ teaspoon salt, divided**
- **4 garlic cloves, minced, divided**
- **2 trout fillets (6 ounces each)**
- **¼ cup pitted Greek or ripe olives, halved**
- **3 teaspoons minced fresh parsley**
- **¼ teaspoon pepper**
- **2 plum tomatoes, chopped**
- **¼ cup white wine or chicken broth**

1. In a large saucepan, combine the potatoes, beans and onions; cover with water. Add ¼ teaspoon salt. Bring to a boil; reduce heat. Cover and cook for 10 minutes or until beans and onions are crisp-tender; drain.
2. Place vegetables in a single layer in a shallow 2-qt. baking dish coated with cooking spray. Top with half of the garlic. Place trout skin side down over vegetables. Sprinkle with olives, 1½ teaspoons parsley, pepper and remaining salt and garlic. Top with tomatoes and remaining parsley.
3. Pour wine over the top. Cover and bake at 400° for 25-30 minutes or until fish flakes easily with a fork.

Seafood en Croute

When I got married, I received this cherished recipe from family overseas. It looks difficult, but it's quite easy. Now that I have children, I can't spend all day in the kitchen. I choose my recipes to impress carefully, and this one's a winner!

—ALEXANDRA ARMITAGE
NOTTINGHAM, NH

PREP: 25 MIN. • **BAKE:** 20 MIN.
MAKES: 4 SERVINGS

- **1 package (17.3 ounces) frozen puff pastry, thawed**
- **4 salmon fillets (6 ounces each)**
- **½ pound fresh sea or bay scallops, finely chopped**
- **⅓ cup heavy whipping cream**
- **2 green onions, chopped**
- **1 tablespoon minced fresh parsley**
- **½ teaspoon minced fresh dill**
- **¼ teaspoon salt**
- **⅛ teaspoon pepper**
- **1 egg white**
- **1 egg, beaten**

1. On a lightly floured surface, roll each pastry sheet into a 12-in. x 10-in. rectangle. Cut each sheet into four 6-in. x 5-in. rectangles. Place a salmon fillet in the center of four rectangles.
2. Combine the scallops, cream, onions, parsley, dill, salt and pepper. In a small bowl, beat egg white on medium speed until soft peaks form; fold into scallop mixture. Spoon about 1/2 cup over each salmon fillet.
3. Top each with a pastry rectangle and crimp to seal. With a small sharp knife, cut several slits in the top. Place in a greased 15-in. x 10-in. x 1-in. baking pan; brush with egg. Bake at 400° for 20-25 minutes or until a thermometer reads 160°.

Flounder Roll-Ups

Here's a surprisingly easy way to show someone special how much you care. It really tastes like you spent all day in the kitchen.

—KATIE SLOAN CHARLOTTE, NC

PREP: 25 MIN. • **BAKE:** 25 MIN.
MAKES: 2 SERVINGS

- **1½ cups soft bread crumbs**
- **⅓ cup diced celery**
- **2 tablespoons finely chopped onion**
- **1 teaspoon rubbed sage**
- **½ teaspoon ground nutmeg**
- **⅛ teaspoon salt**
- **⅛ teaspoon pepper**
- **1 egg, beaten**
- **4 flounder fillets (3 ounces each)**
- **½ cup half-and-half cream**
- **3 tablespoons sherry or chicken broth**
- **1 tablespoon butter**
- **1 tablespoon all-purpose flour**
- **¼ cup shredded Swiss cheese**

1. In a bowl, combine the first seven ingredients; stir in egg. Spread over fillets; roll up and secure with toothpicks. Place seam side down in an ungreased 2-qt. baking dish. Combine cream and sherry; pour over roll-ups.
2. Cover and bake at 350° for 25-30 minutes or until fish flakes easily with a fork and a thermometer inserted into stuffing reads 160°. Remove roll-ups and keep warm.
3. In a small saucepan, melt butter; stir in flour until smooth. Add cream sauce from the baking dish. Bring to a boil; cook and stir for 2 minutes or until thickened. Reduce heat; stir in cheese until melted. Pour over roll-ups.

FLOUNDER ROLL-UPS

EAT SMART

Mediterranean Cod

My friends and I agree that this is one of the best things we have ever eaten. We each take a bundle and eat it right out of the parchment paper. It makes cleanup very easy!

—**MELISSA CHILTON** HARLOWTON, MT

PREP: 25 MIN. • **BAKE:** 15 MIN.
MAKES: 4 SERVINGS

- **4 cups shredded cabbage**
- **1 large sweet onion, thinly sliced**
- **4 garlic cloves, minced**
- **4 cod fillets (6 ounces each)**
- **¼ cup pitted Greek olives, chopped**
- **½ cup crumbled feta cheese**
- **¼ teaspoon salt**
- **¼ teaspoon pepper**
- **4 teaspoons olive oil**

1. Cut parchment paper or heavy-duty foil into four 18-in. x 12-in. pieces; place 1 cup cabbage on each. Top with onion, garlic, cod, olives, cheese, salt and pepper; drizzle with oil.
2. Fold parchment paper over fish. Bring edges of paper together on all sides and crimp to seal, forming a large packet. Repeat with remaining packets. Place on baking sheets.
3. Bake at 450° for 12-15 minutes or until fish flakes easily with a fork. Open packets carefully to allow steam to escape.

PER SERVING *270 cal., 10 g fat (3 g sat. fat), 72 mg chol., 532 mg sodium, 12 g carb., 3 g fiber, 31 g pro.* ***Diabetic Exchanges:*** *5 lean meat, 2 vegetable, 2 fat.*

EAT SMART

Coconut Shrimp with Dipping Sauce

With crispy coconut-cilantro breading and a sweet apricot sauce, these delicious shrimp would be great for any occasion, from an appetizer party to a weeknight dinner.

—**TASTE OF HOME TEST KITCHEN**

PREP: 1 HOUR + MARINATING
BAKE: 15 MIN. • **MAKES:** 5 SERVINGS

- **1 can (13.66 ounces) light coconut milk, divided**
- **1 jalapeno pepper, seeded and chopped**
- **¼ cup minced fresh cilantro**
- **1¼ pounds uncooked medium shrimp**
- **¾ cup all-purpose flour**
- **4 egg whites**
- **¾ cup panko (Japanese) bread crumbs**
- **¾ cup flaked coconut, lightly toasted**
- **⅓ cup reduced-sugar apricot preserves**
- **1 teaspoon spicy brown mustard**

1. Place 2 tablespoons coconut milk in a small bowl; cover and refrigerate. In a large resealable plastic bag, combine the jalapeno, cilantro and remaining coconut milk. Peel and devein shrimp, leaving tails on. Add to bag; seal and turn to coat. Refrigerate for 1 hour.
2. Place flour in a shallow bowl. In another bowl, lightly beat the egg whites. In a third bowl, combine bread crumbs and coconut. Drain shrimp and discard marinade. Dip shrimp in flour and egg whites, then roll in crumb mixture.
3. Place on a baking sheet coated with cooking spray. Bake at 400° for 7-9 minutes on each side or until lightly browned. For dipping sauce, add preserves and mustard to the reserved coconut milk. Serve with shrimp.

NOTE *Wear disposable gloves when cutting hot peppers; the oils can burn skin. Avoid touching your face.*

PER SERVING *324 cal., 11 g fat (8 g sat. fat), 168 mg chol., 316 mg sodium, 30 g carb., 1 g fiber, 23 g pro.* ***Diabetic Exchanges:*** *3 lean meat, 2 starch, 2 fat.*

EAT SMART

Baked Cod and Veggies

This fish packet tastes great whether prepared in the oven or on the grill. It's economical and good for you, too.
—**MONICA WOODS** SPRINGFIELD, MO

PREP: 20 MIN. • **BAKE:** 15 MIN.
MAKES: 2 SERVINGS

- **1 small onion, halved and sliced**
- **1 tablespoon olive oil**
- **1 small sweet red pepper, diced**
- **1 cup sliced fresh mushrooms**
- **1 garlic clove, minced**
- **¼ teaspoon ground allspice**
- **Dash salt**
- **Dash pepper**
- **2 tablespoons sliced ripe olives, drained**
- **2 tablespoons lemon juice, divided**
- **3 teaspoons minced fresh parsley, divided**
- **2 cod fillets (6 ounces each)**

1. In a large skillet, saute the onion in oil until tender. Add the red pepper, mushrooms, garlic, allspice, salt and pepper; cook and stir over medium heat for 5 minutes. Remove from the heat. Stir in the olives, 1 tablespoon lemon juice and 2 teaspoons parsley. Spoon mixture onto the center of a large piece of heavy-duty foil (about 18 in. x 12 in.).

2. Place cod over vegetables; sprinkle with remaining lemon juice and parsley. Fold foil over and fold in the edges twice, forming a pouch. Place on a baking sheet. Bake at 350° for 15-20 minutes or until fish flakes easily with a fork. Open foil carefully to allow steam to escape.

PER SERVING *232 cal., 9 g fat (1 g sat. fat), 65 mg chol., 243 mg sodium, 10 g carb., 2 g fiber, 29 g pro.* ***Diabetic Exchanges:*** *5 lean meat, 2 vegetable.*

BAKED COD AND VEGGIES

Crab Imperial Casserole

PREP: 20 MIN. • **BAKE:** 25 MIN.
MAKES: 8 SERVINGS

- **3 cups uncooked spiral pasta**
- **1¾ cups sliced fresh mushrooms**
- **5 tablespoons butter, cubed**
- **2 tablespoons all-purpose flour**
- **¾ teaspoon pepper**
- **½ teaspoon salt**
- **1½ cups 2% milk**
- **4 cans (6 ounces each) lump crabmeat, drained**
- **1 can (10¾ ounces) condensed cream of mushroom soup, undiluted**
- **¼ cup crushed butter-flavored crackers**

1. Cook pasta according to package directions. Meanwhile, in a large skillet, saute mushrooms in butter until tender. Stir in the flour, pepper and salt until blended; gradually add milk. Bring to a boil. Cook and stir for 2 minutes or until thickened. Stir in crab and soup until blended.

2. Drain pasta. Add crab mixture; toss to coat. Transfer to a greased 13-in. x 9-in. baking dish; sprinkle with cracker crumbs. Bake the casserole, uncovered, at 350° for 25-30 minutes or until bubbly.

Be sure the **canned crab** is labeled "**lump**," which means it contains **large pieces** of crab. Or substitute **1 pound** of **refrigerated** lump crab if you prefer.

CRAB IMPERIAL CASSEROLE

TILAPIA TOSTADAS

EAT SMART

Tilapia Tostadas

Even my non-fish-loving family enjoys this recipe. These healthy tostadas are always a winner in my book.

—JENNIFER KOLB OVERLAND PARK, KS

START TO FINISH: 30 MIN.
MAKES: 4 SERVINGS

- **¼ cup all-purpose flour**
- **1 teaspoon chili powder**
- **½ teaspoon salt**
- **½ teaspoon pepper**
- **¼ teaspoon garlic powder**
- **4 tilapia fillets (6 ounces each)**
- **1 tablespoon butter**
- **8 corn tortillas (6 inches)**
- **2 cups angel hair coleslaw mix**
- **2 tablespoons reduced-fat mayonnaise**
- **2 tablespoons reduced-fat sour cream**
- **1 tablespoon lime juice**
- **1 teaspoon grated lime peel**
- **1 cup canned black beans, rinsed and drained**
- **½ avocado, thinly sliced**

1. In a large resealable plastic bag, combine the flour, chili powder, salt, pepper and garlic powder. Add tilapia fillets, one at a time, and shake to coat.
2. In a large nonstick skillet over medium heat, cook fillets in butter for 5-6 minutes on each side or until fish flakes easily with a fork. Meanwhile, place tortillas on a baking sheet and spritz with cooking spray. Broil 3-4 in. from the heat for 2-3 minutes on each side or until crisp.
3. In a small bowl, toss the coleslaw mix, mayonnaise, sour cream, lime juice and peel. Cut fish into large pieces. On each tortilla, layer coleslaw, black beans, fish and avocado.

PER SERVING *437 cal., 12 g fat (4 g sat. fat), 95 mg chol., 659 mg sodium, 44 g carb., 7 g fiber, 40 g pro.* ***Diabetic Exchanges:*** *5 lean meat, 3 starch, 1½ fat.*

Artichoke Tuna Melt

Artichokes, spinach and a lemony mayonnaise give this melt an advantage over ordinary tuna sandwiches.

—TASTE OF HOME TEST KITCHEN

START TO FINISH: 25 MIN.
MAKES: 6 SERVINGS

- **1 loaf (1 pound) French bread**
- **1 tablespoon olive oil**
- **1 garlic clove, halved**
- **¾ cup mayonnaise**
- **1 tablespoon lemon juice**
- **1 tablespoon Dijon mustard**
- **½ teaspoon garlic powder**
- **½ teaspoon pepper**
- **4 cans (5 ounces each) albacore white tuna in water**
- **1 can (14 ounces) water-packed artichoke hearts, rinsed, drained and chopped**
- **1 cup fresh baby spinach**
- **2 plum tomatoes, sliced**
- **1 cup (4 ounces) shredded part-skim mozzarella cheese**

1. Cut bread in half lengthwise (save one half for another use). Brush bread with oil. Place cut side up on an ungreased baking sheet. Broil 4-6 in. from the heat for 2-3 minutes or until golden brown. Rub cut sides of garlic clove over bread; discard garlic.
2. In a large bowl, combine the mayonnaise, lemon juice, mustard, garlic powder and pepper. Stir in tuna and artichokes.
3. Arrange spinach over bread; top with tuna mixture, tomatoes and cheese. Broil the sandwich for 1-2 minutes or until cheese is melted. Cut into six slices.

ARTICHOKE TUNA MELT

Bonus: Desserts

A **sweet treat** always makes the meal. Whether you need **welcome-to-springtime** strawberry and rhubarb desserts, refreshing **ice creams** and frozen whips, **heartwarming holiday** treats or potluck-perfect **cookies** and **bars**, you'll find a **superstar specialty** here.

Can't Leave Alone Bars

I bring these quick and easy treats to church meetings, potlucks and housewarming parties. I usually make a double batch so we can enjoy some at home, too.

—KIMBERLY BIEL JAVA, SD

PREP: 20 MIN. • **BAKE:** 20 MIN. + COOLING
MAKES: 3 DOZEN

- **1 package white cake mix (regular size)**
- **2 eggs**
- **⅓ cup canola oil**
- **1 can (14 ounces) sweetened condensed milk**
- **1 cup (6 ounces) semisweet chocolate chips**
- **¼ cup butter, cubed**

1. In a large bowl, combine the cake mix, eggs and oil. Press two-thirds of the mixture into a greased 13-in. x 9-in. baking pan. Set remaining cake mixture aside.
2. In a microwave-safe bowl, combine the milk, chocolate chips and butter. Microwave, uncovered, until chips and butter are melted; stir until smooth. Pour over crust.
3. Drop teaspoonfuls of remaining cake mixture over top. Bake at 350° for 20-25 minutes or until lightly browned. Cool before cutting.

Mocha Pudding Cakes

Mini chocolate cakes are the perfect treat for two. My mom used to make these for us when I was a little girl. Now I like to whip them up. It's nice that the recipe uses pantry ingredients.

—DEBORA SIMMONS EGLON, WV

START TO FINISH: 30 MIN.
MAKES: 2 SERVINGS

- **¼ cup all-purpose flour**
- **3 tablespoons sugar**
- **1½ teaspoons baking cocoa**
- **½ teaspoon baking powder**
- **⅛ teaspoon salt**
- **3 tablespoons 2% milk**
- **1½ teaspoons butter, melted**
- **¼ teaspoon vanilla extract**

TOPPING

- **2 tablespoons brown sugar**
- **1½ teaspoons baking cocoa**
- **3 tablespoons hot brewed coffee**
- **1 tablespoon hot water**
- **Whipped topping, optional**

1. In a small bowl, combine the flour, sugar, cocoa, baking powder and salt. Stir in the milk, butter and vanilla until smooth. Spoon into two 4-oz. ramekins coated with cooking spray.
2. Combine brown sugar and cocoa; sprinkle over batter. Combine coffee and water; pour over topping. Bake at 350° for 15-20 minutes or until a knife inserted near the center comes out clean. Serve warm or at room temperature with whipped topping if desired.

Ice Cream Party Roll

People will go crazy for this from-scratch chocolate cake filled with ice cream and a kiss of berry jam. Let each guest top off their own slice with hot fudge sauce and whipped topping.

—**LAURA ANDREWS** MANTEE, MS

PREP: 45 MIN. • **BAKE:** 10 MIN. + FREEZING
MAKES: 12 SERVINGS

- **4 eggs, separated**
- **¾ cup sugar, divided**
- **½ cup cake flour**
- **⅓ cup baking cocoa**
- **1 teaspoon baking powder**
- **¼ teaspoon salt**
- **½ cup strawberry or raspberry jam**
- **2 cups vanilla ice cream, softened**
- **Confectioners' sugar**
- **Hot fudge topping and whipped topping**

1. Place egg whites in large bowl; let stand at room temperature for 30 minutes. Line a greased 15-in. x 10-in. x 1-in. baking pan with waxed paper; grease the paper and set aside.
2. In a large bowl, beat egg yolks on high speed for 5 minutes or until thick and lemon-colored. Gradually beat in ½ cup sugar. Sift the flour, cocoa, baking powder and salt together twice; gradually add to the yolk mixture and mix well (batter will be very thick).
3. In a large bowl with clean beaters, beat egg whites on medium speed until soft peaks form. Gradually beat in remaining sugar, 1 tablespoon at a time, on high until stiff peaks form. Gradually fold into batter. Spread evenly into prepared pan.
4. Bake at 375° for 10-12 minutes or until cake springs back when lightly touched. Cool for 5 minutes. Invert cake onto a kitchen towel dusted with confectioners' sugar. Gently peel off paper. Roll up cake in towel jelly-roll style, starting with a short side. Cool on a wire rack.
5. Unroll cake; spread jam to within ½ in. of edges. Top with ice cream. Roll up again, without towel. Place seam side down on a platter. Cover and freeze for at least 4 hours before slicing. May be frozen for up to 2 months. Sprinkle with confectioners' sugar; serve with hot fudge topping and whipped topping.

ICE CREAM PARTY ROLL

"I combined several recipes to satisfy both the chocolate lovers and cheesecake fans in my family. With a fudge brownie crust, crunchy pecans and a gooey layer of caramel, this gem of a dessert is hard to resist."
—**BRENDA RUSE** TRURO, NS

Caramel Fudge Cheesecake

PREP: 30 MIN. • **BAKE:** 35 MIN. + CHILLING
MAKES: 12 SERVINGS

- **1 package fudge brownie mix (8-inch-square pan size)**
- **1 package (14 ounces) caramels**
- **¼ cup evaporated milk**
- **1¼ cups coarsely chopped pecans**
- **2 packages (8 ounces each) cream cheese, softened**
- **½ cup sugar**
- **2 eggs, lightly beaten**
- **2 ounces unsweetened chocolate, melted and cooled**

1. Prepare brownie batter according to package directions. Spread into a greased 9-in. springform pan. Place on a baking sheet. Bake at 350° for 20 minutes. Place pan on a wire rack for 10 minutes (leave oven on).
2. Meanwhile, in a microwave-safe bowl, melt caramels with milk. Pour over brownie crust; sprinkle with pecans.
3. In a large bowl, beat cream cheese and sugar until light and fluffy. Add eggs; beat on low speed just until combined. Stir in melted chocolate. Pour over pecans. Return pan to baking sheet.
4. Bake for 35-40 minutes or until center is almost set. Cool on a wire rack for 10 minutes. Run a knife around edge of pan to loosen; cool 1 hour longer. Refrigerate overnight. Remove sides of pan.

CARAMEL FUDGE CHEESECAKE

Great Pumpkin Dessert

Here's a crowd-pleasing alternative to pumpkin pie that always garners compliments and requests for the recipe. And it's so easy!

—**LINDA GUYOT** FOUNTAIN VALLEY, CA

PREP: 5 MIN. • **BAKE:** 1 HOUR
MAKES: 12-16 SERVINGS

- **1 can (15 ounces) solid-pack pumpkin**
- **1 can (12 ounces) evaporated milk**
- **3 eggs**
- **1 cup sugar**
- **4 teaspoons pumpkin pie spice**
- **1 package yellow cake mix (regular size)**
- **¾ cup butter, melted**
- **1½ cups chopped walnuts**
- **Vanilla ice cream or whipped cream**

1. In a large bowl, beat first five ingredients until smooth.
2. Transfer to a greased 13-in. x 9-in. baking dish. Sprinkle with cake mix and drizzle with butter. Top with walnuts.
3. Bake at 350° for 1 hour or until a knife inserted near the center comes out clean. Serve with ice cream or whipped cream.

If you don't have **pumpkin pie spice,** you can substitute 2 teaspoons of **cinnamon,** 1 teaspoon **ginger,** 1/2 teaspoon **nutmeg** and 1/2 teaspoon ground **cloves** or **allspice.**

GREAT PUMPKIN DESSERT

Zucchini Cobbler

Here's my surprise dessert! No one ever guesses that the secret ingredient is zucchini. Everyone who tries it says it tastes like apples.

—**JOANNE FAZIO** CARBONDALE, PA

PREP: 35 MIN. • **BAKE:** 35 MIN.
MAKES: 16-20 SERVINGS

- **8 cups chopped seeded peeled zucchini (from about 3 pounds)**
- **⅔ cup lemon juice**
- **1 cup sugar**
- **1 teaspoon ground cinnamon**
- **½ teaspoon ground nutmeg**

CRUST

- **4 cups all-purpose flour**
- **2 cups sugar**
- **1½ cups cold butter, cubed**
- **1 teaspoon ground cinnamon**

1. In a large saucepan over medium-low heat, cook and stir zucchini and lemon juice for 15-20 minutes or until zucchini is tender. Add the sugar, cinnamon and nutmeg; cook 1 minute longer. Remove from the heat; set mixture aside.
2. For crust, combine the flour and sugar in a bowl; cut in butter until the mixture resembles coarse crumbs. Stir 1/2 cup into zucchini mixture. Press half of remaining crust mixture into a greased 15-in. x 10-in. x 1-in. baking pan. Spread zucchini over top; crumble remaining crust mixture over zucchini. Sprinkle with cinnamon.
3. Bake at 375° for 35-40 minutes or until golden and bubbly.

EAT SMART

Old-Fashioned Rice Pudding

This classic dessert is a wonderful way to finish any meal. As a little girl, I always waited eagerly to take the first heavenly bite. Nowadays when I prepare it, my husband likes to top his with a scoop of vanilla ice cream.

—**SANDRA MELNYCHENKO** GRANDVIEW, MB

PREP: 10 MIN. • **BAKE:** 1 HOUR
MAKES: 6 SERVINGS

- **3½ cups 2% milk**
- **½ cup uncooked long grain rice**
- **⅓ cup sugar**
- **½ teaspoon salt**
- **½ cup raisins**
- **1 teaspoon vanilla extract**
- **Ground cinnamon, optional**

1. In a large saucepan, combine the milk, rice, sugar and salt if desired. Bring to a boil over medium heat, stirring constantly. Pour into a greased 1½-qt. baking dish.
2. Cover and bake at 325° for 45 minutes, stirring every 15 minutes. Add raisins and vanilla; cover and bake for 15 minutes longer or until rice is tender.
3. Sprinkle with cinnamon if desired. Serve warm or chilled. Store leftovers in the refrigerator.

PER SERVING *208 cal., 3 g fat (2 g sat. fat), 11 mg chol., 270 mg sodium, 40 g carb., 1 g fiber, 6 g pro.*

RASPBERRY SACHER TORTE

FREEZE IT

Raspberry Sacher Torte

It may look like it took hours to prepare, but this rich and elegant torte has a surprisingly short list of ingredients. A tiny sliver is enough to splendidly satisfy any sweet tooth.

—**ROSE HOCKETT** COLORADO SPRINGS, CO

PREP: 50 MIN. • **BAKE:** 25 MIN. + STANDING
MAKES: 12 SERVINGS

- **4 eggs, separated**
- **5 tablespoons butter**
- **⅔ cup sugar**
- **9 ounces bittersweet chocolate, melted**
- **¾ cup ground almonds**
- **¼ cup all-purpose flour**
- **¼ cup seedless raspberry jam**

GLAZE

- **3 ounces bittersweet chocolate, chopped**
- **2 tablespoons butter**

1. Place egg whites in a large bowl; let stand at room temperature for 30 minutes. In a large bowl, beat butter and sugar until crumbly, about 2 minutes. Add egg yolks and melted chocolate; beat on low speed just until combined. Combine almonds and flour; stir into butter mixture just until blended.
2. In another bowl with clean beaters, beat egg whites until stiff peaks form; fold into batter. Transfer to a greased 9-in. springform pan. Bake at 350° for 25-30 minutes or until a toothpick inserted in center comes out clean. Cool on a wire rack for 10 minutes. Carefully run a knife around edge of pan to loosen; remove sides of pan. Cool completely.
3. Spread jam over top of cake. For glaze, in a small saucepan, melt chocolate and butter; spread over jam. Let stand at room temperature for 1 hour or until set.

FREEZE OPTION *Bake the cake and let cool (do not top with jam); freeze in a heavy-duty resealable plastic bag for up to 3 months. When ready to use, thaw at room temperature overnight. Top with the jam and glaze.*

Grandma's Red Velvet Cake

No one in our family thinks it's Christmas without this cake. I baked the first one for Christmas in 1963, and my mother and I kept the tradition going. It's different from other red velvet cakes I've had, with its subtle hint of chocolate flavor and an icing as light as snow.

—KATHRYN DAVISON CHARLOTTE, NC

PREP: 30 MIN. • **BAKE:** 20 MIN. + COOLING
MAKES: 14 SERVINGS

- **½ cup butter, softened**
- **1½ cups sugar**
- **2 eggs**
- **2 bottles (1 ounce each) red food coloring**
- **1 tablespoon white vinegar**
- **1 teaspoon vanilla extract**
- **2¼ cups cake flour**
- **2 tablespoons baking cocoa**
- **1 teaspoon baking soda**
- **1 teaspoon salt**
- **1 cup buttermilk**

FROSTING

- **1 tablespoon cornstarch**
- **½ cup cold water**
- **2 cups butter, softened**
- **2 teaspoons vanilla extract**
- **3½ cups confectioners' sugar**

1. Preheat oven to 350°. In a large bowl, cream butter and sugar until light and fluffy. Add eggs, one at a time, beating well after each addition. Beat in food coloring, vinegar and vanilla. Combine flour, cocoa, baking soda and salt; add to creamed mixture alternately with buttermilk, beating well after each addition.

2. Pour into two greased and floured 9-in. round baking pans. Bake for 20-25 minutes or until a toothpick inserted in center comes out clean. Cool 10 minutes before removing from pans to wire racks to cool completely.

3. For frosting, in a small saucepan, combine cornstarch and water until smooth. Cook and stir over medium heat for 2-3 minutes or until thickened and opaque. Cool to room temperature.

4. In a large bowl, beat butter and vanilla until light and fluffy. Beat in cornstarch mixture. Gradually add confectioners' sugar; beat until frosting is light and fluffy. Spread frosting between layers and over top and sides of cake.

Saltine Toffee Bark

PREP: 25 MIN. + CHILLING
MAKES: 2 POUNDS

- **40 saltines**
- **1 cup butter, cubed**
- **¾ cup sugar**
- **2 cups (12 ounces) semisweet chocolate chips**
- **1 package (8 ounces) milk chocolate English toffee bits**

1. Line a 15-in. x 10-in. x 1-in. baking pan with heavy-duty foil. Arrange saltines in a single layer on foil; set aside.

2. In a large heavy saucepan over medium heat, melt butter. Stir in sugar. Bring to a boil; cook and stir for 1-2 minutes or until sugar is dissolved. Pour evenly over crackers.

3. Bake at 350° for 8-10 minutes or until bubbly. Immediately sprinkle with chocolate chips. Allow chips to soften for a few minutes, then spread over the top. Sprinkle with toffee bits. Cool.

4. Cover and refrigerate for 1 hour or until set. Break into pieces. Store in an airtight container.

"Get ready for a new family favorite— like brittle, but better. These sweet-and-salty treasures make great gifts, and their flavor is irresistible."

—LAURA COX BREWSTER, MA

SALTINE TOFFEE BARK

FREEZE IT

Cherry Berry Pie

Every time I bake Cherry Berry Pie, folks rave. I'm always looking for new treats to serve my family...but this dessert is one I turn to again and again, especially in the summer months.

—WANDA VAN VOORHIS PLAIN CITY, OH

PREP: 25 MIN. + STANDING
BAKE: 35 MIN. + COOLING
MAKES: 8 SERVINGS

- **2½ cups fresh or frozen pitted tart cherries, thawed**
- **1½ cups fresh or frozen raspberries, thawed**
- **1 teaspoon lemon juice**
- **1½ cups sugar**
- **¼ cup plus 2 teaspoons quick-cooking tapioca**
- **⅛ teaspoon salt**
- **1 package (14.1 ounces) refrigerated pie pastry**
- **1 tablespoon butter**
- **1 egg**
- **1 tablespoon 2% milk**
- **Coarse sugar**

1. Preheat oven to 400°. Combine cherries, raspberries and lemon juice in a large bowl. In a small bowl, mix sugar, tapioca and salt; add to fruit and toss gently to coat. Let stand 15 minutes.

2. Unroll one pastry sheet into a 9-in. pie plate; trim pastry to ¾ in. beyond rim of plate. Add filling; dot with butter.

3. Unroll remaining pastry; cut into ¾-in.-wide strips. Arrange over filling in a lattice pattern. Trim and seal strips to edge of bottom pastry; flute edge. In a small bowl, whisk egg and milk; brush over lattice top. Sprinkle with sugar.

4. Cover edge loosely with foil. Bake 30 minutes. Remove foil; bake 5-10 minutes longer or until crust is golden brown and filling is bubbly. Cool on a wire rack.

FREEZE OPTION *Cover and freeze unbaked pie. To use, remove from freezer 30 minutes before baking (do not thaw). Preheat oven to 400°. Bake as directed, increasing time as necessary.*

WYOMING WHOPPER COOKIES

Wyoming Whopper Cookies

I came up with this recipe while trying to match a commercial cookie that was good, but too crumbly to travel with.

—JAMIE HIRSCH POWELL, WY

START TO FINISH: 30 MIN.
MAKES: 2 DOZEN

- **⅔ cup butter, cubed**
- **1¼ cups packed brown sugar**
- **¾ cup sugar**
- **3 eggs, beaten**
- **1½ cups chunky peanut butter**
- **6 cups old-fashioned oats**
- **2 teaspoons baking soda**
- **1½ cups raisins**
- **2 cups (12 ounces) semisweet chocolate chips**

1. In a large saucepan, melt butter over low heat. Stir in the brown sugar, sugar, eggs and peanut butter until smooth. Add oats, baking soda, raisins and chocolate chips (dough will be sticky).

2. Drop on a greased baking sheet with an ice cream scoop or large spoon. Flatten slightly. Bake at 350° for 15 minutes. Remove cookies to a wire rack to cool.

NOTE *Reduced-fat peanut butter is not recommended for this recipe.*

Maple Carrot Cupcakes

I come from a line of family cooks and have liked to cook and bake since I was young. Mother and Grandmom were always in the kitchen cooking up something delicious. These cupcakes were Grandmom's specialty, and they have become a tradition at family gatherings.

—**LISA ANN PANZINO DINUNZIO** VINELAND, NJ

PREP: 15 MIN. • **BAKE:** 20 MIN. + COOLING
MAKES: 1½ DOZEN

- **2 cups all-purpose flour**
- **1 cup sugar**
- **1 teaspoon baking powder**
- **1 teaspoon baking soda**
- **1 teaspoon ground cinnamon**
- **½ teaspoon salt**
- **4 eggs**
- **1 cup canola oil**
- **½ cup maple syrup**
- **3 cups grated carrots (about 6 medium)**

FROSTING

- **1 package (8 ounces) cream cheese, softened**
- **¼ cup butter, softened**
- **¼ cup maple syrup**
- **1 teaspoon vanilla extract**
- **Chopped walnuts, optional**

1. In a large bowl, combine the first six ingredients. In another bowl, beat eggs, oil and syrup. Stir into dry ingredients just until moistened. Fold in carrots.

2. Fill greased or paper-lined muffin cups two-thirds full. Bake at 350° for 20-25 minutes or until a toothpick inserted near the center comes out clean. Cool for 5 minutes before removing from pans to wire racks.

3. For frosting, combine the cream cheese, butter, syrup and vanilla in a bowl; beat until smooth. Frost cooled cupcakes. Sprinkle with nuts if desired. Store in the refrigerator.

MAPLE CARROT CUPCAKES

Tiramisu

This variation of the popular Italian dessert is so easy to assemble. It's convenient, too, since you can make it the day before your dinner party or potluck.

—**LINDA FINN** LOUISVILLE, MS

PREP: 25 MIN. + CHILLING
MAKES: 12 SERVINGS

- **½ cup strong brewed coffee**
- **2 tablespoons coffee liqueur**
- **2 packages (8 ounces each) cream cheese, softened**
- **⅔ cup sugar**
- **2 cups (16 ounces) sour cream**
- **¼ cup 2% milk**
- **½ teaspoon vanilla extract**
- **2 packages (3 ounces each) ladyfingers, split**
- **1 tablespoon baking cocoa**

1. In a small bowl, combine coffee and liqueur; set aside.

2. In a large bowl, beat cream cheese and sugar until smooth. Beat in sour cream, milk and vanilla until blended.

3. Layer one package of ladyfingers in an ungreased 11-in. x 7-in. dish; brush with half of coffee mixture. Top with half of cream cheese mixture. Repeat layers (dish will be full).

4. Cover and refrigerate 8 hours or overnight. Just before serving, sprinkle with cocoa.

Tiramisu is often made with **mascarpone**, and the cheese filling is sometimes lightened by folding in **whipped cream**. For an authentic taste, use **espresso** instead of strong coffee.

TIRAMISU

"Our kids' most requested cookies are peanut butter and chocolate chip, so I came up with this recipe combining those favorite flavors. The two doughs swirled create a lovely pattern on the cookie. There's no need for additional decoration."
—LORI KESINGER BAKER, MT

FREEZE IT

Best of Both Cookies

PREP: 25 MIN. + CHILLING
BAKE: 10 MIN./BATCH
MAKES: ABOUT 6½ DOZEN

- **¾ cup creamy peanut butter**
- **½ cup butter, softened**
- **½ cup sugar**
- **½ cup packed brown sugar**
- **1 egg**
- **1¼ cups all-purpose flour**
- **½ teaspoon baking powder**
- **½ teaspoon baking soda**
- **¼ teaspoon salt**

CHOCOLATE DOUGH

- **½ cup butter, softened**
- **½ cup sugar**
- **½ cup packed brown sugar**
- **1 egg**
- **1 teaspoon vanilla extract**
- **1¼ cups all-purpose flour**
- **¼ cup baking cocoa**
- **½ teaspoon baking powder**
- **½ teaspoon baking soda**
- **¼ teaspoon salt**

1. In a large bowl, cream the peanut butter, butter and sugars until light and fluffy, about 4 minutes. Beat in egg. Combine the flour, baking powder, baking soda and salt; gradually add to creamed mixture and mix well.

2. For the chocolate dough, in another large bowl, cream butter and sugars until light and fluffy. Beat in egg and vanilla. Combine the flour, cocoa, baking powder, baking soda and salt; gradually add to creamed mixture and mix well.

3. Divide each portion in half. Knead one peanut butter and one chocolate portion together 5-10 times or until it just begins to swirl. Shape into a 10-in. log. Wrap in plastic wrap. Repeat with remaining dough. Refrigerate 3-4 hours or until firm.

4. Preheat oven to 350°. Unwrap and cut into ¼-in. slices. Place 2 in. apart on lightly greased baking sheets. Bake 6-8 minutes or until bottoms are lightly browned. Cool 2 minutes before removing from pans to wire racks.

FREEZE OPTION *Place wrapped logs in resealable plastic freezer bag; freeze. To use, unwrap frozen logs and cut into slices. If necessary, let dough stand for a few minutes at room temperature before cutting. Bake as directed.*

Polka-Dot Cookie Bars

When you're serving a group, these bars are easier to make than individual cookies. For the chocolate lover, substitute semisweet chips for the white chips.

—**ELIZABETH POIRE** KAILUA KONA, HI

PREP: 15 MIN.
BAKE: 20 MIN. + COOLING
MAKES: 4 DOZEN

- **1 cup butter, softened**
- **¾ cup sugar**
- **¾ cup packed brown sugar**
- **2 eggs**
- **½ teaspoon almond extract**
- **2¼ cups all-purpose flour**
- **⅓ cup baking cocoa**
- **1 teaspoon baking soda**
- **½ teaspoon salt**
- **1 package (10 to 12 ounces) white baking chips,divided**

1. In a large bowl, cream butter and sugars until light and fluffy. Add eggs, one at a time, beating well after each addition. Beat in extract. Combine the flour, cocoa, baking soda and salt; gradually add to the creamed mixture. Set aside 1/4 cup chips; stir remaining chips into batter.
2. Spread in a greased 15-in. x 10-in. x 1-in. baking pan. Sprinkle with reserved chips. Bake at 375° for 18-23 minutes or until a toothpick inserted near the center comes out clean. Cool on a wire rack. Cut into bars.

PEACHES AND CREAM TORTE

Peaches and Cream Torte

This is the dessert I make when I'm craving something cool and fruity. It's a lovely ending to any meal. Cream cheese adds zing to the sweet and fluffy peach filling.

—**ELVA ROBERTS** SUMMERSIDE, PE

PREP: 40 MIN. + CHILLING
MAKES: 12 SERVINGS

- **2 cups graham cracker crumbs**
- **⅓ cup packed brown sugar**
- **½ cup butter, melted**

FILLING

- **1 can (29 ounces) sliced peaches**
- **1¼ cups sugar, divided**
- **2 tablespoons cornstarch**
- **1 package (8 ounces) cream cheese, softened**
- **2 cups heavy whipping cream**

1. In a small bowl, combine graham cracker crumbs and brown sugar; stir in butter. Set aside 1/4 cup for topping. Press remaining crumb mixture onto the bottom and 1 in. up the sides of a greased 9-in. springform pan.
2. Place pan on a baking sheet. Bake at 350° for 10 minutes. Cool on a wire rack.
3. Drain peaches, reserving syrup in a 2-cup measuring cup. Add enough water to measure 1½ cups. In a large saucepan, combine 1/4 cup sugar and cornstarch; stir in syrup mixture until smooth. Add peaches. Bring to a boil over medium heat; cook and stir for 2 minutes or until thickened. Cool mixture to room temperature, stirring occasionally.
4. Meanwhile, in a large bowl, beat cream cheese and remaining sugar until smooth. Beat cream until stiff peaks form; fold into the cream cheese mixture.
5. Spread half of the cream cheese mixture over crust. Top with half of the peach mixture; repeat layers. Sprinkle with reserved crumb mixture. Cover and refrigerate for 8 hours or overnight. Remove sides of pan before slicing.

EAT SMART

Iced Tea Parfaits

Here's a parfait that's perfect for a garden or patio party. Tea adds a wonderfully unexpected flavor to gelatin. And kids will have fun finding the cherry at the bottom.

—**TEENA PETRUS** JOHNSTOWN, PA

PREP: 15 MIN. + CHILLING
MAKES: 4 SERVINGS

- **2 cups water**
- **3 individual tea bags**
- **1 package (3 ounces) lemon gelatin**
- **4 maraschino cherries**
- **1½ cups whipped topping, divided**
- **4 lemon slices**

1. In a small saucepan, bring water to a boil. Remove from the heat; add tea bags. Cover and steep for 5 minutes. Discard tea bags. Stir gelatin into tea until completely dissolved. Cool slightly.

2. Pour 1/4 cup gelatin mixture into each of four parfait glasses. Place a cherry in each glass; refrigerate until set but not firm, about 1 hour. Transfer remaining gelatin mixture to a small bowl; refrigerate for 1 hour or until soft-set.

3. Whisk gelatin mixture for 2-3 minutes or until smooth. Stir in 1/2 cup whipped topping; spoon into parfait glasses. Refrigerate for at least 2 hours. Just before serving, top with remaining whipped topping and garnish with lemon slices.

PER SERVING *162 cal., 5 g fat (5 g sat. fat), 0 chol., 48 mg sodium, 27 g carb., 0 fiber, 2 g pro.* ***Diabetic Exchanges:*** *1 1/2 starch, 1 fat.*

Tender Italian Sugar Cookies

These traditional Italian cookies are moist and tender. To tie into the colors of the Italian flag, you could tint the icing, red, green and white.

—**WEDA MOSELLIE** PHILLIPSBURG, NJ

PREP: 20 MIN.
BAKE: 10 MIN./BATCH + COOLING
MAKES: 3 DOZEN

- **¾ cup shortening**
- **¾ cup sugar**
- **3 eggs**
- **1 teaspoon vanilla extract**
- **3 cups all-purpose flour**
- **3 teaspoons baking powder**
- **⅛ teaspoon salt**

ICING

- **¼ cup milk**
- **2 tablespoons butter, melted**
- **½ teaspoon vanilla extract**
- **2½ cups confectioners' sugar**
- **Food coloring and coarse sugar, optional**

1. Preheat oven to 400°. In a large bowl, cream shortening and sugar until light and fluffy. Beat in eggs and vanilla. Combine flour, baking powder and salt; gradually add to creamed mixture and mix well.

2. Shape dough into 1 1/2-in. balls. Place 1 in. apart on ungreased baking sheets. Bake 8-10 minutes or until lightly browned. Remove to wire racks to cool.

3. For icing, in a small bowl, combine milk, butter, vanilla and confectioners' sugar until smooth. Tint with food coloring if desired. Dip tops of cookies in icing; allow excess to drip off. Sprinkle with coarse sugar if desired. Place on waxed paper; let stand until set.

TENDER ITALIAN SUGAR COOKIES

BLUEBERRY ICE CREAM

Blueberry Ice Cream

The wild blueberries on our property spark many recipe ideas. Our 10 children, 19 grandkids and four great-grandchildren think this ice cream is tops for summertime taste.
—ALMA MOSHER MOHANNES, NB

PREP: 15 MIN. + CHILLING
PROCESS: 20 MIN./BATCH + FREEZING
MAKES: ABOUT 1¾ QUARTS

- 4 **cups fresh or frozen blueberries**
- 2 **cups sugar**
- 2 **tablespoons water**
- 4 **cups half-and-half cream**

1. In a large saucepan, combine the blueberries, sugar and water. Bring to a boil. Reduce heat; simmer, uncovered, until sugar is dissolved and berries are softened. Press mixture through a fine-mesh strainer into a bowl; discard pulp. Stir in cream. Cover and chill overnight.
2. Fill cylinder of ice cream freezer two-thirds full; freeze according to the manufacturer's directions. (Refrigerate remaining mixture until ready to freeze.) When ice cream is frozen, transfer to a freezer container; freeze for 2-4 hours before serving.

To create a **luscious treat** that's even richer in **antioxidants**, add some finely chopped **dark chocolate** to the ice cream.

"Are they a brownie or are they a cupcake? There's no wrong answer to this question, I tell my first-grade students. I found the recipe when I began teaching over 30 years ago. My husband and children like this treat, too."
—**CAROL MAERTZ** SPRUCE GROVE, AB

MINT BROWNIE CUPCAKES

Mint Brownie Cupcakes

PREP: 25 MIN. • **BAKE:** 15 MIN. + CHILLING
MAKES: 10 CUPCAKES

- **½ cup mint chocolate chips**
- **½ cup butter, cubed**
- **½ cup sugar**
- **2 eggs**
- **½ cup all-purpose flour**

TOPPING

- **2 cups miniature marshmallows**
- **⅓ cup 2% milk**
- **½ teaspoon peppermint extract**
- **Green or red food coloring, optional**
- **¾ cup heavy whipping cream, whipped**
- **Additional chocolate chips, optional**

1. In a large microwave-safe bowl, melt chips and butter; stir until smooth. Cool slightly; stir in sugar and eggs. Gradually stir flour into chocolate mixture until smooth.

2. Fill paper-lined muffin cups two-thirds full. Bake at 350° for 15-20 minutes or until a toothpick inserted near the center comes out clean. Remove from pan to a wire rack to cool.

3. In a large saucepan, cook and stir marshmallows and milk over low heat until smooth. Remove from the heat; stir in extract and, if desired, food coloring.

4. Transfer to a bowl; refrigerate for 15 minutes or until cooled. Fold in whipped cream. Spread over cupcakes. Refrigerate for at least 1 hour. Sprinkle with additional chocolate chips if desired. Store in the refrigerator.

NOTE *If mint chocolate chips are not available, place 2 cups (12 ounces) semisweet chocolate chips and 1/4 teaspoon peppermint extract in a plastic bag; seal and toss to coat. Allow chips to stand for 24-48 hours.*

Orange Whip

Yogurt adds tanginess to this fluffy orange treat. It's so pretty and refreshing on hot summer days.

—**SUE THOMAS** CASA GRANDE, AZ

PREP: 10 MIN. + FREEZING
MAKES: 4 SERVINGS

- **1 can (11 ounces) mandarin oranges, drained and patted dry**
- **1 cup (8 ounces) vanilla yogurt**
- **2 tablespoons orange juice concentrate**
- **2 cups whipped topping**

1. In a large bowl, combine the oranges, yogurt and orange juice concentrate. Fold in whipped topping.

2. Spoon into serving dishes. Cover and freeze until firm. Remove from the freezer 10 minutes before serving.

ORANGE WHIP

HEAVENLY FILLED STRAWBERRIES

Heavenly Filled Strawberries

Here comes strawberry season! These luscious stuffed berries are the perfect bite-size dessert for a summer party.
—**STEPHEN MUNRO** BEAVERBANK, NS

START TO FINISH: 20 MIN.
MAKES: 3 DOZEN

- **3 dozen large fresh strawberries**
- **2 packages (one 8 ounces, one 3 ounces) cream cheese, softened**
- **½ cup confectioners' sugar**
- **¼ teaspoon almond extract**
- **Grated chocolate**

1. Remove stems from strawberries; cut a deep "X" in the tip of each berry. Gently spread berries open.
2. In a small bowl, beat the cream cheese, confectioners' sugar and extract until light and fluffy. Pipe or spoon about 2 teaspoons into each berry; sprinkle with chocolate. Chill until serving.

Spumoni Loaf

I found this recipe years ago when I was teaching home economics. The blend of nuts, cherries and chocolate in a fluffy filling is delightful.
—**DONNA HANSON** LUSK, WY

PREP: 20 MIN. + FREEZING
MAKES: 10-12 SERVINGS

- **1 cup milk**
- **1 teaspoon vanilla extract**
- **2 jars (7 ounces each) marshmallow creme**
- **4 milk chocolate candy bars (1.55 ounces each), chopped**
- **½ cup chopped almonds**
- **½ cup chopped maraschino cherries**
- **2 cups heavy whipping cream, whipped**

1. In a small saucepan, combine milk and vanilla; stir in marshmallow creme. Cook and stir over low heat until smooth. Transfer mixture to a large bowl; cool.
2. Stir in candy bars, almonds and cherries. Fold in whipped cream.
3. Transfer to an ungreased 9-in. x 5-in. loaf pan. Cover and freeze for at least 4 hours. Remove from the freezer 10 minutes before serving. Unmold and slice.

EAT SMART

Cherry Chocolate Cake

I've had the recipe for this lovely cake for years. It's a chocolate lover's delight! It's so easy to make...and it's easy to take along on potlucks, too. Just spread the second can of pie filling right over the top.
—**ANN PURCHASE** PANAMA CITY, FL

PREP: 15 MIN. • **BAKE:** 30 MIN. + COOLING
MAKES: 18 SERVINGS

- **1 package chocolate cake mix (regular size)**
- **3 eggs, lightly beaten**
- **1 teaspoon almond extract**
- **2 cans (20 ounces each) reduced-sugar cherry pie filling, divided**
- **¾ teaspoon confectioners' sugar**

1. In a large bowl, combine the cake mix, eggs and almond extract. Stir in one can of pie filling until blended. Transfer to a 13-in. x 9-in. baking pan coated with cooking spray.
2. Bake at 350° for 30-35 minutes or until a toothpick inserted near the center comes out clean. Cool completely on a wire rack.
3. Dust with confectioners' sugar. Top individual servings with remaining pie filling.

PER SERVING *187 cal., 6 g fat (1 g sat. fat), 35 mg chol., 253 mg sodium, 33 g carb., 1 g fiber, 3 g pro.* ***Diabetic Exchanges:*** *1 starch, 1 fruit, 1 fat.*

EAT SMART

Frozen Fruit Pops

My grandson, Patrick, has been Grammy's Helper for years. We made these frozen pops for company and everyone, including the adults, loved them. They're delicious and good for you!

—**JUNE DICKENSON** PHILIPPI, WV

PREP: 15 MIN. + FREEZING
MAKES: 1 DOZEN

- **2¼ cups (18 ounces) raspberry yogurt**
- **2 tablespoons lemon juice**
- **2 medium ripe bananas, cut into chunks**
- **12 freezer pop molds or 12 paper cups (3 ounces each) and wooden pop sticks**

1. In a blender, combine the yogurt, lemon juice and bananas; cover and process for 45 seconds or until smooth. Stir if necessary.
2. Fill molds or cups with yogurt mixture; top with holders or insert sticks into cups. Freeze.

PER SERVING *60 cal., 1 g fat (trace sat. fat), 2 mg chol., 23 mg sodium, 13 g carb., 1 g fiber, 2 g pro.* ***Diabetic Exchange:*** *1 starch.*

For a **sweet-tart berry burst**, toss a handful of **raspberries** into the blender before pureeing. This will also give the pops a more **intense pink color**. Experiment with **different** fruit and yogurt **flavors**.

Creamy Lime Sherbet

The lime flavor in this cool, creamy treat is perfect for hot summer days. The pastel color makes it so pretty whether served in a dish or a cone.

—**MARY BETH DELL SPIESS** INDUSTRY, TX

PREP: 15 MIN.
PROCESS: 20 MIN./BATCH + FREEZING
MAKES: ABOUT 2 QUARTS

- **1 package (3 ounces) lime gelatin**
- **1 cup boiling water**
- **1¼ cups sugar**
- **1 can (6 ounces) frozen limeade concentrate, thawed**
- **Dash salt**
- **4 cups milk**
- **2 cups half-and-half cream**
- **8 drops green food coloring, optional**

1. In a large bowl, dissolve gelatin in water. Stir in the sugar, limeade and salt until sugar is dissolved. Add remaining ingredients.
2. Fill cylinder of ice cream freezer two-thirds full; freeze according to the manufacturer's directions. Refrigerate remaining mixture until ready to freeze. When sherbet is frozen, transfer to a freezer container; freeze for 2-4 hours before serving.

CREAMY LIME SHERBET

"This pie is a rite of spring at our house, and we've enjoyed sharing it with many visitors. We love that it's both sweet and tart, with a mild almond accent."

—**JESSIE GREARSON-SAPAT** FALMOUTH, ME

STRAWBERRY-RHUBARB MERINGUE PIE

Strawberry-Rhubarb Meringue Pie

PREP: 45 MIN. • **BAKE:** 50 MIN. + CHILLING
MAKES: 8 SERVINGS

- **½ cup all-purpose flour**
- **¼ cup whole wheat pastry flour**
- **¼ cup ground almonds**
- **½ teaspoon salt**
- **¼ cup cold butter, cubed**
- **2 tablespoons cold water**

FILLING

- **1 egg, lightly beaten**
- **¾ cup sugar**
- **2 tablespoons all-purpose flour**
- **¼ teaspoon ground cinnamon**
- **2 cups chopped fresh or frozen rhubarb, thawed**
- **1½ cups sliced fresh strawberries**

MERINGUE

- **3 egg whites**
- **¼ teaspoon almond extract**
- **6 tablespoons sugar**

1. In a food processor, combine the all-purpose flour, pastry flour, almonds and salt; cover and pulse until blended. Add butter; cover and pulse until mixture resembles coarse crumbs. While processing, gradually add water until dough forms a ball.
2. Roll out pastry to fit a 9-in. pie plate. Transfer pastry to pie plate. Trim pastry to ½ in. beyond edge of plate; flute edges.
3. In a large bowl, combine the egg, sugar, flour and cinnamon; stir in rhubarb and strawberries. Transfer to prepared crust. Bake at 375° for 35-40 minutes or until filling is bubbly. Place pie on a wire rack; keep warm. Reduce heat to 350°.
4. In a large bowl, beat egg whites and extract on medium speed until soft peaks form. Gradually beat in sugar, 1 tablespoon at a time, on high until stiff peaks form. Spread over hot filling, sealing edges to crust.
5. Bake for 15 minutes or until golden brown. Cool on a wire rack for 1 hour; refrigerate for 1-2 hours before serving.

FAVORITE DUTCH APPLE PIE

Favorite Dutch Apple Pie

Everything about this dessert makes it the top request for family gatherings. The delightful crust cuts beautifully to reveal a filling of diced apple. At harvesttime or any time, you simply cannot beat this delectable pie.
—**BRENDA DUFRESNE** MIDLAND, MI

PREP: 20 MIN. • **BAKE:** 40 MIN. + COOLING
MAKES: 6-8 SERVINGS

- **2 cups all-purpose flour**
- **1 cup packed brown sugar**
- **½ cup quick-cooking oats**
- **¾ cup butter, melted**

FILLING

- **⅔ cup sugar**
- **3 tablespoons cornstarch**
- **1¼ cups cold water**
- **3 cups diced peeled tart apples**
- **1 teaspoon vanilla extract**

1. In a large bowl, combine the flour, brown sugar, oats and butter; set aside 1 cup for topping. Press remaining crumb mixture into an ungreased 9-in. pie plate; set aside.
2. For filling, combine the sugar, cornstarch and water in a large saucepan until smooth; bring to a boil. Cook and stir for 2 minutes or until thickened. Remove from the heat; stir in apples and vanilla.
3. Pour into crust; top with reserved crumb mixture. Bake at 350° for 40-45 minutes or until crust is golden brown. Cool on a wire rack.

General Recipe Index

CHICKEN *(continued)*

STOVETOP

CHILI

CHOCOLATE

COCONUT & COCONUT MILK

COFFEE

CORN

CORN BREAD & CORNMEAL

CORNED BEEF

CORNISH HENS

CRANBERRIES

CREAM CHEESE

CUCUMBERS

DESSERTS

CAKES & CUPCAKES

CHEESECAKES

COOKIES & BARS

FROZEN

OTHER

PIES

SLOW COOKER

EGGS

FISH *(see Seafood)*

FRUIT *(also see specific listings)*

GREEN BEANS

GROUND BEEF

OVEN

SLOW COOKER

STOVETOP

HAM & CANADIAN BACON

HERBS

HOMINY & GRITS

HONEY

HOT DOGS

HOT PEPPERS

LAMB

LEMONS

LETTUCE

MAPLE

MEATBALLS & MEAT LOAVES

MEATBALLS & MEAT LOAVES *(continued)*

MEATLESS
(see Vegetarian Recipes)

MUSHROOMS

NOODLES
(also see Pasta & Pasta Sauce)

NUTS
(also see Peanuts & Peanut Butter)

OATS

ONIONS

ORANGES

PASTA & PASTA SAUCE
(also see Noodles)

OVEN

SLOW COOKER

STOVETOP

PEACHES

PEANUTS & PEANUT BUTTER

PEARS

PEAS

PEPPERS
(see Bell Peppers; Hot Peppers)

PINEAPPLE

PORK *(also see Bacon; Ham & Canadian Bacon; Hot Dogs; Sausage)*

OVEN

INDEX

SAUERKRAUT

SAUSAGE *(also see Hot Dogs)*

OVEN

SLOW COOKER

STOVETOP

SEAFOOD

OVEN

SLOW COOKER

STOVETOP

SIDE DISHES

SOUPS
(also see Chili; Stews)

SPINACH

SQUASH
(see Summer Squash; Winter Squash)

STEWS
(also see Chili; Soups)

STRAWBERRIES

STUFFING

SUMMER SQUASH

Alphabetical Recipe Index

D

E

F

G

H

I

J

L

M

N

O

P

Q

R

S

T

U

V

W

Z